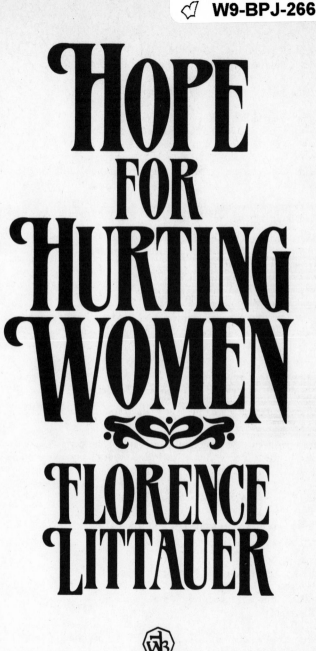

HOPE
FOR
HURTING
WOMEN

FLORENCE
LITTAUER

WORD BOOKS

PUBLISHER

WACO, TEXAS

A DIVISION OF
WORD, INCORPORATED

HOPE FOR HURTING WOMEN
(formerly published under the title *Lives on the Mend*)

Scripture quotations marked KJV are from the Authorized or King James Version
of the Bible.

Quotations marked NAS are from the New American Standard Bible, © The
Lockman Foundation 1960, 1962, 1963, 1968, 1971, 1972, 1973, 1975, 1977.

Quotations marked NIV are from the Holy Bible, New International Version.
Copyright © 1973, 1978, International Bible Society. Used by permission of
Zondervan Bible Publishers.

Quotations marked NKJV are from The New King James Version. Copyright ©
1979, 1980, 1982, Thomas Nelson, Inc., Publishers.

Quotations marked RSV are from the Revised Standard version of the Bible,
copyrighted 1946, 1952, © 1971, 1973 by the Division of Christian Education
of the National Council of the Churches of Christ in the U.S.A., and used by
permission.

Quotations marked TEV are from the Good News Bible, the Bible in Today's
English Version. Copyright © American Bible Society, 1976.

Quotations marked TLB are from The Living Bible, copyright © 1971 by Tyndale
House Publishers, Wheaton, IL. Used by permission.

An effort has been made to locate sources and obtain permission where necessary
for the quotations used in this book. In the event of any unintentional omission,
modifications will be gladly incorporated in future editions.

8 9 0 1 2 3 9 AGF 9 8 7 6 5 4 3 2 1

Library of Congress Cataloging-in-Publication Data

Littauer, Florence, 1928–
    [Lives on the mend]
    Hope for hurting women / Florence Littauer.
        p.   cm.
    Originally published as: Lives on the mend.
    Bibliography: p.
    ISBN 0–8499–3128–2
    1. Women—Conduct of life—Case studies.   2. Women, Christian—
Religious life—Case studies.   I. Title.
BJ1610.L58   1988
248.8'43—dc19   88–10772
                                                                        CIP

This book is dedicated to the fourteen women who graciously allowed me to tell their stories of HOPE to help others.

Thanks to:

Joey Paul and Debra Klingsporn of WORD who first listened to my ideas for this book and encouraged me to write it.

My husband Fred who sponsored and directed the HOPE Conference which provided the tapes for this series and the basic messages for this book.

Kristin James and Kay Keeland for additional research.

Frances Jean Sunderland who provided her cabin in Estes Park, Colorado, for the two weeks I needed to finish this book.

Contents

Common Threads
on the Warp of Life

As you read through this book, you will notice many common threads that teach consistent principles. Take note of these for discussion.

- The pains of the past produce problems today.
- The sins of the fathers are visited upon the children.
- The victim as a child often grows up to be victimized as an adult.
- Abuse victims often become perfectionistic high-achievers.
- A low self-image stems from real or perceived deprivation or rejection as well as abuse.
- Depression takes hold when there seems to be no HOPE.
- Addiction is when you can't live without it.
- Love to a child is transmitted by touch and by eye-to-eye contact and listening.
- Fear is a crippling emotion.
- A child sees divorce as rejection.
- Immature people place blame on others.
- Physical handicaps intensify low self-image.
- Women still dream of living happily ever after.
- Sexual abuse often leads to sexual problems, promiscuity, or prostitution.
- Those who are abused often become abusers.
- Those under pressure look for ways to escape.
- Angry people blame God for their misfortunes.
- Suppressed emotions often lead to physical symptoms.
- Well-meaning people often say the wrong thing.
- In times of grief, it's easier to stay away.
- Suicide is not a snap decision.
- Life isn't fair.
- Pain is a great leveler of people.

- Headaches, asthma, body pain, eating disorders are often symptoms of abuse or emotional problems.
- Abuse victims feel they are to blame.
- Hurting people reach for God in the best way they know how.
- Victims frequently feel they must work their way to heaven.
- Abusers are often respected church members.
- Many need inner healing of the pains of the past.
- Forgiveness is essential for emotional health.
- It's not easy to find appropriate counsel.
- Support groups show that you're not alone.
- We can all be used by God to give HOPE to others.

Coming Apart at the Seams

**Showing that even some fine Christian people
are coming apart at the seams and
are having troubles in their River Cities.**

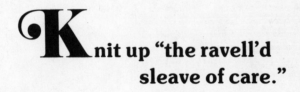

Knit up "the ravell'd
sleave of care."

Macbeth
William Shakespeare

Introduction

"We've Got Troubles Right Here in River City" is a well-known song from the hit musical *Music Man*. And if we take a moment to look around us we can see how true this is—we've got troubles right here in Christian City!

Little did I realize seventeen years ago, when I started teaching Bible studies to country club ladies who seemed to have their lives all together, that many of them were quietly coming apart at the seams. I had just come out of the world—a nice world where I had associated with good people. None of my friends were divorced. They all went to church and I never even considered whether one of them might be unfaithful. When Fred and I dedicated our lives to the Lord and became excited Christians, we moved our friendships to people we found in our evangelical church. If my worldly friends were "good people," surely these new ones would be "*very* good people," perhaps even pious and pure.

When we were asked to go on staff of Campus Crusade for Christ, before we even knew there were Four Laws, I thought we'd died and gone to heaven. Imagine living next door to Dr. Bright, being friends with Hal Lindsey, listening to Howard and Leanne Hendricks, entertaining Dr. Henry Brandt, Eleanor Whitney, Ian Thomas, and other speakers from across the country. Vonette Bright looked like an angel with her halo of golden curls and Barbara Ball spoke in soft saintly tones I knew denoted spirituality.

Certainly I was seated in the heavenlies at the right hand of the Father. I pictured myself growing old on the Holy Hill, content in my rocking chair and wrapped in wisdom, dispatching homilies to the new staff members as they arrived each year seeking higher ground.

How naive I was to think that Christians had no problems, to assume that a rebirth totally wiped out our negatives, and to imagine that God had rolled us all out on that big counter of life and made us into cookie-cutter Christians—all smiling, loving, compassionate, and spirit-filled.

As I began to teach Bible studies to lovely ladies, my rose-colored glasses began to fog up. When I chose Proverbs 31 to examine in weekly studies in my home, I expected to share suggestions based on scripture with saints whose desire was to become virtuous women whose price would be far above rubies.

Instead, I became Mother Confessor as one by one the women shared their hurts with me. Pretenses disappeared, stylish hair was let down, masks were slowly pulled away as heartbroken women cried for answers. They were coming apart at the seams.

Soon I began speaking at women's retreats where I found many who were running away from the troubles in their own River Cities. When I was not on the platform, I was counseling, holding the hands of hurting women, listening to the lament of lonely ladies. Lines formed outside my motel door as I tried to keep one woman from leaving her husband and another from killing herself.

In 1980 I founded Christian Leaders and Speakers Seminars (CLASS) in order to train others how to give HOPE to those in need. Everywhere we looked there were women with buckets of burdens looking for people with armloads of answers. I had assumed the women who came to CLASS would be trouble-free and ready to relieve the trouble-full, but I soon learned that everyone there had some kind of problem in the present or some pain from the past. So we created a "Troubles in River City" chart and asked each participant to check off any "troubles" she had experienced either firsthand or within her family.

The response was amazing. We found in each group that about one-third had alcohol-related problems somewhere in their families. In each CLASS we had incest and rape victims, those who'd attempted suicide, and those who had teens, depressed and on drugs. I soon realized we didn't need to go outside the CLASS of Christian leaders to find those who needed help. We could stay in CLASS for weeks ministering to each other and never run out of cases.

We began to train women to use their background of trials and their steps to survival to give HOPE to others with similar problems and to start mending lives. We taught them to "always be prepared to give an answer to everyone who asks you to give the reason for the hope that you have. But do this with gentleness and respect" (1 Pet. 3:15, NIV).

Christian women are crying out today seeking answers, comfort, sympathy, understanding, still hoping the Christian community will meet their needs.

As the early church gathered for study, for prayer, for sharing and caring, as they came together in fellowship in singing, in praising God, they made it their goal to meet the needs of their people. That's what we must do today: meet the needs of our people. We should not depend on welfare and social services to solve the sad circumstances of our sisters, but we should be ready and willing to comfort those who hurt and to sew up their sorrows.

Robert Schuller states in his church growth seminars that our aim should be to meet the needs of the community within our church and then the community will seek our sanctuary.

Hurting people go where helping people live.

How can we give HOPE to hurting women? How can we mend the broken-hearted?

1. WE CAN OPEN OUR EYES TO THE PROBLEMS IN OUR OWN RIVER CITY. We can become aware of the possible victims in our own pews. A general national statistic indicates that if you know four women, you know at least one who has been sexually molested. We can no longer afford to say:

- "There's no incest in our church."
- "Women who get raped ask for it."
- "If she drinks, she can't really be a Christian."

As we have surveyed our CLASSes of Christian leaders, we've found that their problems parallel those of the world with statistics equal to the national averages: 33% alcohol problems, 25% sexual abuse, 10% incest.

2. WE CAN ASK WHAT JESUS WOULD DO WITH THESE HURTING PEOPLE. Would he be judgmental and jeering? Or would he be

compassionate and caring? He came to save the lost, to heal the sick, to comfort the wounded. He didn't have in mind a Christian community that would become a safe haven for the sanctified, a social center for the saints, but a home for the hungry, a hospital for the hurting.

He saw troubles right there in Jerusalem City. He knew there were hurting people in Judea, Samaria, and unto the uttermost parts of the earth. He dealt with prostitutes, adulterers, and drunkards. He didn't send them to Caesar or the church down the street. He said, "Come unto me all ye that labor and are heavy laden and I will give you rest."

Can we do less?

3. WE CAN REACH OUT AND TOUCH SOMEONE. In October 1984, Fred and I sponsored a HOPE (Helping Other People Emotionally) conference. We invited women who had lived through some of the pressing problems of our time to come and share their stories. One pastor who attended said he learned more in those three days about how to counsel hurting women than he'd learned in his counseling classes in college.

This book will tell those same stories that the pastor heard and will expose you to the inner feelings of a broken heart and the healing that can happen when there is HOPE.

So often we'd be willing to help if we only knew how. This book shows you how to care, how to deal with others according to knowledge, how to reach out and touch someone.

If you are a victim yourself, you'll be encouraged by the lives of women who have been through serious traumas and who have become victorious.

If you have never been a victim, you'll get acquainted with good women just like you, or like your wife or your daughter, who haven't been so fortunate. As you feel their pain and partake in their recovery, you'll have a new understanding and compassion and you will be able to give

HOPE to Hurting Women.

Now, let the Spirit of God speak to your heart as you become a part of these fifteen LIVES on the MEND, as you learn to give HOPE to others, and as you joyfully knit up your own "ravell'd sleave of care."

Stitching in Time

Showing the importance of stopping addictions and emotional instabilities before they start.

Batter my heart,
three-personed God;
for you
As yet but knock, breathe, shine,
and seek to mend.

Holy Sonnets
John Donne

PAULETTE BOYT

Alcoholism

In my family not doing "bad things" made one a "good person." I was brought up to believe that if I didn't smoke, drink, fool around, play cards, or sew on Sundays I would go to heaven. In my entire childhood I only knew one person who drank—Bill the barber who lived in the attic apartment over our store. When Bill would "go on a toot," as my father called it, he'd come home late at night and try to make his way up the narrow stairs that were one thin wall away from our little bedroom. Each time he'd arrive drunk, he would fall down the stairs several times. On the first fall the whole family would be wide awake, and as Bill the Barber would swear loudly, my mother would tell us to block our ears. Mother would stand in her nightgown, with her hair let down from its daily pug, and would wring her hands and weep somewhat like the heroine of old when the villain came for the rent. "What shall we do? What shall we do?"

We did nothing but listen and soon Bill would give up his climb, stop swearing, and sing in loud, happy, off-key tones " 'Twas on the Isle of Capri where I found her." If this went on long enough, Father would get out of bed and drag Bill to the attic, while mother would give us children a nocturnal lecture bemoaning the evils of drink.

If your background is similar to mine and your town drunk doesn't come to church, you might ask why we "good people" need to read about alcoholism. I would have asked the same question a few years ago before I started polling the Christians in CLASS and found that about one-third were dealing with some kind of an alcohol problem. When I asked pastors and counselors, they concurred that about one-half the people who come to them for help have underlying alcohol or drug-related troubles. A Gallup Poll says 81 percent of American adults consider alcoholism to be a major national problem; one out of three families admit alcohol to be a problem in their home (the same average I found in CLASS).

Dr. Anderson Spickard, Jr., in his article "Alcoholism: Even the Church Is Hurting" tells us, "We would all be surprised if we knew the extent of the problem in our home churches. I belong to a large congregation and personally know 5 or 6 members who have been seriously sick with alcoholism. Only God knows how many other closet drinkers there are."[1]

Dr. Spickard defines an alcoholic as:

. . . one whose will has been captured by alcohol, who quite literally can not stop drinking. He or she is in the grips of a progressive and complete destruction of his physical, mental, and spiritual being. Physically he begins to suffer from malnutrition and from serious damage to his liver, digestive tract, and central nervous system. Emotionally and intellectually, he becomes increasingly preoccupied with drinking, with the need to deny that he has a problem, and with frequent occurrence of blackouts—periods of time wherein the alcoholic acts perfectly normal yet later has no recall of any events that took place. Spiritually, the alcoholic drowns in guilt, in fear, and in shame; the more he loses control over himself, the more he is consumed by self-hatred."[2]

In *Alcoholism: A Merry-Go-Round Named Denial*, Rev. Joseph Kellerman says:

Alcoholism is a tragic three-act play in which there are at least four characters, the drinker and his family, friends, co-workers, and even counselors may have a part in keeping the Merry-Go-Round turning. Alcoholism rarely appears in one person set apart from others; it seldom continues in isolation from others.

One person drinks too much and gets drunk and others react to his drinking and its consequences. The drinker responds to this reaction and drinks again. This sets up a Merry-Go-Round of blame and *denial*, a downward spiral which characterizes alcoholism. Therefore, to understand alcoholism, we must look not at the alcoholic alone but view the illness as if we were sitting in the audience watching a play and observing carefully the roles of all the actors in the drama.[3]

Paulette Boyt was the leading lady in her own three-act melodrama. Today she is a petite and pretty lady with huge soulful eyes. She has been an airline flight attendant and comes attractively packaged from Louisiana. She is a trained emotional healing prayer counselor with Lana Bateman's Philippian Ministries out of Dallas and a Christian speaker. If she came to join your church, you'd be thrilled to have her. She could sit in the pews for years and look as if she'd never had a problem.

Paulette's father was a charming man with big dreams of becoming successful, rich, and powerful. Each goal he set for himself seemed to disappear just as he was reaching for it, and these frustrations led him to drink to cover up his feelings of inferiority. His desire to be a hero kept him from showing love to his daughters; he felt it a weakness to hug them, kiss them, or say, "I love you." Always in pursuit of his elusive goals, he had little time for the girls, for listening to their needs, or for getting involved in their lives.

Paulette remembers sitting in the living room and longing for her father to notice her when she was in high school.

His nose was buried in his newspaper and as I looked at him, there was a longing in my heart saying, "Won't you talk to me? Won't you put down that paper and ask me what is going on in my life? Don't you care what I think about?"

Paulette remembers one good year with her father. It was a transition year in his life when he was trying to reestablish himself after a business failure and had to take a job as a fireman. Because there just wasn't enough money, he couldn't drink and he often helped the girls with their homework. But at the end of that year, when he had a few dollars in his pocket, he went back to his old habits and Paulette felt she had lost her father again.

Her mother had been raised by two alcoholic parents and true to what statistics tell us, those raised in an alcoholic home tend to marry alcoholics and in turn breed alcoholics.

Paulette's mother had quit high school to support her parents, and because of their alcoholism, she had become the mother to them both. Robbed of her childhood and receiving no nurturing from her own parents, she grew up with a desperate need to be needed, which she placed upon her own children. She would be a perfect mother, doing everything possible to make them happy. They would depend upon her and her needs would be fulfilled. How many parents kill their children with kindness while binding them helplessly to their side?

With good intentions in her heart, Paulette's mother became a personal maid. She brought Paulette coffee in bed every morning and hovered over her helpfully. Paulette never washed a dish, did one load of laundry, picked up her clothes, made a bed, learned to cook, or handled money. The few times she asked to help her mother, the dear lady would sigh and say, "You probably wouldn't do it right."

Paulette received her mother's message: "You can't do anything without me. I have to do it for you. Even if you tried, you'd fail."

Paulette's sister was able to pull out from under her mother's smothering behavior because of her more choleric personality, but Paulette, with her more melancholy personality, internalized what she felt her mother was communicating and became depressed. She recalls:

I was extremely sensitive as a child, easily depressed, and I took everything to heart. Life was a serious thing to me. I spent a lot of time alone. I was very moody. I was introspective and I would withdraw into myself under pressure. I was not prepared to meet the real world. I was only set to become an emotionally crippled adult, but I didn't know it.

Paulette's father didn't help as he became an alcoholic, was obsessed with being a macho man, and treated the girls like little children even as they grew up. His alcoholism also led to physical problems and when he was dying of cancer, he wouldn't let the girls in to see him in his emaciated condition.

When my father finally died I knelt at the foot of his grave and for the first time in my life felt close to him. I hoped somehow he could see me, if he were in heaven, and would know I was kneeling before him. I had a sense inside of me that the masks were gone, the facade was down. At last I was able to say, "I love you Daddy and I want you to receive my love."

At the age of twenty Paulette, appropriating some of her father's dreams, flew 2,000 miles away to become a glamorous airline attendant. She was extremely naive and expected everyone to care for her as her mother had. She was totally unprepared for the real world. She shared an apartment with two other girls, but it never occurred to her to contribute to the household.

One day a roommate said, "Paulette, I love you dearly, but you are undoubtedly the most selfish, self-centered person I have ever met."

Paulette looked at her in surprise and asked, "What are you saying? I don't understand."

Her friend explained, "Well, you never wash any of the dishes, you never pick up your clothes, you do your own thing and assume that we will do the rest."

How many mothers there are who, for their own hidden needs, wait on a child so completely that they nurture a person who has little sense of basic responsibility.

Paulette was irresponsible in areas other than housework and soon found herself pregnant. Although she didn't love the man involved, the thought of having an illegitimate child was so horrifying to her she could imagine no alternative.

My wedding day was one of the most depressing of my life. When I stood at the altar and told that minister that I would take this man for better or for worse, till death do us part, my heart sank to my feet. I felt, "My God, what have I gotten myself into?"

Well, what I got myself into was two years of agony. We didn't have even one happy moment that I can recall. The young man that I married had been raised in a home exactly like my own and was fresh from his little mommy's side. He too was totally unprepared for the real world.

I had some time to reflect during this marriage and I thought about all the things that had happened to me since I had left home. I had been walked over and plowed under by everyone and everything I had come in contact with. My attitude changed. I decided to fight back. If you can't beat them, join them. And so with the end of this marriage, I set out to do exactly that—to have a good time. I thought I was going to hell anyway because I was divorced, so I might as well enjoy myself on the way.

In Paulette's pursuit of pleasure she met another man who was no more emotionally stable than the first one. In retrospect Paulette says:

We tend to choose a mate according to what we think we're worthy of. An emotionally unhealthy person rarely has the courage to choose a truly healthy mate. So I selected a second one according to what I believed I deserved.

Friends tried to dissuade Paulette from this marriage, but she couldn't handle her three-year-old son alone and this man seemed willing to help. Although she was not in love with him, she was determined to make this marriage work. She needed a success in life and she wanted to live happily ever after.

The pressures of life fell heavily on this person who had never even had to wash a load of laundry. With a three-year-old son, a full-time job, and a new husband, Paulette, who estimates she was emotionally about twelve years old at that time, began taking pills to help her cope with each day.

Paulette already drank plenty when out partying, but until now she wasn't really dependent on it. As long as she had the pills, she could make it through the day. Paulette played hard at the marriage game, deceiving her husband, her friends, and even herself. To keep up this charade of happiness, she found herself needing more pills and more drinks until, with a snowball effect, she became addicted.

She had so little energy for her son that he began to show signs of neglect and cried out for her attention just as she had begged for her father's love. She took him to the doctors where he was diagnosed as hyperactive and given some pills. Paulette never found out if the drugs would help him because she took them herself.

Paulette looks back on this point in her life:

One day I stopped to think about my life. I admitted something to myself I had never admitted before: that people, places, and things were not my problem. I had been saying for years, "It is this husband; if I had a better husband I would be happy. If I had another job . . . It's this town. I need to get out of this town. I need to move. I need a new set of plans." It was always somebody else's fault that I wasn't happy.

Finally, I came face to face with the fact that my unhappiness was inside of me; it didn't have anything to do with those people out there. I began to see the path that I was on and the direction in which I was heading. I was drinking daily and taking more and more pills. I looked down this long road and I saw that if something didn't happen I was going to kill myself. Or did I have a choice? Was there another way?

I was not a very good fighter but deep down inside of me I gathered a strength that I hadn't had before and I chose life. I decided to get well no matter what it took. I chose the very best thing that I knew: a psychiatrist. I went to therapy twice a week for a year and a half. During this time my second marriage ended, but I was not alone for long. I met a man in therapy and we two mixed-up people began to live together.

During her one and a half years of therapy Paulette learned much about herself and why she was so incredibly insecure that she needed drugs and drinks to get through just one more day. She realized for the first time that her craving for her alcoholic father's attention was what led her to such poor choices in men.

The therapist knew she was drinking and taking pills and he showed her in medical books what this abuse was doing to her body and tried to frighten her. No matter what he said it wasn't enough to make her stop. One day he said to her, "Paulette, we've done all we can do for you. It's time you stopped coming."

Paulette couldn't believe her trusted therapist would throw her out into the street. She walked alone down the sidewalks of New York on this bright spring morning. The sky was blue, the sun was shining, and pots of flowers were by the curb. It was the type of day that would make anyone happy, but Paulette thought:

I've tried it all and there's no hope. I've been through therapy to understand myself and now that I know who I am the doctor doesn't want me to come back. I'm thirty years old and I have no joy, no peace, no zest for living. What's the point in staying alive?

Wondering if there was anything she hadn't tried, Paulette suddenly remembered a prayer group she'd heard about that met in a school building. She was convinced she wasn't worthy of a church with all her problems, but a group in a school might be all right.

She didn't know who the people were. She'd been told, "They sing songs to the Lord, praise him, study the Bible, and pray together." Although she didn't want to be rejected by a religious group, she was intrigued. So she took a chance and went.

Paulette observed the people she saw. They were a different group from any she'd been among before. They had a healthy love for each other. Their lives were in order, and they seemed to believe in something. Paulette tells us what happened.

I was desperate for the things those people had. I saw myself as the outcast from God and I had two raging battles going on inside of me. The first one said, "You have gone too far, you have done too much, you have committed too many sins. God can never forgive you." The other side of me thought, "Well perhaps if you could clean it up, maybe straighten out your act you could get going. Maybe if you got good enough, maybe then just possibly God might consider you. But if you could get good on your own, you would have already done it."

One day I met a young minister from an independent church down the street. He was aware of my living arrangement, but he had wisdom and didn't mention it to me. He did, however, say something very important: "Paulette, Jesus wants you right where you are. He doesn't want you to change a thing. He wants you to come to him just as you are."

Nobody had ever said that to me before. I didn't know that was an alternative. I doubted seriously that it could be that easy, but on the off chance that the minister was right, I thought I'd better try it. I asked the Lord to come into my heart even though I had a lot of unbelief and many, many doubts.

About two weeks later I had an opportunity to see a Christian film called The Gospel Road *by Johnny Cash. As I sat there and I saw Jesus hanging on that cross superimposed over New York City, something happened deep in my spirit that I couldn't explain. It pierced my heart and I could hardly wait to get home. I went into my bedroom, closed the door, and hit my knees. I said, "Jesus if you can do that for me, you can have it all."*

I would like to say that I got up from there totally delivered from all my problems, but that just wasn't the case. God's grace and mercy were beautiful in that first week, but I had a big problem. Being so dependent upon men, I couldn't tell this young man that he couldn't live with me anymore, but God took the situation right out of my hands. He brought salvation to that man within one week and made him so uncomfortable he just couldn't stay anymore.

It wasn't quite that easy with the little pills and the drinks. I needed the pills to get me up in the morning so I needed the drinks to bring me down at night. I thought, "What I've got to do is get away from these pills." For five years I had not believed that I could get through a day without them, so I began to pray that God would take away the need for the pills. Within four months God did miraculously take away my dependency on those pills.

But much to my surprise I found that the desire for alcohol didn't disappear. In fact, it probably grew worse because now I realized that I was dependent on it. And so I began to pray in earnest every day, "God, please don't let me take a drink today. Lord, please don't let me buy another bottle." Day after day I prayed and every morning as I would set out for my office I would have this resolve, I am not going to do it today. I'm not going to take a drink today, and I would battle all day with myself but I always knew by the time I left work that I was going to drink again. I was under such conviction that when I would go to the liquor store I would park my little Volkswagen around the back because I was afraid somebody was going to see me that knew me. When I would go in that liquor store I would feel like I had great neon lights, arrows pointing at me, "Alcoholic, drinker; she's got a problem."

Paulette still had a problem. Even though it was only half of her previous problem, she couldn't seem to become victorious. One weekend in February she and a girl friend decided to go on a weekend retreat. They'd never been to one before, but Paulette felt compelled to go even though there was a blizzard. The highway was closed and cars were slipping off the side. Paulette couldn't see ten feet ahead, but she kept driving.

When they arrived, each one was interviewed separately by the minister in charge about their progress on the Christian walk. As he talked with Paulette, he suddenly stopped and asked, "Does anyone in your family have a drinking problem?"

Paulette paused and then said, "Yes, they do."

The minister looked her straight in the eye, "Do you, by any chance, have a drinking problem?"

"Yes, I do."

He handed her a booklet from Alcoholics Anonymous and continued, "That is why God is always sending me people with drinking problems. I'm a recovered alcoholic myself."

"I'm not an alcoholic!" Paulette stated emphatically. "I just have a drinking problem."

The pastor nodded in understanding and poured out so much compassion and concern for her that weekend that she was able to go home and pour out her alcohol.

The prayer group sustained her and represented the Light of Christ to her. Even though they knew she still took a drink now and then—to show herself she wasn't an alcoholic—they encouraged her and told her she was going to make it. She was still fearful and one night told them she felt as if she were holding onto the hem of Jesus' garment and that any day the world would pull her so hard she'd let go and lose it all.

It was her mother who pulled her. She became ill and Paulette had to return to her home town to care for her. She left her support group behind and was far away where no one but her son seemed to care whether she lived or died. Her father was gone, her sister had left town, and within a few months her mother died. In her loneliness and depression she began to drink again. She had trouble sleeping at night and so she took some pills to help. Soon she realized what she was doing. She would kneel at the foot of her bed, shake her fist at the cross of Christ, and cry out:

How could you do this to me, God? I loved you, I trusted you, I leaned on you and this is where you have brought me. Why have you done this to me?

Paulette moved to Dallas where she sought help at an Alcoholics Anonymous group. The cure was not easy and she didn't sleep for one whole month. Each day she had to go to the group for support. When she felt she was going to die, someone would say, "If I made it, you can too." She couldn't face the reality of life without a drink.

Paulette also had a new job at a bank, but she could hardly stay awake. She couldn't tell her boss she was sleepy because she was trying to get sober. So she'd return to her group for sympathy and they'd send her home to take a warm vinegar bath. They had lots of empathy, but little sympathy.

During these difficult times Paulette met Lana Bateman (see chapter 15), who led Paulette through a time of counseling and prayer. The sense of God's forgiveness gave her emotional freedom for the first time. Lana taught her that God the Father was not like her father and that he loved her unconditionally, just the way she was. She began to accept the love of God and understand that he was not out to get her.

Lana recalls her initial meeting with Paulette:

> I will never forget the first time I saw Paulette. I opened the door and took a deep breath as I looked into a pair of large brown eyes filled with frenzy and pain. There was almost a sense of hopelessness about her and I expected this fragile soul to apologize for breathing before she had even gotten over the threshold.
>
> Our first hours together were filled with stories of futility and heartbreak. She had given up drugs and alcohol, wasn't that enough? Why was there such a deep well of emotional pain? If God wouldn't bring release, she didn't want to go on living.
>
> In God's time Paulette experienced emotional healing. She prayed and the process of stability began. It's been a mountain climbing experience for this frail beauty, as the bodily ravages of drugs and alcohol are not surmounted without dedication and difficulty.
>
> The struggles, however, have made the woman. Paulette now experiences victory upon victory as a life once turned inward reaches out to help the broken-hearted. Those who once avoided her eyes filled with agony and anger are now drawn to her sensitive servant's heart. Caring compassion for others has replaced distorted self-pity, and Paulette's continual growth and assurance are a miracle to behold.
>
> She's come a long way from that helpless, lonely, forlorn child and her growing confidence and stability make her a beacon of hope to all who've feared there might not be a road to release. Paulette's life parallels the legend of the thornbird, whose greatest hours of agony produced its most beautiful song. The melody of her life extends help to the hurting.

> A failure—the world might exclaim.
> A jewel in my crown, the Savior proclaims.
> For God turns our ashes to gold.
> And that which was helpless, transforms
> and makes whole.[4]

Paulette's reach for recovery has not been an easy one, but with God's transforming power and her determination she has overcome her double addiction. Today she dedicates much of her time to helping others through speaking, working as a prayer counselor for Philippian Ministries, and doing multi-level counseling for her church.

She concludes:

I was certainly not beautiful. I was anything but strong. And yet God has given me beauty and joy. He has put a song of praise in my mouth and has made me a strong and graceful oak for his own glory. My God changes not. What he has done for me he will do for anyone.

Paulette is always available to give HOPE to those whose lives are coming apart at the seams.

GEORGIA VENARD

Drug Addiction

From the time Dr. Timothy Leary told college students they could use mind-altering drugs to take trips to paradise, there has been a wild rush to high places. We adults would like to imagine that these flower children are still wandering barefoot through San Francisco, harmlessly tossing rose petals off the Golden Gate Bridge. We'd like to think drugs are not our problem; we'd like to look the other way.

Occasionally, we hear that a young person in our church is on drugs. We console the parents with Proverbs 22:6 and say, "You've brought him up right, he'll snap out of it when he's older." Seldom do we consider that some *adults* might be addicted and certainly it would never happen to us. But statistics show that the flower children have grown up, have responsible jobs, and many still use drugs.

Statistical information gathered by the Texas War on Drugs relates these shocking facts:

1. The illegal drug industry ranks in size with Mobil Oil as our second largest business—only Exxon is larger.
2. Cocaine is now the leading cash flow drug at 26–32 billion dollars a year.
3. The U.S. spends almost as much money on marijuana—18–26

31

billion a year—as it spends on imported oil. Marijuana is California's largest cash crop.[1]

According to a professional organization of pharmacists, Pharmacists Against Drug Abuse: "One-third of all kids in America use illegal drugs. In fact, one out of every eighteen high school seniors is using marijuana every day."[2]

Adults, perhaps some you know, are using drugs to pep them up and slow them down. The newest major problem is cocaine, derived from the leaf of the coca bush. There are 24 million estimated cocaine users in the United States, and Cocaine Anonymous—a spinoff of Alcoholics Anonymous—celebrated its second birthday on November 19, 1984 with about thirty chapters in the Los Angeles area.[3]

The June 4, 1984 issue of *Newsweek* notes: "All chemical addictions are different faces of the same demon, a craving so strong that it cannot be controlled despite its destructive consequences."[4]

Lest we think we are immune, Dr. Colter Rule writes in the May 1983 issue of *Good Housekeeping:*

Some addictions may be the result of a desire for love and attention that was not met, particularly in childhood. If the deprivation was too painful and pervasive, we may react by losing the ability to distinguish between our wants and our real needs. What's more, the hunger for love and attention may be pushed down into the subconscious where it may grow stronger and eventually emerge in the guise of an addictive urge.[5]

Recently I saw David Wilkerson, author of the bestseller *The Cross and the Switchblade,* being interviewed on a national telecast. The host asked him, "Give us some spectacular accounts of your heroin and cocaine addicts in the streets."

David answered, "I am more concerned with the many women who are on Valium and who are coming to me and saying, 'I don't know what to do.' They use drugs suggested by a doctor but abused by the person."

Any user of any drug risks becoming seriously involved but certain types of people are more susceptible than others. The *Los Angeles Times* states that there are:

So-called addictive personalities, who are characterized by traits such as impatience, perfectionism, loneliness, and compulsiveness. In a general profile, addicts also tend to be young—20–40—and upwardly mobile, fueling their fast-paced lives with the drug's chemical energy.[6]

Today's drug users are not only those lying around on park benches, they are business men and women, doctors and nurses, successful, ambitious, pressured people like you and me. One day in El Paso, while hiding away in a hotel to write, I talked with the breakfast waitress. She was efficient but seemed embittered. I asked, "Is this a bad day for you?"

"Every day is a bad day for me."

"Would you like to tell me about it?"

For twenty minutes she stood with coffee pot in hand and told me her troubles. She had come over from Germany and had married a charming American who, although she had not known it, had played around with drugs from the time he was nine years old. "He always seemed such fun and he was so relaxed" she said. "I had no idea he was an addict. He had a good job in Dallas, and we lived in an attractive apartment." She explained that she learned of his habit when he needed more expensive drugs and was spending over $200 a day. He quit his job and stopped supporting her and their baby. Since a regular salary couldn't handle his habit, he had to start dealing in drugs and smuggling cocaine over the border from Mexico. Soon he and his drug buddies were gathering in the apartment and she found stained spoons and used matches scattered everywhere. When she objected, he beat her up and she barely escaped with her life.

In tears she told me how she begged him to get help, but he always denied he had a problem. "I'm getting along fine in life and I have all these friends. It's you who's not social. Why don't you get help?"

Finally, when she was working two waitress jobs to feed the baby and save up money to protect herself, the landlord came with the bill for back rent. She pulled together what she had saved, paid the rent, and bought a one-way ticket to El Paso.

I would have done anything to help him, but he blamed everything on me and would never accept responsibility for his own actions. Since

I left I found out he beat up the lady next door and she died, so I guess I'm lucky I'm still alive. It's left me a bitter woman and I'll never love or trust anyone ever again.

Our case history for this chapter is Georgia Venard, an attractive, intelligent nurse from Phoenix who could be the woman sitting next to you in church. You would have no idea she had a problem. You would smile; she would smile. "Praise the Lord, Sister."

One Sunday before church, the Sunday school teacher, having heard of Georgia's drug difficulties, called and boldly asked her to address the class of well-dressed, secure Christians. He planned to use a video about addictions and thought she would add a live touch to the program. "Take twenty to thirty minutes to share your testimony and tell the people what happened to you."

Georgia prepared a message for the allotted time but when she got to church, the teacher had decided to limit her to fifteen minutes. During the church service she mentally adjusted what she would say, cutting her message in half. As she walked into the class, the teacher said, "I think ten minutes will be enough."

The video was shown and the teacher, obviously wishing he'd never brought this subject up at all, introduced Georgia and said she could have two minutes to tell about drug addiction. "Two minutes? What happened to the thirty minutes? What can I possibly say in two minutes?"

As these questions flashed through Georgia's head, she moved quickly up the aisle, talking as she walked.

I know what you are thinking, "Why do we need a message on drugs?" Let me tell you why. It can happen to you. If you were like me, you grew up with the idea that drunkards and addicts were just people in the streets, down in the gutter. They were staggering, wore tattered clothes, and had blurring eyes. "Wait a minute," you say. "We are in the church, we are all Christians here. We dress nicely, we shave, we comb our hair." I know, but it can happen to you. You say, "How do you know?" I know because I sat beside you in this church for eight long years and not one of you knew. I sang in your choir, I played the piano, I did special music, I knelt at your altar. As I sat in the pew of this church I'd often think, "If they only knew."

Georgia's two minutes were over and she walked out the door wondering if she had really said anything of significance. A woman walked up to her hesitantly, grabbed her by the arm, and with tears in her eyes said, "I probably shouldn't tell you this, but I am a nurse and the same thing is wrong with me."

Before the week was out three more people quietly identified themselves to Georgia as having drug-related problems.

How did a good Christian lady like Georgia get herself in trouble? She grew up in the church and was there every Sunday morning and evening. On Wednesdays she attended prayer meeting. She went to church camp and recommitted her life at every revival. From sixth grade on she went to Christian schools and even majored in theology in college. Georgia sang in a trio with her sisters from the time she was a child and she followed all of her denominational instructions. In spite of her near perfect Christian life, Georgia never felt she was good enough for God.

I can't tell you the times I went to the altar and begged God's forgiveness. I followed all the rules they gave me, yet I still had this empty, hollow place that kept hurting and I felt unforgiven and unaccepted. I sang "Jesus Loves Me, This I Know," but I didn't really know.

I soon found growing up that I didn't fit anywhere. I repeatedly cried myself to sleep at night because I was sure no one loved me. I felt rejected as if there was something wrong with me. Somewhere along in my early teen years, I decided that I could do nice things for people and that would obligate them to love me. They would have no choice. I began conforming to what others wanted me to do. If I could achieve and prove that I wasn't bad, then someone would love me. In my childhood and my teen years, my parents fought a lot and I thought it was my fault.

There's one example that is very vivid in my mind. I was a small child and I remember my mother and father had a fight; I don't know what it was about but they weren't sleeping together that night and my mother informed me that I had to go sleep with my father in their bedroom while she stayed in mine. I was scared; I had seen my father angry many times and I didn't understand what this fight was about. I remember going several times down to that bedroom trying to get the nerve enough to go in there and get in bed with him but I couldn't make it. After a few tries I went back and said to Mom, "I can't do it." She said, "You've got to do it, now just go down there and get in bed." I made one last try. I got to the door, got on my hands and knees, and crawled across that floor. As I did, my father jumped out of bed, scaring me half to death, and ran into the bedroom and started fighting with Mom again. He grabbed the shotgun and said he was going to kill himself. He started out with my mother after him. They struggled on the stairs, both fell down, and he ran out into the night still waving the gun.

I huddled, terror-stricken, at the top of the stairs, wondering if I'd ever see my father again. As my mother turned and saw me, she called up, "It's all your fault. If you'd done what I told you in the first place this never would have happened!"

Surely, the mother in her own hurt and anger did not mean to place the blame for her problems onto Georgia. And it probably didn't pass through her troubled mind that Georgia would never forget those words, "It's all your fault." How easy it is for parents to blame their children, not realizing at the time how indelibly their words are written.

In Georgia's quest for acceptance and affection she fell in love with a boy named Bill who looked just like her father. Georgia was excited to have a father-figure who would really love her. At eighteen Georgia became engaged and began plans for the wedding. Imagine someone to care for her forever. Then came the night when she caught Bill kissing her best girl friend and the engagement was over.

It must have been my fault, she thought. *If I'd done what I should have done, this never would have happened.*

As Georgia was working to recover from this heartbreak, her mother chose a young man for her to marry. He was just what her mother wanted for a son. But when Georgia wouldn't agree to be his wife, he married her youngest sister. Later when they divorced, Georgia was told, "If you'd married him as your mother had instructed you to do, this never would have happened to your sister." Once again, it was all her fault.

Georgia's mother became ill with cancer and was given one year to live. Georgia couldn't bear the thought of losing her mother and she cared for her carefully and lovingly. Within the first month of illness, her mother suddenly died. Georgia had given her a needed injection an hour before and a relative stated, "If you hadn't given her that shot, she'd be alive today."

Yes, Georgia, it's all your fault.

Georgia's life was wrapped in a cloak of guilt. She kept looking for someone who would accept her as she was and stop putting the blame for life on her. Finally, at twenty-one, Georgia met Carroll Venard, whom she married on Christmas Day. She would now live happily ever after.

Within a year she had a baby boy and five years later they adopted a little girl. She had three people to love and three people who needed her attention. In trying to show God how good she was, Georgia became heavily involved in church activities. She bought clothes for the poor and distributed them. She took charge of the church music and played both the piano and the organ. She was the youth director for several years and a substitute teacher at the Christian day school.

Georgia still didn't feel she was doing enough to benefit mankind. So, while her children were still young, she went to nursing school. What better profession in which to minister to those who really needed her, whose very lives depended upon her touch? Where else would people be so obligated to give love and credit for her care?

Georgia never wanted to hear "It's your fault" again, so she studied, worked, cared, and loved her way through nursing school. She found she had a natural healing spirit—she could walk into a hospital room and calm the crying patients, leaving them in comfort.

Georgia was a high-achiever. Such behavior is often the sign of a hidden, almost desperate, need for acceptance and approval. "I'll do everything bigger and better. It'll never be my fault again."

Georgia was chosen for the executive board of the Lupus Foundation and became its educational director while she was working full-time as an RN in a Phoenix hospital. She counseled patients and families of the terminally ill and taught at Phoenix College. She and twenty other nurses perfected a new dialysis treatment and she was in charge of the equipment. She wrote an article on this new method which was published in an international nursing magazine. A staff doctor was so impressed with Georgia's ability that he volunteered to put her through medical school and set her up in practice afterwards.

What more could Cinderella want? Surely she would live happily ever after.

At this high point in her life, Georgia checked into the hospital for some surgery. To ease her discomfort during the painful recovery, Georgia was given the common pain-killer Demerol. Not only did this relieve her pain, but it gave her a feeling of confidence, of well-being. Because she was a nurse, Georgia had convenient access to this drug. And because of the relaxation its use provided, Georgia kept giving herself shots of Demerol. She recalls:

Long after the physical pain of surgery was past, I was using that drug to cover other pain.

Being extremely careful of where and when she used this drug, Georgia hid her growing addiction from her co-workers. While her husband knew she took Demerol occasionally, he had no idea how often. As Georgia became aware of her growing need for this drug, she began to feel guilty. God would surely get her for this. She told herself she didn't really need Demerol and she could stop anytime; therefore, she didn't really have a problem.

Georgia thought of telling her pastor, but she knew he'd been brought up like her. He'd be so shocked she'd feel more guilty. She felt like an unsaved sinner sitting in church, but she was afraid not to go for fear God would condemn her.

One day Georgia decided to call the local hot line for drug abuse, but as she reached for the receiver she remembered her friend Barbara was one of the counselors. What if she answered and recognized her voice?

Georgia didn't want to discuss her problem with her husband who was on the local police force. He spent time apprehending local drug addicts and surely she didn't want him to know he was living with one of them.

Then, on Christmas Day 1980, Georgia looked at her husband and sensed she was losing him.

There were no words exchanged between us, I just looked at him and something in his eyes told me he was through. I didn't blame him and I knew it was all my fault.

Georgia tried to figure out how to end this charade. She could leave. There was no reason to stay. The family could live without her—except for her two-year-old grandson. How could anyone explain to him where Grandma had gone? Georgia called out to God, *Whatever's wrong with me, help me at any cost!*

Overwhelmed with guilt, Georgia reached for the only answer to her hurt and shame, more drugs. During the next six weeks she took heavy doses that could have killed her had she continued. As with so many good people who never intended to get into trouble, Georgia's compulsion led her to steal from the hospital pharmacy and to cover her problem. Georgia thought no one would know what she was doing, but one night as the clock turned twelve, Georgia turned a corner in the hospital and ran into a wall made up of the pharmacist, the doctor on duty, the head of the hospital, and the state narcotics officer. As she stood before them, they stripped her of her job and her purpose for life. They arrested her for stealing drugs from the pharmacy. She stood emotionally naked. The humiliation, the shame, the remorse, the guilt! It was all her fault.

At three o'clock in the morning, the arresting officer called Georgia's husband and said, "We've got your wife on narcotics charges. We need you to come and get her." Georgia was so ashamed to stand before Carroll and admit she had stolen drugs. The officer said to Carroll, "She's going to need lots of love."

When Georgia heard this she thought:

No one's ever loved me when I was good, how can he love me when I'm so bad? If only I hadn't done this, I wouldn't be in the mess I'm in. It's all my fault.

All the way home Georgia waited for her husband to "let her have it," but he said nothing. When they entered their living room, Carroll sat down in a large chair and held out his arms. Georgia fell into them and felt his warm love around her as she'd never felt it before. He wrapped her up as a father does a little child and suddenly she sensed he loved her as she was, as a sinner totally to blame for her situation. He loved her unconditionally.

For the first time in forty-one years, Georgia felt forgiving love. Carroll had tried to love her before, but her guilt-sick soul had never been able to receive it.

That night Carroll became to her an image of God the Father, forgiving and loving with no strings attached.

In her rehabilitation program at St. Luke's Hospital, Georgia learned that drugs were not her problem. They were the symptoms of a life in which she had always felt at fault and in which she had carried the burdens of everyone else's mistakes. The counselors showed her the collection of resentments she had strung together and she realized the weight of guilt she'd carried. She'd caused her father's anger, her sister's unhappy marriage, and her mother's death. For the first time she saw these problems weren't her fault; she saw that she had been driven to achieve to show God she wasn't all bad.

Georgia says she cried for weeks, but many of her tears were floods of relief.

While in the hospital Georgia befriended a young addict named Tommy and she shared the gospel of Jesus Christ with him and told him of God's love and forgiveness. One afternoon Georgia was so tense, she headed for the chapel to beg God for release. As she went to the door, twenty-four-year-old Tommy, addicted to heroin and cocaine, asked if he could go with her. When they got to the chapel, Georgia threw herself on the altar and sobbed and sobbed and sobbed. Tommy didn't know what to do, but he had compassion and he put his arms around her.

"What's the matter, Georgia?"

"I need to be forgiven, Tommy, I'm so bad. I need forgiveness."

"Don't you believe what you told me just two days ago? You gave me a verse that said if I'd confess to God, he'd forgive me."

As Georgia cried, Tommy went to the back of the chapel, picked up a Gideon Bible, handed it to her and said, "Here, find that verse and read it to yourself."

Georgia opened to 1 John 1:9 and read out loud, "If we confess our sins, he is faithful and just to forgive us our sins, and to cleanse us from all unrighteousness" (KJV).

As Georgia and Tommy knelt together they both trusted that God would forgive them and cleanse them—from all unrighteousness.

From that point on, Georgia knew she was going to make the long uphill struggle. She went back through her life and forgave those who had placed guilt upon her. She began a healing process that will never end. Georgia recalls:

There was a gradual knowledge of God's love and then this over-whelming sense that God accepts me unconditionally. After those years of not being able to feel forgiveness and love, this new freedom from fear was something I can't describe. Sometimes it still hurts, sometimes there's a cramp of resentment from the past, sometimes a shooting pain of guilt. But I am reminded of God's love and what he has done for me.

You may not have experienced the agony of drug addiction or feel that there is a need for the church to address this issue, but Georgia has found an overwhelming reaction to her testimony and to her heartfelt desire to minister this hope to the Body of Christ.

She recently spoke at a church retreat, intending to bring three messages on the anguish of and victory over drug abuse. As she completed her second session, the audience responded with such intense need that Georgia was forced to cancel her last address and simply minister to those hurting hearts and answer their questions. One could almost feel the relief that swept through the audience as many realized for the first time that someone understood, someone cared, and someone had walked the same road of defeat and desperation.

How badly we all want to say, "Not in our church. It doesn't happen to good people." How quickly we crash into a heap when the reality hits home that our upstanding congregation does in fact contain some who are victims of this insidious bondage.

Georgia's story is not unique. There may be both men and women in your church buried behind painful expressions and frightened silence thinking no one would understand. The church often adopts a system of denial not unlike that of the addict. "If you ignore it, it will go away." Sadly, this is not true and those who are struggling among us sink ever deeper into futility and despair.

Georgia's message calls believers to accountability and pleads with God's people to reach out, to help, to comfort, and to love those who are drowning in the raging storm of drug abuse.

As for yourself, check what you're putting into your body. Those harmless pills that make you happy, that smooth out the rough edges of life, could become habit forming. Put the pills away for another day, for in the area of addictions, a stitch in time saves more than nine.

3

PATSY CLAIRMONT

Emotional Instability and Fear

Emotional instability can be caused by any of the *present* stresses in our lives or any of the *past* situations that were not dealt with at the time. National figures vary from one out of six to one out of three women who are in some way unstable. Often emotional problems lead to fears, which, carried to extremes, become phobias. A recent government study states, "About 20% of American adults suffer from some form of mental illness in any given 6-month period. 13.1 million suffer from anxiety disorders or phobias."[1]

Since I have never been a fearful person, I had no idea that some people were afraid to go out of the house until I met a pastor's wife who suffered from fear at one of our CLASSes. Her husband had to sit with her in the same room and she had not driven a car in fifteen years. She had summoned up every ounce of courage she had to attend CLASS, and for the first time she tearfully shared her fears in the small group session. Her parishioners had not known of her problem. They had felt she was cold and aloof because she socialized with no one. As this hurting woman poured out her need, the ladies quickly changed their criticism to compassion and the first step to her healing had begun: She admitted she had a problem and needed help.

Newsweek calls the 80s the age of anxiety and proclaims phobias the disease of the decade.

What schizophrenia was to the 1960s, what depression and burnout were to the 1970s, phobias are to the 1980s—not just a diagnosis, but a metaphor for the human condition, a frame of reference for viewing a whole landscape of human emotion and behavior. Robert L. DuPont, director of Washington's Center of Behavioral Medicine, calls phobias the malignant disease of the what-ifs, the exponential growth of imaginary disasters that can choke off rational thought. It is not surprising, therefore, to find them flourishing in an age in which the future itself dangles from a conditional clause.[2]

One in nine Americans has some kind of phobia, making this the country's second most common mental-health problem after alcoholism. "This statistic becomes even more impressive when one considers that many alcoholics are suspected of being phobics who merely mask their problem with drink."[3]

The National Institute of Mental Health states that one adult in twenty suffers from the most serious variety of this disease —agoraphobia. This composite word is derived from the Greek words *phobia*, meaning "fear" and *agora* meaning "marketplace."[4] Agoraphobia is literally a fear of the marketplace. Is it coincidental that so many agoraphobics have their first panic attack in a supermarket?

One woman said, "The food around me seemed piled so high, as if the aisles were closing in, and my head would start to swirl, and I'd just have to leave my cart right where it was and get out of there."[5]

As I became more aware of the grip of phobias on so many lives today, I began to study and listen to comments which might give me added information on this problem. On March 13, 1985, I turned on a TV talk show, "Alive and Well" out of Los Angeles. Dr. Cary Hamlin defined agoraphobia as "unexplained intense fear symptoms." And the location of a person's first panic attack becomes a place of dread and fear. He will not return there and soon he will go nowhere.

Robert Vaughn, one of Dr. Hamlin's patients, explained that he had his first panic attack in a supermarket. He thought he was going to die right there. An ambulance took him to the hospital where he stayed three weeks "dying of heart attacks." For ten years he had repeated "heart attacks" and his whole family became fearful that he might die at any minute.

After these years of misdiagnosis, which Dr. Hamlin said is common, someone took Robert to Dr. Hamlin who began to treat him with drugs and therapy. As the doctor said, "It is a brain chemical abnormality which needs medication. Inderal stops panic attacks and ten million people in this country take it."

Others say it is a self-centered problem that keeps the person focused on what might happen to him and indifferent to relationships with others. *Newsweek* says:

A phobic is as egocentric as a cat. People who spend years trudging up and down stairs because they are deathly afraid of elevators don't mind if their beloved children ride in them. A phobia is fear looking at itself in the mirror.[6]

George Sweeting, president of Moody Bible Institute, wrote in his column "Talking It Over":

Life was meant to be an exciting adventure; yet for millions of people, the adventure is haunted by fear. God is against the kind of fear that burdens—the one that chills, freezes, and ultimately kills. Again and again in scripture God's first words are "Fear not" or "Don't be afraid." The key to overcoming such fear is faith. God loves you, and He holds the future. If we fear, we do not have faith. If we have faith, we cannot live in fear. For years David was hounded by King Saul. But God's servant found help: "I sought the Lord, and He answered me, and delivered me from all my fears" (Psalm 34:4). In the same psalm, David adds, "The angel of the Lord encamps around those who fear Him, and rescues them" (v.7). Put God first in your life and He will deliver you from fear.[7]

Now that I've given you an overview of emotional instability, let's look at the life of Patsy Clairmont, a close friend and staff member of CLASS.

I first saw Patsy at a retreat in Michigan. I was sitting in the audience awaiting my time to speak and looking over the women sitting in a straight line of chairs on the stage. There was a similarity among these attractive Christian ladies with one exception. One of the women looked so little up there, so unsophisticated, so blank-faced with no make-up. Her hair seemed the same color as her skin and so did her dress. She seemed somehow out of place and I wondered what she was going to do. As the program began I couldn't take my eyes off this home-spun girl who was soon introduced as "Patsy Clairmont, who will now do our book reviews."

At the sound of her name it was as if a master switch had been thrown and Patsy was turned on. I'd never seen such an instant transformation. She jumped up from her chair, grabbed a pile of books, and rushed to the lectern, which swallowed her up until she almost disappeared. After settling her books, she stepped out to the side where we could see her and began speaking. Her first line was so hysterical it brought applause from the three thousand women in the auditorium. As my mother would say, "I sat up and took notice."

Patsy's face was like Red Skelton's. It seemed made of rubber as it quickly changed from one humorous expression to another. I was fascinated with her comic talent and great sense of timing. Each book she reviewed sounded more compelling than the last and I could hardly wait to rush to the book room and buy them all. Her hilarious closing line brought a wave of laughter that started in row one and swept up through the balcony, followed by a second wave of excited applause. I knew I had seen the birth of a star. As Patsy sat down, the switch went off and she blended quietly into the backdrop.

I invited Patsy to come to California to attend the first CLASS we'd ever done. Such talent needed to be seen outside Kalamazoo, Michigan.

"Would you like to attend a seminar for speakers?" I asked.

"I have been looking for direction in my speaking. I would love to come."

I was excited at the prospect of working with Patsy for I had seen a magic button that had turned on an entire audience. Patsy came to CLASS and everyone who met her fell in love with her engaging personality and unique humor. Patsy quickly learned to outline her messages, to turn her humor into deep truth, and to reach the hearts of the people. She became my first CLASS staff member because she learned my material quickly and delivered it with her own special style.

As our staff grew, petite and precious Patsy became our pet. As long as there was an audience she was the CLASS clown, entertaining on stage or in the motel room with equal ease. But when attention would be turned away from her, Patsy's switch would turn off and she would drop behind a quiet wall. We began to wonder if we knew the real Patsy.

I knew Patsy liked spontaneous speaking, so one day I asked her to come up and help me with a CLASS lesson. We were to explain to the group the value of using examples from your childhood to give color to your message. Patsy's mind seemed to go blank and she told me later, "I can't remember my childhood, not one Christmas or one birthday."

As we discussed Patsy's lack of memory, Lana Bateman (see chapter 15) explained that this loss could mean either an emotional trauma had taken place or her childhood was personally so negative for some reason that Patsy's memory blanked it out. Patsy appeared to be two different personalities: a hilarious *Sanguine* when "on stage" and a withdrawn *Melancholy* when "turned off."[8]

Lana led the questioning and we learned that Patsy had lived the past dreaming of a future that never came.

As a child I dreamed that one day I'd be a ballerina or a stewardess, but what I grew up to be was a failure.

When Patsy was in high school, she dropped out and ran away from home. Her rebellion led her into many negative situations. To show she could control her own life, she started smoking, drinking, and dancing the nights away. Her favorite song was "Born to Lose."

Then Patsy met Les. He seemed so strong and she sensed his stability would bring emotional balance to her life, so Patsy became a teenage wife. But instead of being swept off to a castle by Prince Charming, Patsy found herself in a terrible tenement complete with rats for pets. When her Aunt Elvira came to visit she grabbed everything she owned and went home with her. Patsy had run away again. Les left for military duty in Germany, and they weren't reunited until eighteen months later.

Patsy remembers the birth of her first son, Marty.

When they placed that baby in my arms I looked at him and thought, "Patsy, this is the first right thing you have ever done." I looked again and knew in the very depth of my heart that there had to be a God for a creation to be so perfect. I counted every toe and every finger and checked the ears and was amazed at this little life that I held.

The next week, I went back to church, walked up to the front, and asked God to take over my life. There was an initial change;

there was a hope that came into my heart. I can remember the day so clearly because when I left that church I thought to myself, "I have never seen the sky so blue. I have never seen the grass so green."

My mom lived on a lake and I had always hated that lake because I felt it was cold and ugly. Somehow it frightened me and I never would go near it. I went home that day to her house and walked around to the front. I looked out and, for the first time, I thought it was beautiful. There was such excitement in my heart as I antici-pated new hope for my life. "Maybe I can make it." Soon I fell back into the old habit patterns, things that consumed the very joy of Jesus in my life.

Patsy had made a sincere commitment to the Lord, but the "everydayness of living" overwhelmed her. She was still an emo-tional child trying to live an adult existence and it wasn't working. She had a low self-image and she didn't think life was fair.

What she didn't realize was that she had a deep need to be in control of her life, yet she made choices that put her into slavery. She began to blame God for her circumstances and her emotions fluctuated between anger and fear.

One day she grabbed up Marty's little chair and threw it at her husband. Les caught the rocker just before it hit him in the face. Patsy was startled at what she'd done; she began to tremble with fear and she sank into her first panic attack.

Remembering this time in her life Patsy says:

There are two types of people: Those who when they wake up in the morning say, "Good morning Lord!" and those who wake up and say, "Good Lord, it's morning." I was one of the latter and I skipped a lot of the mornings of my life because they made the day too long.

My doctor told me, "You're like an ostrich; every time it gets hard you want to go in and cover up your head." It was the only way I knew to escape the dread, the disorder, the depression—the dread of another fear-filled day, the disorder and chaos in my home, the depression of hopelessness in life.

Oh, how hard that was for me to wake up in the morning already filled with fear, this ominous thing that I could not touch but that seemed to surround me on all sides. I would think, "I haven't even done anything yet and already it's hard for me to open my eyes and face yet another day." The dread was consuming my energy, the disorder was obvious in my home, in my mind, and in my emotions, and the depression was like a constant companion that had moved in and become my roommate.

Patsy's panic attacks increased and Les would rush her to the hospital where the doctors would give her injections to calm her down. No diagnosis was ever made so Patsy tried to analyze her problems. She realized her anger and her fear were partners, one followed the other closely.

The panic attacks were so frightening that I began to feel like I was allergic to my anger, so I tried to push the anger down. As I pushed down the unresolved anger and my unrelenting guilt, what came forth from my life was unreasonable fear.

The anger had been seething within Patsy from childhood, when she had first realized she was not in control. The guilt had been added when she became a Christian and knew she should be living a clean and joyful life. But instead of depending upon the Lord, Patsy became more dependent upon people and medication. Because of her constant fear, Patsy soon became addicted to tranquilizers in an effort to keep herself calm, stable, and free from attacks. She also became a heavy smoker. Patsy would do anything that would blot out reality if only for a short time. Her mother came to help Les take care of her and soon Patsy was strangling them both, draining them of any life of their own. She was grabbing onto their stability and trying to ingest it into her own spirit.

I seemed to be spiraling down deeper and deeper into this darkness. As I would have one fear and give in to that, it would call its friends, "Over here, you guys!" There would be more and more and more and so it went from being afraid of heights and storms and riding in cars and hospitals and elevators and crowds of people and being all alone. Soon I was not driving a car anymore and I found myself afraid to leave home.

Although the term "agoraphobia" was unknown to Patsy at that time, she was surely in its grips. She had withdrawn from normal life and for two years seldom left her home. She was a self-imposed prisoner with her mother and husband alternating as wardens. At this point in her life, Patsy drank ten pots of black coffee a day, smoked two packs of cigarettes, and took four Librium to keep herself under control. When her anger threw her into a panic attack, she would get so enraged she couldn't breathe and would have to go to the hospital. Here she would be given a shot of Demerol which would knock her out and arrest the attack.

People in her church were concerned but they didn't know what to do. The pastor had no experience dealing with instability and agoraphobia and after awhile the parishioners just avoided the problem.

Patsy grew worse and her doctor finally suggested she attend a meeting of Recovery, Inc., a self-help program founded by a Jewish doctor, Abraham Low. This was a difficult thought as Patsy feared having a panic attack and having to make a quick trip to the hospital. One night Patsy, in desperation, had Les take her to the Recovery class.

Although her church had no answers, there were some who criticized her going to a secular program conducted by a Jewish doctor. But it was in this warm, accepting group that Patsy found help. The first night the people in the program explained that her situation was distressing but not dangerous. Somehow that simple thought seemed to settle Patsy's emotions. They gave her a plan and offered her HOPE. She remembers them saying, "Nervous people strive to be exceptional but fear that they are not even average."

That statement made sense to Patsy. Because she had run away from home and never finished high school, she felt below average. Her suppressed anger and guilt had led to fear and her self-worth had died a slow death. She had tried to be somebody, but her efforts had failed and she had reached for people and pills to make her forget how insignificant and unstable she felt.

From that first meeting of Recovery, Patsy knew there were people in the world who were like her and who really understood what she had been going through. One of the great values of any recovery or support group is that welcome flood of relief when you first know someone else has been there and really understands.

There was no instant cure, but the group provided stability and suggested positive thoughts to replace her fears. As her emotions began to stabilize, Patsy emerged from her self-exile and dared to see some of her old friends again. She recalls:

People initially liked me, but in the long haul they couldn't deal with me. They couldn't handle the ups and downs, the roller-coaster emotions, the changes in my personality. There were too many extremes. My highs were too high and unstable, my lows were too deep and too dark. It had become difficult and people had moved away.

After I began to get a handle on my symptoms, my friend Mary Ann called and with sensitivity said to me, "Patsy, I don't want you to answer this question or give me a first response. I'm going to present an idea and I want you to ask God what he wants you to do about it." I suddenly became responsible to God instead of just to Mary Ann. I could have said no easily to her but I had to be a little more careful about talking to God. She asked me if I would go to a weekend retreat.

For someone with agoraphobia that was a major decision—to leave the safety of my home, to make sure I had enough tranquilizers to be in control of the situation, to purposely put myself in the midst of over three thousand women. Just the thought of hours in a car to reach my destination frightened me, because to go from my home to the grocery store was a major trip and I could only go if my husband drove me.

When Patsy took this situation seriously to the Lord, he answered, "Go!" This thought so frightened her that she searched for a safer solution, "I'll ask Les," she thought.

"He'll not want to release a treasure like this."

As she asked, Les was singing, "I deserve a break today," and he instantly said, "Yes." Les encouraged her to go and he was so hopeful that Patsy might be able to leave the house for a weekend with friends without having a panic attack.

Patsy took her first big chance since starting Recovery and went to the retreat. She stuck close to Mary Ann and listened intently to the speakers. She heard in Romans 12:2, "Do not be conformed to the world but be transformed." How she needed that wand of transformation. The verse said she could have a "renewed mind that would prove the good, acceptable, and perfect will of God."

During that weekend Patsy learned for the first time how to appropriate the word of God into her own life and pray for a renewed mind. Within a year Patsy quit smoking, cut down on coffee, and was easing off the tranquilizers. She was not hospitalized for panic attacks again and she was studying the Bible and reading every Christian book she could find.

In the past, Patsy had tried to tell Les that he should be a Christian like her, but when he looked at her life, he'd ask, "Why?" At the end of that year, as Les saw the dramatic changes in Patsy, he knelt down in their living room and asked the Lord Jesus to come into his heart and make him the kind of man God wanted him to be.

A transformed life is a greater witness than the most eloquent of words.

When I first met Patsy, I had no idea she was working to overcome her large collection of fears. I didn't know her first trip to California took every ounce of courage and constant prayer to even get her on the plane. She jokes about that first flight now and remembers how she looked up before boarding and saw "A.A." on the side of the plane. "Dear God," she said, "make that American Airlines and not Alcoholics Anonymous!"

As I became aware of Patsy's problems and as the CLASS staff fell in love with her delightful personality, our combined concern and compassion gave her the freedom to verbalize her fears and the willingness to share her progress with others. Patsy has put together her "Seven Steps to Stability" so that others will have a plan to follow and HOPE for victory.

PATSY'S STEPS

There are always miraculous stories of people whose addictions or fears were removed overnight and we should always pray for this to happen. However, accepting miracles as the norm not only prevents the patient from proper counsel, but also heaps new guilt upon their present guilt by making them feel God didn't find them worthy of this healing power.

Many good people have somehow gotten into trouble. What can be done about these hurting women? Where can they turn for help and for hope? *Good Housekeeping,* in the May 1983 issue, asks:

Do you ever feel paralyzed with anxiety or troubled by excessive guilt? Are you often tired, dejected, unable to think? Are you afraid of heights or elevators or crowds? If so, you are not alone. In fact, if you don't feel some turmoil in today's world, you are not normal. Anyone who thinks she can get through life free of emotional problems is kidding herself.[9]

If YOU have a problem today,
If YOU are hurting,
If YOU need help and HOPE, read and apply Patsy's "Seven Steps to Stability" and start your life on the mend.

STEP 1: SEEK GODLY COUNSEL

It's human nature to want to fix our own problems without letting anyone know we have them. To seek counsel seems to be an admission of weakness. If you are full of fear, it is almost impossible to tell another person how you feel for fear he or she will laugh at you, or worse yet, tell you it's all in your head and you should snap out of it. The agoraphobic already knows, "It's all in my head" and the fact that pills won't cure it is even more frightening. Patsy describes the feeling this way.

Picture a child in a little house that has only one window and that window has a crack in it so that everything she sees is distorted. She knows no other view and all of life has a big crack in it. That's what it's like for those of us who are emotionally upset. We view life through the fragmentation of our mind and our future has a fearful crack in it.

How do we repair the crack before the whole window disintegrates? Patsy started with the Recovery program that let her know she was not alone, that others really did understand how she felt. One of the greatest benefits of any support group is the relief found when the troubled person realizes, perhaps for the first time, that she is not the only person in the world with this affliction.

Next, Patsy went to the retreat and learned from godly women how to make the words of the Bible come alive in her own life. She put into practice what she learned and began to see changes. She read what others suggested and prayed with those who cared.

Paulette, whose story is told in chapter one, went to Alcoholics Anonymous where she found supportive people who held her up when she didn't think she could live another day. She received love, encouragement, and prayer from a Christian group who continued to pray for her even after she had moved away.

Georgia, whose story is told in chapter two, stayed in St. Luke's Hospital where trained nurses moved her through the painful steps of withdrawal. Almost as soon as she came home, people sought her counsel and she started her "Tuesday Group" for mutual support, which still meets each week.

We should note that even though each of these hurting women was an active Christian at the time of her great need, the first and most important counsel in each case was not found within the church.

As you can well imagine from knowing about Patsy's past diet of coffee, cigarettes, and tranquilizers, her health was far below normal. She had allergies to everything, she had pains that rotated throughout her body, and she was exhausted much of the time. She had ulcerative colitis, and upon entering a room she would check for the nearest ladies' room and sit close to that exit.

One day, at a conference, I dared mention her health and her lack of stamina. She was immediately defensive and told me her doctor said there was no hope for her ever being better and she just had to live with her ailments.

I asked her if she taught in her Bible study that with God all things were possible and she replied, "Of course."

"Then don't you think God could do something with your body?"

I told her of my nutritionist in California and suggested she go to see her the next time she was in town. Patsy's reaction was, "Well, I know it wouldn't work." How natural it is for us to shrug off advice we don't like with the assumption that "it wouldn't work."

Patsy went back to her room and prayed to God for wisdom. His reply? "Sing a new song."

Before checking out of the hotel the next day, Patsy left a note on my pillow, "Thank you for loving me enough to give me advice when I didn't want to hear it and for reminding me that 'with God all things are possible.' "

Patsy went to Dr. Starr, who put her on a program to restore her body and she has been climbing slowly ever since.

Paulette says, "If a person has been on alcohol or drugs for long, they probably have physical problems that need help. They must be put on a sound nutritional program to help heal their damaged bodies."

As Patsy saw the benefits of being open to suggestions, she became excited about having my daughter Marita do a color analysis for her, help her establish a style in clothing, and show her how to use make-up.

A counselor friend of mine in El Paso, Sharon Ferrell Rios, feels personal appearance can have a direct impact on one's mental health. So she assists her clients with inner growth as all therapists strive to do. Part of Sharon's therapy may include helping her client choose a new outfit, a new hairdresser, or new make-up. Sometimes she also helps them work on improving their speaking voices or on minimizing distracting mannerisms. "Improving outer appearance," says Sharon, "may be just the catalyst needed to initiate the change process. A troubled mind should first focus on simple areas of improvement."

Although Patsy was already an avid reader and book reviewer, she recognized her lack of education had left her without a background in English grammar and vocabulary and she asked for instruction. I taught her one principle at a time. Once she was using it correctly, we'd move on to the next. As she gained confidence in her use of the language, she studied *Word Wealth* to increase her vocabulary and began reading *Bartlett's Familiar Quotations* for pleasure.

Oh, what God can do with an open mind! Whatever your problem may be today, know that with God all things are possible. Whether it's your mind, your body, your clothing, or your education, there is HOPE for you. When you seek godly counsel, counselors will appear. When you have a teachable spirit, teachers will arrive.

STEP 2: SETTLE YOUR PAST

Because I didn't have a traumatic childhood and because I have what is called a strong denial system, I never felt it was important to spend much time reliving the past. I had no concept that repressed anger and deep hurts kept bottled up inside us could lead to unexplainable symptoms such as Patsy's fears, ulcers, and colitis until God sent Lana Bateman to CLASS (see chapter 15). Lana began, with one person at a time, to work with the staff and help them pour off the pools of pain from their pasts.

As Lana counseled Patsy, she was able to show her the power that anger had played in her past and how the suppression of her feelings had led her into fear attacks and bodily ailments. Lana led Patsy gently through the childhood incidents that had caused her anger. Patsy was able to see and feel for the first time how hurt she'd been and how she'd had no control over her circumstances. She learned to relieve the blame she had placed on others and how to accept herself as a worthwhile human being. With the Lord at her side and Lana leading in prayer, Patsy was able to forgive those she'd held grudges against and most important, free herself from overwhelming guilt.

Lana found that Patsy's extreme high and low swings of behavior, which appeared to be a *Sanguine-Melancholy* personality split, was a masking of her true *Choleric,* "born-leader" nature that had been both repressed and depressed.[10] As Patsy found her true temperament and dared to exert some of her leadership traits, her mood swings lessened. Patsy still "turns on" when she hits the stage and fireworks burst forth, but the lights stay on much longer.

According to *Good Housekeeping,* May 1983:

> Most of our problems begin in childhood. Because as youngsters we are vulnerable and dependent on other people, we develop all sorts of childish fears—of being unworthy, unloved, even abandoned. If we don't outgrow these fears, or if we bury them, they continue to influence our behavior. It's these childhood fears that may later cause the emotional problems that made some of us workaholics or compulsive cleaners or prone to psychosomatic symptoms such as headaches, high blood pressure or stomach ulcers.[11]

How many of us are playing roles in life, not really sure of who we are? No matter what our problem, it will be helped when we are willing to seek godly counsel and to settle the past.

It was when Paulette went through the same kind of counseling with Lana that she found her drinking was the cover-up for her deep feelings of inadequacy in life and for her poor choices in both men and medication (see chapter 1). Paulette writes:

> Most alcoholics begin to seriously drink because they are covering something up. They are burying something. It is either something they did, something that was done to them, or a traumatic incident in their life that at the time they just couldn't cope with. They couldn't deal with it and so they buried it in the bottom of a bottle. You must deal with those things in your life that you have buried deep down or you will never get completely well.

Georgia, as she read Osborne's *Art of Understanding Yourself,* realized she had shut out her past and denied she was bearing the blame for her parents' problems (see chapter 2). She says:

> I would be reading this book in the middle of the night and suddenly a certain example would cause me to think "why that same thing happened to me." You see, I had shut everything off and I couldn't remember my childhood. By reading and then writing what came to mind, I was able to work through my past and begin to deal with the present, one day at a time.

Step 3: Speak the Truth

All of us "good people" think we tell the truth. We don't really lie, cheat, or steal, but often we are not honest with ourselves or with our God. We quote scripture and appear saintly while inside we are seething. We say,

- "That didn't hurt me at all."
- "I have joy in adverse circumstances."
- "I forgive seven times seven."
- "I can do all things through Christ who strengthens me."

These statements are all true, yet often we mouth them with little meaning.

Before we can hope to overcome any problem, we must get honest with ourselves and say to the Lord,

- "I'm not all that charming."
- "I didn't really like what she said."
- "I may say I've forgiven, but I'll never forget."
- "I'm not happy and I want my own way."
- "I'm an alcoholic."
- "I can't live without these pills."

God answers, "Finally, you're being honest and you've stopped making excuses. Now we can move on to bigger things."

My friend Terry told me recently that her mother-in-law always boasted about how spiritual she was and how forgiving. "I just never hold a grudge and I always forgive." Having heard this lie for years, one day Terry asked, "Then how come you haven't spoken to cousin Helen since she said your son was lazy?" The dear spiritual giant became instantly irate, stormed from the room, and hasn't spoken to Terry since.

God knows our heart and he wants us to be honest with him.

No matter what our problem, until we face it straight on, get honest with God, and admit we can't overcome with our own strength, his power in our lives will be short-circuited. As Patsy began to speak the truth to herself and to God, she no longer needed to hide in the house, wrapped up in her fears. She was able to look out of uncracked windows and open the door to a new life.

Step 4: Saturate Yourself with God's Word

Both Patsy and I were brought up "in the church" and were "good girls." We could recite a few verses and sing "The Old Rugged Cross," but it was not until we committed our lives to the Lord and began to devour his word that we felt God's loving control of our lives. There is no substitute remedy for the pains of life; we must saturate ourselves in the Scripture.

As Patsy studied hour after hour, God's Word began to move in and take up residence in her mind. The fears that had controlled her were crowded into the corners and a new light went on in her life. Sometimes she would read a verse over and over searching for meaning, but God would gently remind her, "Don't worry if you don't understand it now. I'll pull it out and make it real when you need it."

Patsy remembers one experience in which God put his words into action.

I went to a hotel in downtown Detroit to stay for a weekend retreat. I had only thought about the hectic ride down and had been praying that I'd live through the trip. It never entered my head that it would be a big hotel and we would be on the 22nd floor! The girl at the front desk said, "The elevator is right over there."

The elevator? I was deathly afraid of heights and panicked at the thought of an elevator. "I'll take the steps," I mumbled. "To the 22nd floor?" my friend asked. "Don't be silly." I didn't want to tell her that I was afraid of this little box that went up and down so I walked over to the door and tried to claim every promise I could think of. "I can do all things through Christ who strengthens me—even get on an elevator." The door opened and a lady got off saying "That's the fastest elevator I've ever been on."

"Oh," I thought, "who asked you to speak? Don't you know

you're not supposed to talk to strangers?" My friend pushed me in and I found the lady was right. I didn't even have a chance to work up a good healthy fear before I was on the 22nd floor. As we opened the door to the room I looked straight across and there was a big window. I mean that window was the whole wall! I thought, "What kind of person would make a window on the 22nd floor from the ceiling to the floor from wall to wall?" My friend ran across the room and said, "Oh look isn't it a beautiful view!"

She had her face all pressed against the glass while I stood sick in the doorway. As I gripped the door frame I felt like I was balancing the whole building from tipping over. My friend, not noticing my fear, said, "I've got a great idea, why don't you and I sleep in the bed closest to the window?"

I replied weakly, "Won't that be fun?" I did manage to get into that bed and I dreamed that I rolled out of bed and right out of that window. As I jumped up awake I thought, "Oh Lord, I know you haven't brought me this far to throw me out a window." Suddenly, scripture came up in my heart, "There is nothing that will separate us from the love of God. Not even heights nor depths." I began to move closer and closer to the edge and before the weekend was over I was able to look out the window and retain lunch. I still don't rush to mountaintops and say "Isn't this fun!" but I do know now that if a mountaintop is where God takes me I can do all things through Christ who strengthens me.

When we saturate ourselves with God's word, he will bring the message to our mind when we need it most.

STEP 5: SET YOUR MIND

So often we set our minds against something, dig in our heels, and vow heaven and earth could not move us. In Romans 8:6 Paul labels such an attitude as a mind set on that which human nature dictates and suggests it will lead to disaster. But he says, "The mind set on the spirit is life and peace."

We have a choice to make. We can focus on getting our own way no matter what; or we can set our minds on the spirit and Jesus will lead our lives toward the path of peace.

Patsy's mind had been set on herself and her fears for many years and that had led her literally to the brink of death. She had to willfully set her mind on the spirit, on God's control of her life, before she could let go of her friendly phobias and let God lead her to peace.

STEP 6: STABILIZE YOUR EMOTIONS

In order to stabilize your emotions you have to stand tall, plant your feet firmly on God's earth, and stop leaning on other people. Patsy had been teetering on emotional cliffs for years, hanging on to a thin slice of life by her fingernails, counting on people and pills to keep piecing her back together. One day she said:

I'm sick of myself. I'm sick of being sick. I'm sick of giving in to fear. I'm going to promise you God, by your power, to become your person.

As Patsy threw herself before God, she saw that her life was a shambles. How could she raise children and be a decent wife when her emotions were in such turmoil she couldn't even do simple chores in the home? When you see someone who lives in an outward mess, you can know they were first in an inward mess. Patsy recalls:

In my chaos the first thing that God assigned me to do was make my bed. "Make my bed every day, Lord?"
He replied, "When you're faithful in the little things, then I will entrust you with more."
I didn't know how making beds would help my mind but I decided to "be faithful in the little things" and to restore order in the areas of responsibility that God had given me.
I began to make the bed every day, do the dishes, and cook the meals. I did that which was right there before me, those things that had been totally out of order for so many years. God is not the author of confusion, and I began to set things straight in those drawers and in those closets. My self-esteem began to rise.
Have you ever cleaned out a closet or a desk drawer and become so excited with the results you wanted to invite in the neighborhood to see? That's how I felt as I accomplished these simple tasks. Our self-esteem is built as we make the very best choices for our life whether or not we feel like it. We may often say, "This would be the easy thing," but we must quickly counter, ". . . but for me this is what I must do."

Paulette looks back at her pampered childhood and realizes how she never learned the simple tasks of life. Because she couldn't cook, sew, clean, or do a wash, she felt insecure; this lack of ability contributed to her instability and inadequacy which she covered up with drink and drugs. As she worked to stabilize her emotions, she had to stop depending on false supports and her need for people and begin leaning on the Lord.

Georgia (see chapter 2) thought she had no emotional problems because she had buried her past and denied she had any feelings, but as she began to know who she really was, her emotions came to the surface. As she began to stabilize, people who once thought her cold and aloof dared to talk with her. One nurse said, "I always thought you were this well-put-together person, but now I see you are human."

Georgia counsels, "Once you've dealt with your emotions, people see a warmth in you; the love of the Lord shines through. They may have a totally different problem but they recognize the past pain in you and seek your help."

One lady wrote to Georgia:

Your story has given me insight to some ghosts in my own past and the strength to resolve some long ago but not forgotten issues that had kept me bound up and useless. You have given me an awareness of what is going on in my life and have developed in me an empathy for hurting people. You have given me the courage to admit and honestly confront some of my thoughts and problems and to make changes. You have given me hope to work for good solutions to undesirable situations that occur in my life. Thank you for being open and available.

STEP 7: SELECT YOUR THOUGHTS

Whatever we feed is what grows the fastest. If we feed our fears they will multiply and soon we'll have a whole family of phobias; conversely, if we feed our faith with God's word, it will soon be strong enough to capture that scary collection. Patsy tells how she learned that lesson.

I can remember a time when I was home alone late at night while my husband was out helping my parents. We lived on 650 acres owned by the Boy Scouts of America, and I was a mile from my nearest neighbor. As our dog kept barking I imagined spooky things surrounding the house. Soon I was so frightened I got up and began to look for a weapon to defend myself. I found a part of the Kirby vacuum cleaner and took it back to bed with me. I put the phone in bed also and opened the phone book up to the emergency page. As my heart was thumping, I had one hand on the receiver and the other waving my Kirby sword back and forth looking from the door to the window. My face swung around too far and I caught a glimpse of myself in the mirror. I thought, "Boy, do you look stupid." God's Word says, I don't give you that "spirit of fear, but of power, and of love and of a sound mind" (2 Timothy 1:7, KJV). He promises he'll be a shield and a fortress and a hiding place, and here I am trying to protect myself with a vacuum cleaner!

I laid down my Kirby sword and I picked up the sword of the Lord. I began looking into this living, life-changing, lasting Word of God and I was reminded of who God wanted to be in my life. As I relaxed, I was able to fall so soundly to sleep I never heard my husband when he pulled up, when he entered the house, or when he came into the bedroom until he shook my foot and said, "What's the vacuum cleaner doing in bed with you?!"

How easy it is to feed our fearful thoughts and yet how quickly God can jump into control when we ask. Patsy then developed a plan for selecting the right thoughts.

1. REFUSE any impure, unkind, compulsive or frightening thoughts in the name of Jesus based on 2 Corinthians 10:5: "Casting down imaginations, and every high thing that exalteth itself against the knowledge of God and bringing into captivity every thought to the obedience of Christ" (KJV).

2. REPLACE it with a positive godly thought based on Philippians 4:8: "Whatsoever things are true, whatsoever things are honest, whatsoever things are just, whatsoever things are pure, whatsoever things are lovely, whatsoever things are of good report, if there be any virtue, and if there be any praise, think on these things" (KJV).

3. REPEAT these steps over and over until your mind is renewed and your vain imaginations put aside.

Whether you are recovering from emotional problems, fears, drugs, or alcohol, remember the control your mind has over your body. The results of Patsy's "Seven Steps to Stability" will cause you to *stand fast*. To go from being an emotional cripple to running the race of life with patience and endurance takes time and determination. You have to keep your eyes on the goal, discipline for training, and even "buffet your bodies with blows." But the victory is worth it, so stand fast and don't get weary.

So often the emotional cripple wants God to straighten his foot and his path and wants people to carry his burdens for a while.

Patsy took her first solo step of faith when, after years of living with fears, she agreed to speak at a women's retreat. As she waited to be introduced, her phobias grew legs, ran up her arm, and whispered in her ear, "Run!" As panic overtook her, she started for the door. A friend grabbed her just as the introducer, obviously a little frightened herself, announced, "Please welcome Clutsy Pairmont." The audience broke into laughter. Patsy relaxed and began to speak while the Lord swept up her fallen fears and threw them away.

Yes, there's HOPE for each one of us with phobias and emotional fluctuations. "Stand fast therefore in the liberty wherewith Christ hath made us free, and be not entangled again with the yoke of bondage" (Gal. 5:1, KJV).

Patsy has stood fast. I've watched her **seek** godly counsel and move steadily through the healing process, **settling the past** as stability replaced fragmentation. I know she **speaks** the truth and she has so **saturated** her mind with Scripture that she inspires audiences with large selections of God's Word from memory. She has **set** her mind on God's goals for her growth and has been faithful in the simple chores of life, giving God the space to **stabilize** her emotions. She **selects** her thoughts knowing "if there be any virtue" she should think on these things. The result is that today Patsy stands fast knowing that God gives not "the spirit of fear, but of power, and of love, and of a sound mind."

Some may limp, some may stumble, but someday we'll all march on to victory!

Are you afraid? Do you have a friend who is emotionally limping and stumbling through life? Be assured that God does not give the spirit of fear, but he knocks, breathes, shines, and seeks to mend.

Tending the Mending

Showing how we need loving understanding for those who are trying to mend their lives.

**To wake the soul
by tender strokes of art,
To raise the genius,
and to mend the heart.**

Prologue to Addison's *Cato*
Alexander Pope

BONNIE GREEN

Adultery

Committing adultery is not a goal in the Christian life. If nothing else, we all know the essence of the Ten Commandments and we have surely heard—loud and clear—"Thou shalt not commit adultery." Since we all intend to live by the great commandments and the golden rule, why do we Christians need to look at this question, "Is there life after adultery?"

In my book *After Every Wedding Comes a Marriage,* the chapter on "The Other Woman" has received the most attention. Yes, unfortunately, there is infidelity in our River City.

There are two extremes on this subject. The world says, "Do your own thing"; "if it feels good do it." In Los Angeles, psychologist Cynthia Silverman has a popular workshop for married women who are having affairs.

She gives practical advice. 1–Remember to cover absences with excuses your husband can't check. 2–Don't confess, because a "white lie is better than a black truth." 3–Choose married men, who also must be discreet.[1]

We have gone through a pitiful moral landslide in the past twenty years that has focused on self-fulfillment no matter what the cost to others. The "me generation" has venerated the sexually active male as macho and the Mae West, "come up and see me sometime," female as liberated. Those of us who don't wish to be fulfilled are filed away with pictures of little old ladies crocheting afghan squares. Articles tell us that infidelity improves ailing marriages and variety is the spice of life.

On the other end of the spectrum is the extreme Christian view which I call the "door-mat dogma." We women are nothing more than common chattel and it is our duty to love, honor, and obey no matter what our husband might be doing. So many women I listen to, whose husbands may abuse them or openly run around, talk of going for Christian counsel only to be told that submission is their cross to bear. Many women with little children are locked into abusive marriages because of financial need or a fear of letting anyone know how desperate they are.

Gratefully, there has been a trend away from the "door-mat dogma" in vital Christian communities and aid is being offered to the victim before it is too late. Instead of recognizing the dear sister as "hanging in there" and proclaiming her noble, Christian writers and counselors are now giving advice on how to administer "tough love." Dr. James Dobson's book *Love Must Be Tough* gives examples of adultery cases and how they were solved.

What leads a person into an extra-marital affair?

Sex is the first thought and is surely a result of most infidelity, but surveys show companionship, the relating socially and intellectually of two people who listen to and respect each other, is more often the first desire. Ann Landers recently polled women and found more preferred a good dinner in a fine restaurant to sex.

Dr. Ruth Neubauer, a marital therapist, suggests:

People often cheat as a way of increasing self-esteem. A new lover may flatter the cheater's ego and a new romance may regenerate the cheater. Infidelity often can be activated by a desire for sexual adventures and more variety.[2]

Many men feel they have outgrown their wives who have been too busy tending to the home and raising children to keep up with the times. In her book *The Infidelity Report*, Wendy Leigh interviews hundreds of "cheating spouses" across the country and quotes "Richard" as saying:

I cheat because my wife doesn't have enough interests. If she were interested in some of the things I am, then I wouldn't cheat. I enjoy relationships with women who are intellectual, who are interested in travel, law, the stock market. If I were married to a woman like that I would be faithful.[3]

I bet you would Richard! Or would you then get interested in polo, pottery, or planting petunias?

Usually those who are unfaithful are looking for something in another person that fills a need they feel is ignored at home. How exciting it would be if we could sit down before infidelity strikes and assess each other's needs. In Philippians we are asked to "look out for each other's interests and not your own." So often women I counsel know what it is their husbands want but just refuse to give in because they won't reciprocate. Few advances are made by pulling back.

Wendy Leigh says:

The extramarital affair prevents cheaters from confronting the deficiencies in their primary relationship. Instead of confronting what is wrong in the marriage and dealing with it, the secondary relationship cheater sidesteps the issue by going elsewhere.[4]

Because Christians aren't supposed to have marriage problems, we often let the horse escape before shutting the barn door.

If you, or some friends, are victims of an unfaithful mate, is there any hope? Is there life after adultery?

Bonnie Green phoned me one Sunday afternoon to ask if I'd be willing to come to her home for lunch and speak to a few of her friends. She had listened to the tapes Fred and I had done on marriage and she wanted me to share some concepts with a group from the Hollywood set she planned to invite. I agreed to meet her at Los Angeles Airport as I flew in from a Phoenix engagement. I asked how I would recognize her.

She laughed and replied, "It'll be easy. I'll be the only woman in the baggage claim area over six feet tall." She was right. As I entered the claim area I looked across the crowded room and there was a strikingly beautiful and elegantly attired woman that I knew in a wink must be Bonnie. Her smashing figure and flawless face belied her sixty years and even her soft silver page-boy hair seemed youthful.

As I introduced myself she flashed a radiant smile exhibiting perfect teeth. She hugged me warmly and we became instant friends. On the way to the restaurant where we were to meet her husband, Bonnie told me she had been "Bunny Waters" in the heyday of MGM musicals and had been used as a prop of pulchritude for her height and her beauty. It took little imagination to picture "Bunny" posed next to Esther Williams in *Bathing Beauties* or adorned in maribou and sequins as a Glamazon.

Because of Bonnie's height I was stunned when we arrived at the French restaurant in Beverly Hills and I met Johnny Green. If you wished to cast a part for a typical composer/conductor you would have chosen Johnny: short, slim, slightly stooped, thinning hair, big glasses, and a carnation in his lapel. As he reached up to kiss Bonnie, it looked as if she'd have to pick him up to make their lips meet. I pictured her carrying him over the threshold!

Johnny moved quickly to seat us both and began a brisk round of witty repartee that had us all in laughter within seconds. An obvious genius, Johnny had graduated from Harvard at nineteen and holds earned and honorary doctorates in both music and law. He serves on the ASCAP board and has been chairman of many Jewish philanthropies.

As he answered my queries about his life, he asked, "Bonnie, whom does Florence remind you of?"

She looked me over and said, "Betty Furness."

As I seemed surprised he added, "If anyone ought to know what Betty Furness looks like, I should. She was my second wife."

Johnny then asked Bonnie to tell me her life story. Whenever she'd take a breath, Johnny would jump in and explain what Bonnie had clearly said as if I needed an interpreter.

Bonnie grew up as a shy and sheltered girl with a low self-image because of her height. This liability was turned into an asset when she won a contest right after high school and was awarded a trip to New York and an opportunity to work in a popular night club on the great Broadway. Little did she know it was a hangout for the Mafia; in fact, she didn't know what the Mafia was. While the bright lights of old Broadway were exciting, Bonnie was too reserved to appear nude in the show as the director expected and she refused to go on stage without some veiling and feathers.

As she became acquainted with her show-biz friends, she found most of them were "kept women," a term she at first didn't understand. It seems if you are immersed in anything long enough, you take on the color of your surroundings. Even though Bonnie had arrived in New York "pure as the driven snow," she soon shaded into a tint of grey. She recalls:

In that atmosphere I eventually became amoral with no sense of responsibility whatsoever. I felt that I wasn't very smart or clever and if a man was nice to me and generous all I had to give him was myself. Thank God, there weren't too many very nice and generous men around!

Because Bonnie felt guilty doing what others took on as a matter of course, she began attending a church. Several of her friends were Catholic, but after they went to confession they continued to live the same lifestyle as before. So Bonnie chose another religion that said there was no such thing as sin, just "mistakes." This relieved her conscience and she even planned to become a minister.

Bonnie first met Johnny Green through her friend Betty Furness, before Betty became his second wife. Bonnie instantly disliked him because he had "such an ego!"

At twenty-seven Bonnie felt lonely and unfulfilled. She wanted to get married and have children because it seemed the normal thing to do. She had a deep urge to belong to someone and a yearning to be needed by some special person. On the heels of rejection by a man she felt was her Prince Charming, Bonnie ran into Johnny again. They were both under contract to MGM and Johnny was depressed over his divorce from Betty.

Bonnie wanted to be Johnny's savior and redeem him from an affair with a married woman and too much drinking. Bonnie sat by the hour as Johnny poured out his thoughts to her. She was a good listener and didn't think she had much to offer in conversation. She encouraged his assumption that she was a person of virtue and they appeared to fill each other's needs.

Three and one-half weeks after their first date the tall and the short were married. Bonnie had no preparation for this new supposedly selfless life. Within two months of the wedding John got drafted, Bonnie got pregnant and sick, and John's only brother was killed in the war.

Because John's mother was grief-stricken and heartbroken, she came out to California from New York and moved in with them. Bonnie didn't understand how John and his mother could be so consumed with sorrow, so she retreated from them and shut out

John in his time of need. This was the same Bonnie who just a few months before had wanted someone who needed her, but evidently not someone who needed her quite this much.

Her lack of compassion for and her aloof attitude toward her grieving new mother-in-law caused the lady to return to New York where in her loneliness she later jumped out of a hotel window and killed herself.

Johnny, always a workaholic and on his way to five Academy Awards, treated Bonnie as an art object to be shown off to friends. Because he was so well-known and revered, Johnny and Bonnie were on the "A" party list in Beverly Hills and traveled with the top names in Hollywood. Although Bonnie had thought being a wife and mother would make her happy, John insisted they have a cook and governess freeing her to party, play golf and tennis, and go to the mountains skiing. As he worked, she played. Soon she felt that John didn't really need her and that he looked at her as more of a sex object than a real person. While he thought their marriage was healthy, she was sick of being alone so much and sought validation of her value in the adoration of other men.

John called Bonnie illogical and stupid. And behind his back Bonnie ridiculed John as Mr. Perfection and a know-it-all.

As they drifted further apart and Bonnie sought pleasure and affirmation from others, her conscience bothered her and she was saddled with guilt and fears. Her devious life excluded being a loving wife or a resident mother.

One night she and some friends went to see a play produced by Moral Re-armament, a group committed to searching for and following the will of God. She saw on stage a divided family like hers and watched them become loving and united. Maybe there was hope for her. She sought out some people at the Moral Re-armament building in downtown Los Angeles and was challenged to become a woman of God. That idea sounded good, but how did you go about becoming one? The people prayed with her and sent her home to listen to God for counsel and instruction. Bonnie had no concept of how this might work but she was faithful in praying.

God showed her she was not setting good standards for her two teenage girls. She was teaching "Do as I say, not as I do." Bonnie told me:

Setting that one right was where I needed to start. I was smoking three packs of cigarettes a day and drinking far too much; so, with a purpose far bigger than my own self-indulgence, I stopped both smoking and drinking at the same time. That I felt better physically is obvious. But much more important, I felt the beginnings of an inner strength, peace, and contentment that I had never known.

The next thing I actually heard God say to me was that I needed to get honest and ask forgiveness of everyone in my family. I began with my girls. One just said, "OK, Mom." But Kim, the youngest, said she would never forgive me because I would go on being the same "screaming witch" and never change. It took her over fourteen years to forgive me. Then I went to John. I thought I would tell him only what I wanted to, and he would understand and all would be well. Oh, how wrong I was! He wanted to know everything as far back as I could remember. He probed me for several weeks while I drove us in my car . . . I just couldn't sit and face him. Needless to say, I nearly drove over a cliff several times. It was so painful, not only for me, but for John as well.

When everything was out, all the guilt and the fear were gone; there was nothing left buried. I felt free, but John was deeply hurt and angry and barely tolerated me. He never gave me a birthday or Christmas card, a gift . . . a hug or a kiss. He didn't even touch me for six long years. This was a time to ask God for his guidance and listen for his voice. But I didn't. I started doing it my way again—differently—but my way.

I became a self-righteous martyr. I let our help go and took on running our house myself. I stopped wearing make-up and became a drab drudge and a loner. I resigned from every volunteer job, gave up my beloved sports, and began attending a Christian church.

John jumped in at that point in her story and said to me, "You wouldn't believe what she was like in those days. She went from being a free spirit to an overnight frump. She was so virtuous no one could stand her and all our friends dropped us. My prestige in the Hollywood community was important to me, but Bonnie didn't care as long as she had her religious friends."

Although John was deeply hurt, he didn't leave Bonnie and one day he called out in his frustration and pain, "YOU think you have all the answers to everything! It's YOUR fault that no one likes us anymore." Shortly after that outburst, Bonnie's pastor consoled her, "When God puts his hand on your shoulder, he cuts away the people who are holding you back!"

At this point in Bonnie's path to piety, John received an offer to go to England and make the film *Oliver*. To Bonnie's surprise, he asked her to go with him. Two years away seemed like the answer to their marriage problems and so Bonnie went ahead to choose a home. In the quaint Kensington section of London, she found a typical English townhouse. The kitchen and dining room were on the ground floor, the living room took up all of the first floor, the second floor was their bedroom and bath, and the top floor, which had been a nursery, became John's home office and studio on the weekends. During the week he left home at 7:00 A.M. and didn't return until 10:00 P.M.

Bonnie was grateful to have a fresh start and she was determined to put John first and do everything to please him. "I never mentioned God or the Bible," she told me, "nor did I leave spiritual literature around for him to read."

Since the European center for Moral Re-armament was in London, Bonnie quickly made new friends. On weekends she would be out with them in the day and be back home by 4:00 each afternoon to bring tea to John and his young English secretary. Bonnie recounted:

About six months into our stay I was taking the tea tray up and, as I got to the top of the stairs, I heard sobs coming out of that room. The door was open a crack and through it I could see John on his knees, holding his secretary in his arms. With tea cups rattling, I went down to my bathroom, which was my prayer closet, and got on my knees to ask God what that meant. Very clearly he told me to ask what was going on—not to point an accusing finger, but to ask.

I prepared a beautiful, candle-lit dinner for after she had gone, waited until the end of the meal, and then very shakily, but gently, asked John if there was a serious relationship between them. He jumped to his feet and said, "Yes, I love her very much, and I have laughed more with her than with any woman in my life." I told him he had better go and tell her I knew. Again, I thought everything would at last be OK, and we could get on with our marriage. Oh, what a fool I was! God's timing isn't our timing and he knew that both John and I needed much more tempering first.

John then jumped in to tell me how he left that night to go let the girl know they had been found out. When he came back to Bonnie at 5:00 in the morning he opened the door and announced, "I'm willing to try if you are. I want three nights a week with her—no questions asked—and you can have the other four."

Bonnie's first impulse was to say, "No way," but instead she agreed to try. For her four nights Bonnie did her best to make their English home a welcome haven for her husband. She prayed in the big bathroom, kneeling by the step to the tub, and asked God to give her a light touch and the gift of laughter, realizing that humor had been one of the first things to leave their marriage. She prayed for strength to swallow her pride and for new understanding, wisdom, and compassion.

Her Moral Re-armament friends listened without judgment to her new marital arrangement and to her self-pity and tears. They neither sympathized nor gave advice, they just listened and sent her home to get down on her knees and give it all to God. Through these new friends, who really cared without condemning and gave compassion without counsel, Bonnie learned for the first time what real friendship was all about and that the joy of living is found in Jesus Christ.

Bonnie was excited when she discovered that her four days with John included Christmas. When John asked her what she wanted to do she suggested a trip to Caux, Switzerland, the World Headquarters for Moral Re-armament. When they landed in Geneva, John ran to the phone to let his "other woman" know he had arrived safely. Bonnie stood quietly by. She didn't want to ruin Christmas.

Half-way up the mountain above Montreux, they looked up to see an enormous castle rising amidst the snow-covered trees. Their room had a balcony where they stood and viewed the Alps and all of Lake Geneva. In the room was their own live Christmas tree with candles, chocolates on the table, and huge feather comforters on the beds. Carolers strolled through the halls each morning and there was a children's pageant in the Great Hall on Christmas eve. As the two of them sat by the floor-to-ceiling tree and little ones lit candles, Bonnie prayed under her breath, "God tell me what gift I can give John that *she* can't." Very clearly she heard, "Tell him he can go call and wish her a happy Christmas."

"I can't do that . . . I don't want to . . . This is *my* time!" Still, God was adamant and his instruction was the same. She finally put her hand on John's knee and said, "Honey, go call her. It's my gift to you." John leapt out of his chair and, as he flew to the phone, Bonnie wished, "God, please don't let her be there!" When John came back, grinning from ear to ear, Bonnie thought God had failed her, but no, he is faithful. John reported the other woman hadn't been home, but he had been able to leave a message. He told Bonnie how grateful he was for her Christmas gift. She had learned a lesson in *obedience* to God.

Another lesson Bonnie learned was her need to become forgiving. "After all," God said to her, "you were the first to sin. It didn't even have to be the act, but it was the dissatisfaction and selfishness in your heart that was the beginning of the sin. Now learn to be compassionate, forgiving, accepting, and loving—and then forget the pain."

When we are willing God is able.

The big question in Bonnie's mind was whether John would choose her or the other woman when it was time to return to the United States. He'd often say to Bonnie, "I can't bear to hurt her."

He tested Bonnie's love in many ways and one night asked her to give him some good reasons why they should stay married. She poured out her love for him in a way she had never done before and it was that night he made his decision.

"A man would have to be a fool to walk away from such love. I'm no fool, and this is where I'm meant to be!" John now says that Bonnie's life became the ministry and the witness that made him want to change. Actions, not words, are what mean the most.

Johnny and Bonnie left England together. They talked and cried more than they ever had in all of their years together. Neither had anything left to hide. Pride had been stripped away. One thing that still hurt Bonnie was John's feeling *so guilty* about what he had done to the other woman. She let him talk about it and listened without condemnation as she had learned from her friends in England.

As Bonnie thought about their marriage she realized:

John had always been sentimental and affectionate, but those elements were lacking in me. They embarrassed me. Humor and laughter have always been an integral part of John's very being; but that capacity, too, was missing in my make-up. I can honestly say that I'm grateful to the other woman, because, only through her, did I begin to learn how very important are sentiment, touching, caring enough to be able to listen and hear, a light touch and laughter, and fully accepting John no matter what. And also, I learned how good it feels to forgive.

In 1975, John was given a bicentennial commission to compose the dedication work for the grand opening of the new Symphony Hall in Denver. He wanted it to be an especially meaningful work that would bring a feeling of anticipation and hope to both its performers and its audiences in contrast to the mood of pessimism and futility that characterized contemporary art at that time. But for months he couldn't come up with a single idea that sparked him. Then suddenly at 4:00 one morning, he awoke not only with the subject matter and the title, but also with a clearly defined schematic of the entire work entitled *Mine Eyes Have Seen*. It would be a one-movement symphony motivated by direct parallels and contradictions like the relationship between both testaments of the Bible and a three-hundred-year spectrum of American history. John joyfully proclaimed that God had been the architect who had given him the plans which were now his to execute.

Bonnie recalls:

My Harvard husband is an American history buff, but the Bible? That was something else again. A friend of mine who was a true Christian and a great Bible teacher literally laid his life down for five months taking John by the hand through the Bible three to five hours every day. By the end of this time, with deep searching and study, John had become convinced that Jesus was indeed the Messiah prophesied throughout the Old Testament and rejected by his own people. And John gave his life to the Lord.

Later, in an interview with *New World News*, John said:

In my own case, examining myself required the deep x-ray look at my own spiritual anatomy. When I finally examined the plates, I got a rude and shattering shock. I found that all my attitudes toward Bonnie were anchored in a self-serving pride, in the conviction of my special intellectual superiority and my divine right to deal with Bonnie from Mount Olympus. I came up from Mount Olympus. I came up head-on against the awful truth that I was the original male chauvinist pig. But God gave me the light to see what a blessed thing our marriage could be if I could find the sheer guts to change, to get on my knees and apologize to Bonnie for the stupid arrogance with which I had deprived her of her God-given fundamental rights of full partnership. It hasn't been easy, but I am still trying and God has given me my life's greatest blessing, far more important than my moderate talents as an artist, Bonnie's forgiveness. Thank you Bonnie for giving me that.[5]

Now, John and Bonnie are growing in every way. Together they do a Bible study each morning in John's bathroom while he shaves, and they spend at least an hour in intercessory prayer, reading scripture, discussing and thinking aloud with God and with one another.

In Bonnie's words:

If your mate is having a serious affair, nothing you say will actually change anything. Just keep in mind, "There but for the grace of God, go I!" Remember that none of us is ever free from temptation.

Always remember to keep praying and, while you are praying, change what God tells you to change. Keep asking God to show you where you need to be different and constantly ask him to help you accomplish this most difficult task.

Grow in spirit by calling on elderly or ill people, and comforting them in their loneliness. Grow in mind by taking classes in useful and interesting subjects. Grow in health by caring properly for the cathedral of your soul, your body! This trio carries an unlimited warranty of feeling better, much, much better.

Make the achievement of forgiveness a major project. Keep saying, "With God's help, I forgive not only others, I forgive myself and, in forgiving, I forget. I do not suppress the guilt; I forget the wrong!" Learn to trust.

For eight years Bonnie taught a marriage class and here are some of the steps she still shares.

1. Constantly give God praise and thanks for every joy, for lessons learned, for friends, for his goodness and his presence.

2. Ask God to love the other person through you. Admit that, at this moment, you alone can't love; but you do know that he can. Before you are even aware, you, yourself will be able to love again.

3. Practice believing in your mate, and make it your business to find ways to show that you do believe in him or her.

4. Give up everything in your life that you know is wrong. You must not, you cannot compromise or rationalize. Eliminate from your heart forever all resentment, bitterness, hatred, anger, jealousy, and fear. Easier said than done I know, but well worth the effort, I promise you!

5. Make a real, personal friend of Jesus Christ. Talk with him often. He understands everything and is truly the best friend you'll ever have. "If any man be in Christ, he is a new creature: old things are passed away; behold, all things are become new" (2 Cor. 5:17, KJV).

6. When your mate is telling you something, listen with all of your being and attention.

7. Do romantic little things without being embarrassed. Surprise him or her with a candle-lit dinner, a few fresh flowers on the table—they don't have to be roses—daisies will do nicely if you put them there.

8. Take walks together and hold hands—touching is so important.

9. Put little love notes or cute, funny cards in his pocket or her purse.

10. Tell good jokes or cute anecdotes, so you can laugh together. You don't have to be Bob Hope, just be yourself, but contrive to bring laughter to your marriage relationship.

11. Stop taking yourself and life so deadly serious—hang a little looser. If you're a homemaker, keep your home neat and clean, but don't be a fuss-budget or a perfectionist.

12. Remember, it's the glow from within that creates beauty.

That night in the French restaurant, when I first heard the Bonnie and Johnny story from their own lips, I was touched with the poetic words they used to express their love and with the romantic twinkle they still have for each other. I was overwhelmed with the power of God to mend lives and rewrite our script. As I went to their home that evening and looked up to the five gold Oscars on the mantle, I knew God would give them one more Academy Award for the best roles in their own hit show, "There Is Life after Adultery!"

MONA VAN BRENK KERN

Divorce

Is there anything that hasn't been said about divorce? When I first started writing eight years ago, divorce was a new subject for Christians. But in this short time it has broadened to such a degree that one pastor apologized to me for his "divorced Sunday school class" because it had more members than any other. In another church I spoke to a similar group of over seven hundred people.

When we survey our CLASS, one-third of the participants are divorced and many are involved in bitter court battles, fights that continue forever as permanent pain without decisive victory.

The dictionary defines divorce as the end of a marriage—too simple a statement for so complex a problem. California law describes divorce as "a judgment decreeing a dissolution of the marriage which restores the parties to the state of unmarried persons."[1] It may legally restore them but they will never be the same again; there will always be a severed segment in one's soul, the wistful wonder of what might have been.

According to *U.S. News and World Report*, marriages are being dissolved at the rate of one every twenty-seven seconds. The numbers exceed one million every year, more than twice the divorces of two decades ago.[2] *U.S. News and World Report* also states that many women are paying an unexpected price for their movement of the last twenty years toward sexual equality. Spouses who once might have received lifetime payments now get them only long enough to find a job. The modern trend is toward putting women right to work. Many attorneys support this feeling, saying it is healthy for the wife to become independent and self-supportive. Unfortunately, many of these women are becoming the nation's new poor. The support laws have become sexually neutral in most cases, and in California, divorces studied by Stanford University showed that men's standard of living after the first year of divorce rose by 42 percent while that of women and children dropped by 73 percent.[3] Couples are being divorced not only after a few years of marriage, but often after twenty, thirty, and forty-year relationships. We need to be aware and prepared to deal with divorce. We can't think this type of tragedy only touches others for it may come close to home anytime.

Women of divorce may find their settlements do not provide for a continuance of their normal lifestyle. Many new and frightening experiences are encountered as they struggle alone in a strange and different world from what was familiar in their marriage. In the desperate desire to become liberated, today's women may have cut themselves out of the old patterns where the support courts always protected the female with arrangements maintaining her previous lifestyle. The courts no longer give "everything" to the woman. We must be aware of the serious struggles she may face simply trying to meet the most basic needs.

A California attorney tells me that spousal support awards today reflect the expectation that both men and women are intended to work. Permanent spousal support awards are rapidly decreasing and are considered only in marriages of long duration. The theory for support today is that one party in the marriage, usually the wife, has sacrificed a career to raise a family and has not acquired specific job skills. Assistance would, therefore, be awarded to that person only temporarily while he or she brings a job skill up to market level enabling self-support. Many factors influence spousal support awards but we need to be aware that the woman is not always automatically taken care of as was previously thought. If she can come into court on her own two feet and raise her right hand, she is considered fit to go to work.

I am frequently startled and shocked to hear of the positions many women are faced with as men find ways to win all. It seems unbelievable that once generous, concerned mates may become selfish and greedy individuals when faced with the division of property and money. The scriptures predicted these problems today.

In 2 Timothy 3:1–3 Paul said that in the last days people will be greedy and many times will act selfishly. Some will be insulting, ungrateful, violent, and fierce. Many women encounter these offensive and distasteful demonstrations of human behavior when these characteristics suddenly become a part of their dissolution experience.

Marion was a rape victim whose husband couldn't handle what she'd been through. He refused to go to counseling—it was *her* fault—and he told everyone who'd listen that his wife was having repeated affairs and was in fact sleeping with her therapist. In his role as church elder, he told the pastor his pathetic story of personal piety versus his wife's unfaithfulness and inspired the pastor to write a condemning letter to Marion without checking the truth. Although she was innocent, she could see she was fighting a losing battle and finally gave up and moved out. No sooner had Marion pulled her car out of the driveway than her husband moved in his mistress. Apparently he had been having a closet romance during the time he was spreading rumors about his wife who had been faithful through it all.

In the divorce Marion was held responsible for one-half of the considerable debts her husband had run up during his affair, the sum of which took what she might have received. She is now struggling to support herself while he remains an elder and appears in church with his new partner.

In another example, a Christian lawyer put his assets in his girl friend's name and suddenly divorced his wife, making her responsible for enough of his debts to leave her penniless. Because he needed money to pay off back income taxes he had purposely ignored, he was awarded his wife's family home that her mother had left her the year before.

Yet another lawyer forged his wife's name and divested himself of all their property without her knowledge. At the divorce settlement he was so poor there was nothing for her to receive. Shortly thereafter he bought the new woman in his life a $300,000 home.

Even sensible, spiritual men seem to be losing their heads. I received a letter from a girl telling me of her sister's plight.

Dear Florence,

Ann was a pastor's wife for ten years before her husband became involved with his secretary. Her husband put her and their three children out of their church and convinced an entire congregation she was crazy, manipulative, and obsessively jealous. She kept her fears inside so long that when she finally sought help, she was put in a mental ward because of her suicidal tendencies. The church is now closed, and God has vindicated her completely. Her husband stole thousands of dollars from his church to buy a small business in town, and the secretary works for him. Even though they have not married, they have a new baby.

God has been so precious to put her life back together. It was a big sacrifice for Ann to arrange to go to CLASS, but we believe God has very special plans for her to minister to women.

One dispossessed wife of a wealthy church leader went to her pastor for help. He suggested "Get out of town and try to forget you ever knew him." She's still in town but has never heard from anyone in the church. Her ex-husband remains in good graces with the group.

The brokenness borne of an unnatural, unwanted death of a marriage is immensely painful to those involved. Many Christian families are tormented by such tragedy touching their lives, and agonizing adjustments must be made.

Another painful and startling fact is that divorce goes on forever! A legal paper in the hand does not heal emotions. The person left behind in the dust needs your help and understanding. Caring, concerned Christian people can really make a difference in assisting those suffering from this grievous and devastating change in their lives.

None of the women I mentioned wanted to be divorced. Each was forced into it by a deceptive mate, stripped of her substance, and sent out to pick up the pieces alone. We must make a difference and offer the HOPE so desperately needed to merely survive. Hebrews 13:20 tells us that we will be equipped with all we need for doing his will. We know it is his will that we help one another and be kind, not critical (Eph. 4:32). People who are hurting need help.

A part of following our Lord Jesus means that we take up the tasks he began. We, as a Christian family, must be willing to take some responsibility and dare to be a part of the healing which the Lord makes possible. We must trust him in choosing to make us a part of his plan to help heal the lives of others, just as we must accept the help that others may give to us in our time of sorrow. Compassionate concern for each other is what really makes a difference in lives, and churches that provide this love are the magnets of their community. As in the early New Testament, our church families should be able to provide for human needs and our churches should be places where all of us can find help. Just because a lady drove a Mercedes last month doesn't mean she has a dime for the bus today. John 13:34 commands us to love one another. Loving is doing! Is there some hurting person to whom you could show love today?

If you could meet Mona personally you would want to show love to her today. She has a bright, honest face with twinkling eyes. When she speaks in soft syllables her language has a lilt and her phrases are poetic. When I first met Mona she was in the audience at a women's seminar. She waited until everyone was gone before she came to me with this touching story of her life.

Mona was the all-American girl who lived a "Leave It to Beaver" existence. She was the virginal heroine dressed in white chiffon, standing, wide-eyed and innocent atop a hill looking out to sea, holding a handful of daisies.

Mona was born into a secure traditional home and had perfect attendance ribbons from Sunday school. Her Mom and Daddy hugged her, loved her, and told her she was wonderful. She was talented and was encouraged to study music, tell stories, and participate in church productions. At eleven she began teaching Sunday school, and from then on she wrapped herself up in the protective robe of Christian friends. She had committed her life to Jesus as a child and knew no other style but steady sanctification.

It was only natural that she enroll in her denominational college where she enjoyed the fellowship of other saintly people from similar backgrounds. At the right time, in the right place, she met tall, dark, and handsome Mr. Right. It was love at first sight and they were married in a perfect little wedding back in the old home church. Mona recalls:

He was the kind of husband that met all of my needs. He was my best friend. We communicated. He took the time to care where I was and he listened to me. He even took special days off so we could do things together. My mother thought he should be hanging in a frame because he was almost too good to be true.

From this storybook romance came two little boys. First Bryan, brown-eyed, sensitive, grown-up, and serious from the start. He accepted the Lord when he was eight years old and held to his youthful convictions. He went off to Christian school and traveled with his trumpet one summer with a Christian group.

Loren was as noisy as his brother was quiet. He seemed to be performing in the hospital before he was taken home. He too accepted the Lord early in life and started teaching piano when he was only twelve years old. He then traveled with his mother as a ventriloquist doing children's crusades. What more could any parents want?

Mona and her husband, after going back to Bible college, were sent to Seattle to start a church from scratch. They rented a bingo hall and had to go at night after the games were over and clean the place up for the Sunday service. Tables and trash had to be removed and beer barrels rolled out. Mice ran in and out freely.

It was exciting to be called of the Lord to start a new fellowship, and the family had fun working together. As the years passed the group grew and built a beautiful sanctuary. On the day the five-bedroom parsonage was completed, Mona thought she'd died and gone to heaven. Her boys bought her the record "I'm the Happiest Girl in the Whole USA" and she would listen, sing along, and feel like the heroine in a fairytale.

The whole family traveled to other churches presenting both music and message, and a ministry emerged which they called "Transmitting Love." Mona and her husband shared with others the principles they had learned about the secrets of wedded bliss.

Looking back at this time in her life, a time when she did not know much about sorrow, Mona sees the lessons she has learned. Today she speaks to those of you who have not suffered as some have.

May I say to you today, do not take those joys for granted. Do not get caught in the ungrateful trap of feeling that it is your right because you are serving the Lord to have good and wonderful things come unto you. You see, he is using these days of giving you joy to shape and mold you. He has a purpose for what he wants you to be at another time in your life. Sap every day for all that it is worth. Enjoy every second of excitement and beauty that it holds, grasp every moment of joy and happiness you can, and hold it in

*reserve; it is not an accident. This is the day the Lord has made,
I will rejoice and be glad in it.*

As a pastor's wife Mona counseled many women with deep hurts.
She sat at bedsides, held the heartbroken in her arms, and whispered,
"I understand." Since she had never had a serious problem, there
grew in her heart a tiny seed of smugness. She never verbalized
these thoughts to others, but inside she felt, "If they've got these
problems, they must have been doing something wrong—there's
sin in their lives." Mona knew that when you do things right in
God's sight he will reward you.

Mona was blessed in her speaking ministry and remembers the
spring of 1980 when she stood before a large group of women at
a retreat and closed her message by saying, "I am ready to face
the rest of 1980 and whatever it holds with a quiet and confident
heart believing in the God I serve."

That August her oldest son Bryan brought home his princess
and they were joined in Christian matrimony in a storybook wedding. Could any mother ask for more?

Six days after the wedding Bryan's bride, Teresa, fell ill and
was unable to care for herself. Bryan lost his job and couldn't
find another one. Instantly things changed; life turned slightly gray.
Disease and depression dealt the couple a losing hand, and they
felt they had no alternative except to return to Seattle and live
with Mona and her husband. Here the devastated couple could
receive medical and financial help, while Bryan helped his dad at
the church.

On Christmas Sunday 1980 Mona awoke to find an empty bed.
Her husband was gone. She searched and called but there was
no response. "He must have gone to church early," she thought,
but he wasn't there. Time for the Christmas sermon came and
there was no pastor. Search teams and police tried for days to
find him without success. Not knowing if he was dead or alive,
Mona became so emotionally exhausted she couldn't even find the
strength to go up the stairs. For ten nights she slept on the couch
while ladies from the church took turns sleeping on a mat on
the floor beside her. Finally the call came. The pastor had not
been kidnapped or killed; he had left Mona, the children, the
church. He wouldn't tell them where he was and Mona was left
in shock to pack up and pull out of the parsonage. There were

bottles of dreams and crates of memories, but there was no "happily ever after" anymore. Mona states:

A many-sided breakdown took my pastor-husband from our home. What was to follow those first devastating hours would be days and weeks and months turning into years of heartbreak, fear, darkness, and a lot of questions. Those months were like a roller coaster— for one minute there would be hope of some restoration and healing only to be shattered again and back to the pits of despair. It went that way for many, many months and culminated in a divorce that I didn't want in the spring of 1982.

The family moved to a tiny house in the country, a sad replacement for the beautiful parsonage, and things just seemed to get worse. Teresa's health deteriorated, the family had no income, and Mona's emotionally ill mother-in-law, for whom she was completely responsible, passed away, leaving a number of details for Mona to take care of. At this point, partly because of the trauma and problems within the family, Loren went through some spiritual darkness and made some decisions that caused the final breaking of his mother's heart.

At moments it felt like every point, every security, everything in my life that had brought me happiness had been reduced to nothingness. I felt like someone had taken out my heart, tramped it, smashed it, beat it with a sledgehammer, and put it back inside this body. It still beats, but it beats a little crooked.

Mona shares a story she once heard that symbolizes what God has done with her broken heart.

There was a beautiful garden in the center of the magic kingdom. In the cool of the day the master of the garden often walked. Of all the dwellers in the garden the most beautiful was the noble bamboo tree. Year after year Bamboo grew more lovely and yet more noble and gracious, conscious of her master's love and watchful eye. One day the master himself drew near to contemplate his beloved tree, and Bamboo, in the passion of adoration, bowed her lovely head to the ground. The master spoke, "Bamboo I am ready to use you." It seemed the day of days had come, the day for which the tree had been made.

Bamboo's voice came low, "Master, I am ready; use me as you will."

"Bamboo," the master's voice was grave, "I must take you and cut you down."

"Cut me down? Me, when you, Master, have made me the most beautiful tree in all of your garden? Cut me down? Not that! Use me in your way dear master, but do not cut me down."

"Beloved Bamboo, if I do not cut you down, I cannot use you." The garden grew still; even the wind held his breath. Bamboo slowly bent her glorious head, "Master, if you cannot use me as I am, cut me down. Do what you must."

"Beloved Bamboo, I must cut your leaves and branches from you too."

"Oh, Master, spare me. Lay my beauty in the dust but don't take my leaves and branches too!"

"Unless I cut them off I cannot use you." The sun hid his face, a butterfly glided fearfully by, and Bamboo, shivering in the expectancy, whispered low, "Master, cut."

"Bamboo, I will divide you in two and cut out your heart for if I do not I cannot use you."

Bamboo without hesitation bowed to the ground, "Master, then cut." So did the master of the garden cut down Bamboo, hack off her branches, strip her leaves, divide her in two, and cut out her heart. He carried her to where there was a spring of fresh, sparkling water in the midst of the master's dry field putting one end of broken Bamboo in the spring and the other end into the channel of his field. The master gently laid down his beloved tree and the spring sang a welcome. The clear sparkling waters raced joyously down the channel of Bamboo's torn body into the waiting fields. The rice was planted, the days went by, the shoots grew, and the harvest came. Bamboo, once so glorious, was put to use in her brokenness and humility. For in her beauty she had life abundant for herself, but in her brokenness she became a channel of love for her master's world.

Mona had always been a beautiful tree, a shining example for all who were struggling to grow around her, but it is in her brokenness that God has made her a channel of love to a hurting world.

God is not the author of sin, but he's not surprised by it. He is never caught off guard and he always has a plan to use each one of us when we're willing. Mona is a victim of circumstances she didn't cause and couldn't control. Her prayers, her pleadings, and her penitence could not bring her husband back, but God has made something even more beautiful out of her life. The pain is still present but it doesn't hurt quite so much. There are some nights when that drowning feeling threatens to overwhelm her and there is one out there she will always be burdened by and praying for. The Lord says, "I know my plans for you and they are plans for your welfare, not your calamity, that you might have a future and a hope" (Jer. 29:11, NAS).

Mona's future is to give HOPE to others—to those of you who didn't deserve what you got, and to those of you who have suffered and could now be helping others. Mona has a few basic principles to teach us all no matter where we stand today.

PEACE IS NOT THE ABSENCE OF PAIN. So often we are taught in our churches, at least by implication, that if we are good Christian people we will live happily ever after. The prosperity doctrine is appealing as long as we are prosperous, but what guilt falls upon us when life falls apart. "Peace is not the absence of pain," Mona says:

But the strength and the vitality that comes up within you, giving you the courage to get up and go on. It's the presence of the Holy Spirit that fills you and somehow your legs still move.

LIFE ISN'T FAIR. So many of us were brought up to believe firmly that life is fair and if it isn't, Mother will make it so. Mona states:

Life isn't fair. Don't teach your children that it is. Don't be running down to the school all the time, trying to fix up your daughter because she didn't get to be cheerleader and she should have been. Or your son didn't win the band contest when he was the best and you know it! Or the teacher gave him a low grade when he really deserved a higher one. Don't spend your life trying to get your kids all fixed up because the minute you can't be with them, they are going to learn that life isn't fair.

Church isn't fair. We make mistakes and we give the wrong kids prizes in Sunday school contests and we let Mary Lou's kid *play the piano when it should have been Susan's kid's turn to play.*

Life isn't fair, but the Lord can give us an attitude of love and forgiveness in life's unfairness. Don't waste precious time moaning over the unfairness of the situation when you could be spending that same time getting well.

Mona didn't deserve what happened to her but she's pulled herself together and is giving help and HOPE to others.

Jesus Is Enough. In those lonely months Mona was put to the test: When all else is stripped away is Jesus enough? She remembers how empty she felt. Those days of overwhelming rejection were so depressing she avoided looking in a mirror.

I would find myself walking along a street and crossing to avoid the sight of me in a plate glass window. I felt ugly, fat, frumpy, and rejected. Then I would spend times with Jesus and I found the one who knows me best, loves me most. My times in tears with him would restore my wholeness and my reason to live. The Bible became a love letter personalized to Mona. I would mark down the date of each promise beside the verse and as the healing came I could go back and remember how dark it had been when I'd first found that promise.

Lean Hard on Others. When you are in a time of trial and trouble don't be afraid to let other people minister to you. Find a friend who will let you talk and share how you really feel. Don't bottle it up inside; let it out at the right time with the right person.

Let Others In to your home to help you. Don't be too proud to let them cook and clean or just sit next to you quietly and hold your hand.

Stay Put. Don't move away too quickly, as many do to remove themselves from memories, but stay close to friends and your pastor until you feel clearly led to change. Mona had poured her life into the church people for so many years and they were faithful to give back those years in loving support.

Look for Laughter and do some frivolous things that will remove inner tensions for a little while. Mona had a friend who took her to Disneyland and they rode the merry-go-round together. Mona says, "You cannot worry on a merry-go-round."

DON'T CRITICIZE your former mate and let the children hear how horrible their father or mother was. Mona tells:

We choose in our time of heartache what mark will be left on our children. We can tear down all the good they ever knew and tell evil, ugly things, but all it does is ruin us and send our bitterness to scar the next generation.

CONTINUE TO MAKE MEMORIES. Don't stop all the traditions because a member of the family is gone. Even though it is difficult, do special things on special days. Because Mona's husband left at Christmas and called on Valentine's to say he was divorcing her, those holidays are reminders of her pain, but she has continued to celebrate them. She will not let the beauty of life disappear.

For those of you who find a Mona in your church, what can you do to help and minister to her needs?

LISTEN, let her pour her heart out to you and don't repeat a word of what she's said to anyone else.

DON'T JUDGE or suggest what she could have done in the past that might have made things better.

DON'T GOSSIP or pass on any information you wouldn't be willing to say in front of her.

DON'T RUSH the time of grieving or assume everything will be under control within a month.

DON'T EXPECT the children of the suffering family not to hurt because they're young. Think of some special treats you can do for them, especially at holidays and birthdays.

DON'T CRITICIZE the one who's left with words such as, "I never did like him." "I even know some things about him you don't know." She chose him and lived with him and when you say negatives about him you hurt her even more.

Does Mona's storybook life have a happy ending? Yes it does. Her sons are both victorious Christians and Teresa is slowly getting well after years of living with a debilitating illness. God has made beauty out of ashes and Mona is a bride! God brought her another pastor and has put her in another parsonage.

When I asked Mona what she would do differently if she could start again, she quoted an anonymous friar who said:

> If I had my life to live over again, I'd try to make more mistakes next time. I would relax, I would limber up, I would be sillier than I have been this trip. I know of very few things I would take seriously. I would take more trips. I would be crazier. I would climb more mountains, swim more rivers, and watch more sunsets. I would do more walking and looking. I would eat more ice cream and less beans. I would have more actual troubles, and fewer imaginary ones. You see, I'm one of those people who lives life prophylactically and sensibly hour after hour, day after day. Oh, I've had my moments, and if I had to do it again I'd have more of them. In fact, I'd try to have nothing else, just moments, one after another, instead of living so many years ahead each day. I've been one of those people who never go anywhere without a thermometer, a hot-water bottle, a gargle, a raincoat, aspirin, and a parachute. If I had to do it over again I would go places, do things, and travel lighter than I have. If I had my life to live over I would start barefooted earlier in the spring and stay that way later in the fall. I would play hooky more. I wouldn't make such good grades, except by accident. I would ride on more merry-go-rounds. I'd pick more daisies.[4]

It's never too late to start, for God can mend a broken heart.

6

SHELBY PRICE

Single Parenting

God ordained the family. He intended it to have a husband who loved his wife as Christ loved the church, a wife who would revere her husband, parents who would not provoke their children to wrath, and children who would be obedient to their parents in the Lord. We were to be filled with the Spirit, speaking to one another in psalms, hymns, and spiritual songs, singing heartily and making music to the Lord.

What a beautiful picture of the ideal family, painted in oils, framed in gold, and hung over the mantle. Is it anything more than a memory? Not since "Father Knows Best" didn't know enough, "Our Miss Brooks" went up the river, and "Leave It to Beaver" left, have we viewed even a caricature of what normal life might be.

What happens to women who meant well, who established a godly home, who tried to please God, husband, and children, and suddenly found themselves against their will being a single parent in a lonely world where they no longer fit in?

"According to Census Bureau Statistics for 1984, single parents headed 25.7 percent of the families with children under eighteen in the U.S." Experts predict that this will increase significantly by 1990.[1]

The Institute for Social Research at the University of Michigan reports that in 1940 only 8 percent of the households were people living alone, while 1980 showed about one in four. Beyond this change they state, "The true social isolates are women who are single parents."[2]

Sociologist Duane F. Alvin says of single parents: "Even though their circumstances of living bring them into contact with neighbors and relatives, their lives appear to be severely restricted in terms of opportunities for much social contact with friends."[3]

Parade had an article "How to Live Alone" that said:

America has always been a country of loners, of rugged individualists, of solitary heroes. At the same time, however, the family unit has always been the mainstay of our society. This appears to be changing. . . . Most experts agree that there is an emotional drain to being alone. In response, what they term "the loneliness industry" has sprung up to provide books, dating services, and other coping devices. There is, too, a physical drain in that, from laundry to finances, those who live alone must perform all the nuts-and-bolts chores of life, rather than sharing them. "It is probably a more tiring lifestyle," says Dr. Michael Vaught of Rutgers University.[4]

Because so many singles groups exist in the world and because so many churches would prefer not to dignify this unscriptural situation by treating it, thousands of lonely ladies go seeking companionship outside of the Christian community. Shelby Price is one outstanding and courageous woman who has been instrumental in starting singles groups within her church and who is now a lay counselor to single women in a group that numbers three hundred members. Shelby has gone from being part of the problem to being part of the solution.

Shelby grew up in a low-income family in Southern California where she, as the oldest of four, was a victim of sexual abuse. Because her parents both worked, she had placed upon her the responsibilities of caring for the younger children. While her parents had no interest in going to church, they felt it was good for the children and sent them to Sunday school, choir, and Wednesday night services. As Shelby remembers, "If the doors were open, we were there."

Her church attendance did two positive things for Shelby: she learned scripture verses so she could win memorizing contests, and she saw normal families, an observation that gave her the desire to have a loving home, two children, plus material possessions she had never enjoyed. She wanted to live happily ever after.

Oh, how many of the women in this book, including me, really thought we could marry Prince Charming and ride off to the castle to be happy forever and ever. Amen!

Because Shelby had good grades in high school and was from a "needy family," she was awarded a scholarship to the University of California in Riverside. Since no one encouraged Shelby to continue her education, and since her parents had divorced and she needed money, she left college at the end of two years to go to work.

At twenty-one, Shelby met the man of her dreams at church. He fit her image: tall, intelligent, good-looking, and a Christian. She knew he would provide well for her and the two children they would have.

Nine months after Shelby and her Prince Charming married, Debra was born. Then, on their first anniversary, they moved into a small apartment in Chicago over 2,000 miles from home and away from any friends and family. Shelby was lonesome and unhappy. Inwardly she blamed her husband for taking her away from California, but they never discussed her feelings because he was working sixteen hours a day and had little time for her.

With most victims of sexual abuse, intimacy in marriage is very difficult. Old feelings of fear resurface and the victim tends to put responsibility for the past on the present mate. Victims invariably have a built-in low self-esteem. If they'd been worth anything, no one would have abused them. If anyone had really loved them, they would have stopped what was going on. As Shelby sat alone waiting for her husband to come home at night, she assumed his preoccupation with his job was because he didn't find her company of value.

In Chicago they didn't go to church and so Shelby was robbed of fellowship, spiritual growth, and positive role models. Shelby had put all her HOPE in marriage and she was miserable. Even with the numerous hours her husband put in on the job, the move didn't work out as he had hoped and they moved back to California at the end of one year.

Shelby was grateful to be in the sunshine again and she celebrated by having a son, Doug, as she had always planned. Two years later at twenty-eight years of age, Shelby's husband lost his business. Everything they had accumulated was stripped from them: their house, two cars, and everything they were purchasing on credit. For Shelby who had grown up longing for the things she had been deprived of in childhood, this loss of possessions was a devastation of her hopes and her worth.

Her son developed asthma, often a sign of extreme emotional stress, and they had to move to Santa Rosa to find some clean air. By this time they had moved twelve times and Shelby had given up "the good life." Her husband continued his long working hours and spent much of their income in making himself appear to have a lofty lifestyle. He paid little attention to family activities and never attended one school event.

In his pursuit of pleasure, he took flying lessons and Shelby, in an effort to create some kind of a bond between them, signed up for lessons too. She remembers the first time she soloed. "I talked to God a lot. I asked him how on earth I'd ever gotten here and what was I going to do." The words came to her mind, "You're in this by yourself and you're going to land it alone."

In March 1974, just before Shelby was to get her pilot's license, her husband called and asked her to pack a suitcase for him. He was flying to Fresno for the weekend in the company plane. Shelby looked forward to a quiet few days and decided she'd tackle some sewing projects she had postponed. He came for his bag, kissed her good-bye, and left on business. On Sunday he called to say he had to stay longer—and on Monday and on Tuesday and on Wednesday. On Thursday a neighbor who always seemed to be the sage and seer of the community came to tell Shelby that her husband was not coming back.

Shelby couldn't accept this report; she jumped into her car and raced to his office. She burst in the door and there he was behind his desk, as usual. There seemed to be nothing wrong. She blurted out what the neighbor had said, expecting a refutation. As she waited, he swallowed, looked her in the eye and said, "It's true. I know it's wrong but I'm not coming back to this marriage ever."

Shelby was stunned. She couldn't believe her ears. At thirty-five years old and after thirteen and a half years of marriage, she was being tossed away like a used Kleenex. What had happened to her dreams? She says:

I couldn't imagine this was happening to me. I didn't know where to turn. How were the bills to be paid? His business always had problems. There was no money in the bank. I hadn't worked in twelve years; I had no skills; I had a valueless education. I was frightened. I was angry. I was hostile. I didn't deserve this. I had done everything that I knew how to be a good wife and mother and I blamed God for taking away my ideals and my dreams of creating and having a beautiful family and a loving lifestyle.

I was irrational. I would get up in the middle of the night, make sure that my children were asleep, and then drive down to the area that I thought my husband was in and search the driveways and parking lots for his car because I still did not know where he was. I called friends asking for help. None of them knew what to do. I called a judge we knew. I called an attorney we knew. I called the insurance man. What do I do; what do I do? Where do I go? None of them offered me help.

I asked around for counselors. No one knew one. I leafed through the yellow pages and found a name. As I sat down in his office and talked, I took a real good look at him. He was sloppy, about seventy-five pounds overweight, and had a crewcut in a time when everyone wore long hair. He smoked a pipe and no matter how startling a statement I made to him, he simply nodded his head. I thought, "This man is from nowhere; he has more problems than I have. I'm not staying here." I dropped that counselor immediately.

Shelby went through the typical panic for help and could find none. How great it is today that so many of our churches are prepared to assist people like Shelby, to offer Christian counseling, to suggest honest legal aid, to provide temporary funding for those in need.

Shelby couldn't eat; she couldn't sleep. She felt as if her blood was running madly in circles through her body and she couldn't rest. Several times she cleaned her house from top to bottom in the middle of the night. She couldn't think of anything else to do. Some nights she wanted to run away but she couldn't leave the children, so she walked in circles around the dining room table. Around and around and around.

One time she borrowed a friend's camper and took the children on a long drive to Sacramento. They loved the campground but didn't know their mother never slept.

Shelby was exhausted, alone, helpless! Maybe another counselor would help even though the first one was a mistake. She hunted up another name in the phone book. This counselor seemed positive and cheerful, but he recorded everything Shelby said and she felt she was going to be one more case history in his book of records. He came up with some logical sounding advice. "Locate the other woman that your husband is living with, explain the family financial situation, and she'll probably pull out." How simple!

Shelby had no idea who this woman was or where they were living so she went to her all-knowing neighbor who gave her the facts. Shelby was eager to straighten this out once and for all. When she arrived at the door of the apartment, she was let in. The woman listened to Shelby as she explained about her family's financial state and reminded her that she and her husband were not yet divorced. But the woman stated she was going ahead with her choice regardless of the circumstances. She had no bad feelings about being part of a family breakup. She was in love.

The next day Shelby parked her car in a public garage, and as she rounded a corner, she ran right into her husband. He had followed her there and she was terrified. "He's going to kill me," she thought. "I'm ready Lord. I'm ready for heaven. Here I come."

"It's a nice day, isn't it?" he asked.

"Yes, just lovely."

"How are the children?"

"Fine."

"I hear you're looking for a job."

"I *have* a job!"

As Shelby backed toward her car, he concluded, "By the way, I didn't like what you did yesterday. Don't do it again."

"I won't. I won't."

Wrong advice again. She began to ask everyone she met what she should do. The advice was often the same.

- "This is not unusual. A lot of people are in the same boat."
- "Everyone's getting a divorce."
- "Cheer up, it could be worse."
- "Forget about your marriage."
- "Move on. Set up a new life."
- "Statistics show a man who leaves for another woman never returns."
- "The worst thing you could have done was to go visit her."
- "Establish new relationships."

- "Be discreet with other men until after your court appearance.
  You wouldn't want to look bad for the child custody question."

No one seemed to have any thought as to how she might put this marriage back together. The advice was always: Forget it and move on.

Shelby tried to move on even though she couldn't forget it. One morning she got up early and decided, "I will get a job today! I can't go on circling the dining room table forever." And she did.

She dressed up, practiced a smile in the mirror, and started driving around town. She went first to a store she had worked in years before, but they had no openings. She drove into Santa Rosa and as she turned a corner she had a definite leading, "Go in there." She looked up to see "there" and it was a bank. She said to herself, "You don't know anything about banks except that you have trouble in them." She drove by and parked down the street. When she got out she was by another bank, so she went in. No hope. That feeling was still there so she walked down to the first bank and went in. The manager came out, asked her a few questions and said, "Wanda quit this morning. You can have her job."

This was the first dot of light at the end of her dark tunnel. Shelby started to go to church again and she began to feel better even though she had severe swings in moods. One day she'd feel she was going to make it and the next day she'd be suicidal.

She thought, "There must be someone somewhere that I can talk to."

She asked at church and was referred to Gary, a Christian counselor. Up to this point Shelby had been in shock, with some denial, and had not cried. But when she sat before Gary she dissolved into sobbing tears.

When I saw a man I could trust, who grieved with me over my situation, I fell apart. For three sessions I did nothing but cry.

Gary told her that God didn't like divorce. She might have to move on without her husband, but it wasn't because God didn't care. Gary helped her to get back into reading the Bible after her years in the spiritual wilderness. Shelby chose a life verse: "Show me your ways, oh Lord, teach me your path. Guide me in your truth and teach me. For you are God, my Saviour and my HOPE is in you all day long" (Ps. 25:4–5, NIV).

Gary showed Shelby that her children had been in limbo. She had fed them but had ignored them emotionally. He told her she had to take charge again and be a parent. She had to discuss her problems with them on their level but not drop burdens upon them that would be too heavy for them to bear.

Shelby joined a singles group at church and began to relate with others who were working through similar problems. She tried to show interest in her children's activities again and was able to smile proudly when Debbie was crowned Honor Queen of Job's Daughters.

Then came the holidays! All people who are going through a divorce find these first holidays the hardest.

The children were with their father, and Shelby cried for four days. It was bad enough to have no husband, but she had no children either.

Gary helped her to see that holidays would never be the same, but they could be different and still be good. Gary promised her that he, his wife, and five children would take Shelby next year to a grove of giant redwoods in the center of a forest and set up a Thanksgiving banquet table. They did. It was not the same, but it was good.

Christmas changed also. Shelby invited a group of singles to her home. She provided the turkey and they brought the other dishes. One year she adopted a destitute family from a service agency and took them food and a Christmas tree. A few years later Shelby was able to spend Christmas alone.

She was grateful to God for some time to herself. She lit a fire, unplugged the phone, didn't turn on the TV, and never got out of her pajamas. She relaxed, meditated on her life, and thanked God for Jesus' birth and her salvation. She praised him for how far he'd brought her and remembered his words in the airplane, "You're in this by yourself and you're going to land it alone."

Christmas will never be the same but it can be different and still be good. Gary also led Shelby through some counseling of her past, going back to her abuse as a child. He showed her how she had put such a desperate price on having money and needing things that she had failed to put her trust in the Lord. As he helped her heal the pains of her past, she began to put the present in perspective.

Because Shelby had to work, she couldn't be home with her

children and she counted on the Lord and her neighbors to watch over them. The children were ten and thirteen at the time of the divorce and there was one neighbor who provided the eagle-eye watch for the community. She would call Shelby at work and say, "Do you want Doug out playing in the storm drain in the middle of the street?" "Do you really want Doug on the roof again?"

Shelby would dial home and let her phone ring and ring. Finally Doug would answer and she'd say, "I don't want you on the roof anymore."

Doug was so impressed with his mother's psychic powers that he stopped doing anything too bad. It wasn't until years later that Shelby told him how she always knew what he was up to.

Shelby knew she had to get more education in order to be promoted, so she enrolled at Santa Rosa Junior College and earned an associate's degree. The classes were late at night and many times as she walked to her car in the rain she would cry out to God, "Is this really what you want me to do?"

When Debbie chose San Diego State as the college she would attend, Shelby moved there also and began going to a large church with a new singles ministry she helped develop. Doug had stayed with his father for a year after which living with Shelby looked much better. He returned and began attending a high school youth group at the church. He made friends in this new area and soon committed his life to the Lord Jesus. The youth pastor helped Doug develop his cartooning and comedy skills and he established new and life-changing goals.

One of the most important things that happened for Doug in those days was the formation of a group in their church called "The Good Shepherds." These were dedicated men who took the sons of single mothers out once a month on a special outing. They would go to the beach, the mountains, an amusement park, or a ball field. They became substitute fathers and positive role models for these young boys deprived of normal family life.

I recently talked with a single mother who was having problems with her son. I asked her, "What would be the best thing this church could do for you?" She answered instantly, "Have some of the good men pay some attention to these young boys without fathers." What a fulfilling ministry it could be if "good men" would pour their lives into those of boys in need.

Any woman who has been divorced knows how quickly her self-esteem drops, but if she has also been a victim as a child, she may never recover. Shelby realized that she needed help in raising her inner spirits, so she took time out of her work to attend seminars that would be meaningful and relevant to her own needs. It was at this point in Shelby's life that I met her at our very first CLASS. In those intervening years I have seen Shelby change from a shy person with little confidence or concern for how she dressed to a sharp, attractive speaker. At our HOPE Conference she stood before the group with calm assurance and told the story of her life with depth and humor. I could hardly believe the difference.

Shelby attended seminars other than CLASS and learned from Psalm 139:14, "I am fearfully and wonderfully made" (kjv). She found that God felt her "works are wonderful" and he wanted her to be able to accept herself as he made her.

She urges others in her position to seek help everywhere it is available: from friends, family, counseling, pastors, books, seminars, and courses. Then get out and help others. Shelby says, "Believe me it will not take much looking to find someone who is worse off than you."

In Shelby's church some of the single parents formed a support group called GLUBs. Curious people asked, "Does that stand for 'God Loves Us Best,' 'God Looks Under Beds'?" "No," Shelby replies, "we are 'God's Little Unclaimed Blessings.' " These little unclaimed blessings meet monthly and their aim is to become the women God wants them to be, with or without husbands.

There were many difficult days for Shelby as she tried to bring up her children and herself alone. Days when the car wouldn't start, when her son was in the emergency room, when they went three years with no TV because they couldn't afford to replace the one that broke. *That was really a good thing for our family as we used that time to get out of doors and we spent evenings talking to each other.* Shelby encouraged her children to discover and develop their unique talents. Debbie got a degree in business finance from San Diego State and Doug is a speech major at Point Loma College.

In her search for every kind of help available, Shelby discovered that the bank she worked for had a trust fund for women. Because of a class action suit, they had set up a million-dollar trust fund exclusively for women's education and advancement. Shelby applied and was approved. She has studied hard and has wisely used the $10,000 she received to attend National University where she proudly received both a B.A. in Business Administration and a master's degree in Human Behavior. Because of these degrees she was part of the management trainee program in the bank where she is now a Financial Services officer. She is also studying to be better equipped in counseling others in need.

Shelby suggests that other women who need a direction search around and see what grants and fundings are available. Some of these programs are set up for specific reasons, and you might be the one to qualify.

Most of all, Shelby says:

Don't waste time and energy in being bitter over the bad deal you got in life. I have lived through sexual abuse as a child, desertion and divorce as an adult. I have lived through discrimination both as a female and as a middle-aged person looking for a job. I have raised two children to be productive adults by myself. Additionally, I have experienced the death of my younger sister through cancer and my own serious hospitalization with typhoid fever. Yet I believe God wants me to use all of this experience and the knowledge of his delivering power to help others. He can't do this if I'm sitting in self-pity or anger. I have learned that the acid of bitterness only eats away at the container.

Are you one of God's little unclaimed blessings? It's so much easier to give up and sit around in justified self-pity, but God can open amazing doors of opportunity when you reach out for the handle. He alone can brighten the corner where you are.

EMILIE BARNES

Family Stress and Crisis

When Fred and I decided to put on the HOPE Conference and we began the selection of those women whose lives would be victorious examples to others, I thought of Emilie Barnes. Her ministry of helping women have "More Hours in My Day" has brought practical change into the lives of more women in Southern California than any other I know.

Emilie and I met fifteen years ago when I was teaching a Bible study in Riverside where Emilie lived. From the moment I learned that she grew up in three rooms behind her mother's dress shop and compared her background to my living in three rooms behind my father's store, I loved her as a sister. We have many other traits in common. We both love to teach and train, to decorate and entertain. We're both born leaders who innately take charge of any situation and fill leadership vacuums. As we began to travel and speak together, we would alternate weeks of being in charge. On Emilie's week she would decide where we ate and who would go first through revolving doors. As we developed our FEMINAR and wrote materials, our aim was to make the life of Christian women more fun and less work, more uplifting and less stressful. I taught on understanding our personalities and overcoming depression, while Emilie showed women in practical terms how to get their home, heart, and handbag in order.

These exciting years were God's preparation for the separate ministries he had in mind for us. Throughout this time we grew together and became best friends, and I had the joyful opportunity of observing Emilie's home and habits and seeing that here is a role model of a Christian woman who does practice what she preaches. If Emilie hasn't lived it, she won't teach it.

Because of my high respect and admiration for Emilie, I called her and explained we were doing a seminar where women would tell the traumas of their lives and the steps to their solutions. Her typical quick reply was, "If I can conjure up a trauma in the next few minutes, I'd love to be a part of it."

I explained, "Emilie, we don't need another victim or an alcoholic, we want you to tell the discouraged mother of young children that she can make it, to relieve the stress of women trying to be all things to all people. Would you be willing?"

As we discussed the stress upon the average woman today, the wear and tear on her emotions, we knew there was a need for some answers. During the years when Emilie and I were raising our children, the word "stress" had not come into style. We didn't even realize what emotional handicaps we were living under and that our feelings and frustrations had a name; but now stress is the disorder of the decade.

Dr. Hans Selye, a Nobel Prize winner, was the inventor of the word "stress" as we use it today and came up with this comforting thought: "Complete freedom from stress is death." This maxim may encourage some of you who have been struggling for the rewards of the stress-free life.[1]

Dr. Selye wrote that the secret of life is the successful adjustment to ever-changing stress. "There are two roads to survival," he said, "fight or adaptation. And most often adaptation is the more successful."[2]

Planning for Health, a bulletin published by a medical care program in Southern California, Kaiser Permanente, states, "Intense and constant anger, fear, frustration or worry that is bottled up inside can threaten health. It is this build up of emotional stress without release of tension that leads to trouble. Physical distress can often be a kind of 'body language' to express emotional troubles that have been repressed. Some of our most common expressions show that we all know something of this body language of the emotions. 'He burns me up . . .' 'This is more than I can stomach . . .' 'That makes my blood run cold . . .' These are only a few of the many examples of the awareness that is reflected in our everyday speech."[3]

Because Kaiser's aim is to keep people out of its hospitals, they suggest that you not bottle up your feelings but find someone to talk with who will care. In our stressful society it is not easy to find an unstressed person who wants to hear about your stresses, so perhaps prevention could be a preferable solution.

Since we know stress may cause depression, heart disease, asthma, diabetes, lower back pain, skin rashes, accidents, digestive complaints, substance abuse, allergies, and mental illnesses, we want to avoid whatever pressures possible. We are advised to stay in the sunshine and away from noise. We should lose weight, give up smoking and drinking, cut down on salt and caffeine, take more vacations, exercise daily, relax, meditate, and give up pills. We should realize stress decreases protein level, retains sodium, raises cholesterol, and wipes out vitamin B-2.

Dr. Richard Hart, director of the Center for Health Promotion at Loma Linda University says, "In the past, hospitals have run health education programs. But merely disseminating information isn't sufficient. Even with the right information, most people don't change their lifestyles."[4] How true it is that even knowing what we should eat and how we should live, few of us want to change until faced with a personal crisis.

Loma Linda, a Seventh Day Adventist medical center, has very successful programs on stress management, cardiac enhancement, diet and nutrition, smoking cessation, and weight loss. These programs all have a spiritual emphasis and help people change their approaches, attitudes, and behavior patterns rather than encourage use of drugs.

"We need to plug into something outside of ourselves that reaffirms us," says Dr. Hart. "It's a rare individual who can do it on his own. It's usually the one who thinks he doesn't need [anything besides himself] who needs the most.

"Until a person can wade through that, they're not going to have success. Many Christians in the country are reaffirming their concept of God. That reaffirmation is a tremendous tool for motivation or change that many people don't tap into."[5]

Emilie Barnes is one who has had many stresses in her life, but she has disciplined herself to eat correctly, exercise daily, and tap into that supernatural strength that is available for each one of us. Let's find out what it is that makes Emilie the healthy, organized, dynamic leading lady she is today.

Emilie grew up in a Jewish home in Los Angeles with a typical Jewish mother and an alcoholic father. When her father drank he became violent and often abused her mother and younger brother. Although he never laid a hand on Emilie, she lived in fear of the day when he would strike out at her. She remembers walking alone to school one day when she was eleven and saying to herself, "I wish my father would die." When she got home that afternoon, her father was dead. Guilt swept over her and she wondered if God would punish her for her wish.

There was little time for remorse or introspection as Emilie was given the entire responsibility of running the home. There was no insurance, there were hospital and funeral expenses to be paid, and there was no available income. Debts had piled up and her mother, Irene, had no idea what to do for work. Irene's sister, who was successful and solvent, loaned her enough money to open a tiny dress shop in Los Angeles and the three of them moved into three little rooms behind the store. Because her mother had to work all the time to earn enough for them to eat, Emilie took charge of the daily duties. At eleven she was doing the washing and hanging the clothes out on a clothesline strung on top of the roof. Emilie hung the washed clothes carefully because if she dropped one piece on the tarpaper roof it would have to be washed again. She planned the meals carefully to save money and did the marketing and cooking. When Emilie wasn't in school or doing housework, she was working in the store and learning the dress business. There was no time for play.

When her hard-working, energetic mother decided to feature her fashions in some local shows, she sent Emilie to modeling school so she would always have a built-in model available at no cost. Emilie was not typical model material, but it was then that she met her friend Esther who was. Emilie was short and slight with big brown eyes that matched her hair. Esther was tall, blonde, and voluptuous and seemed to attract boys wherever she went.

The summer before her junior year in high school, Emilie extracted a promise from Esther. "If one of us gets a date we won't accept it unless the other has one too!" Emilie knew this might be a one-sided problem, but Esther was agreeable.

Bill, a college senior, wanted to date Esther. She smiled and said, "I'd love to go out with you, but you'll have to find a date for little Emilie." Bill looked Emilie over and remembered his identical twin brother Bob owed him a big favor. Bob had no choice so he agreed on the blind date.

Emilie, at fifteen, fell in love with this college man and he seemed to enjoy her too. They had the perfect summer romance spent bicycling and boating, picnicking and partying. When fall came, Bob packed up to return to college and said to Emilie, "It's been a fun summer and I like you a lot. See you around."

See her around? Around where? And when?

Bob was not about to let his fraternity brothers know he'd dated a little high school girl so he went back to school free of any confining relationship.

Emilie was the heartbroken heroine, virtuous and faultless, yet spurned by the man she loved. "I may be young," she thought, "but I know how to run a home. I can wash and iron, cook and sew."

As Bob looked over the crop of girls at college, not one had the sparkle of Emilie's big brown eyes, the sense of humor that made him happy, the drive and energy that gave him excitement. He had to admit, "I miss the kid."

Bob started coming home weekends and Emilie knew she was in love. One evening after they had been out on a date, Bob brought her back to the little apartment behind the store. They sat down on the sofa and as he moved over toward Emilie, he became still and serious. He looked into her startled eyes, held her face in his hands and said, "Emilie, I love you, but I cannot ask you to marry me."

She couldn't understand what he meant and she asked, "If we love each other, then why can't we get married?"

Bob replied, "Emilie, you know that I am a Christian." She knew he was a Gentile, but she didn't know what a Christian was. As she sat confused, Bob explained, "If God wanted to communicate with his people, how do you think he would do it? Picture if there was a snail on the ground and you wanted to talk with that snail. How would you do it?" Emilie had no idea. She'd never wanted to talk to a snail! Bob answered for her, "You would have to become a snail wouldn't you?" If she'd not wanted to talk to one, she surely didn't want to become one. Bob went on, "That is what God did. He wanted to talk to his people so he became a person in his son Jesus Christ, your Messiah. He came on this earth to love and to teach his people, but most of all he came to die for our sins."

Emilie looked up at Bob and said hopefully, "That is a wonderful thought, but I am not a sinner. I am a good little Jewish girl. I have been confirmed and I have been to Hebrew School."

Bob asked, "Do you know what sin is?" As Emilie thought of a string of bad things, he went on, "Sin is when you say, 'I want to lead my own life, go my own way, and make my own decisions.' " Emilie realized she was leading her own life, going her own way, and making her own decisions. She believed in God, but he was not a part of her life. Bob quoted the Bible, "For all have sinned and fallen short of the glory of God" (Rom. 3:23, NAS). "For the wages of sin is death, but the gift of God is eternal life through Jesus Christ" (Rom. 6:23, NAS). "I am the way, the truth, and the life, and no man comes unto the Father but by me" (John 14:6, NAS).

Emilie had never had a boyfriend who sat on the couch and quoted Bible verses. Bob continued, "Emilie, what you need to do, when you're ready to receive the Messiah into your life, is to open the door of your heart and invite him to come in. When you do, that's what will make you a Christian. At the very moment you invite him in you have eternal life. Eternity begins at that very moment and when we die, it's merely a change of address. You see, Romans says that "God demonstrated his love toward us that while we were yet sinners he died for us" (Rom. 5:8, NAS). He takes us exactly where we are. He went to that cross and he took upon himself the sins of the world, past, present, and any one we'll ever commit in the future. He died for those sins. He conquered that death and he rose again. When we receive him that's what makes us a Christian.

When Bob left that night he told Emilie he loved her and he would be praying for her. Bob had been raised in a Christian home. He had learned how to share his faith as a child. He knew if such a situation arose in his life he would be equipped to handle it. He knew that God would answer that prayer in his perfect timing. "I love you and I'll pray for you."

As Emilie went into her tiny bedroom that night she realized that if she didn't become a Christian, she wouldn't be able to marry the man she loved. She was also smart enough to know that she couldn't just fake it and say she was a Christian for the rest of her life. She thought of the many times that she had been in Bob's home and how never once had his family ever said anything about her being of a different faith. She knew they loved her, they were concerned for her, and most of all, they prayed for her. That night in the quietness of her room Emilie asked God, "Did you have a son? Is his name Jesus? Is he the Messiah that our people are waiting for? I want to open the door of my heart; I want that completion; I want that fulfillment." Emilie stepped that night into the family of God. Her eternity began at that very moment.

When Bob and Emilie announced their engagement, the aunt and uncle who had originally loaned Emilie's mother the money to go into business were terribly upset. Bob wouldn't marry Emilie unless she was a Christian but her relatives wouldn't accept her if she was. They tried to bribe her by offering to send her to Europe, "We'll give you a car, a wardrobe, plus an unlimited expense account, if you will not marry this young man." It was everything in the world a sixteen-year-old would love to have. More than Emilie had ever dreamed of having. It was at that point that God proved to Emilie, "I do have a son; his name is Jesus; he is our Messiah, a free gift with no strings attached." Emilie chose the Messiah and Bob, with no strings attached, instead of her aunt's gifts with qualifications.

Because Emilie's Jewish relatives would not come to a church wedding, Bob and Emilie were married in a friend's home. As Emilie was starting her senior year in high school, Bob was beginning his first year of teaching. He had to sign her report cards during her senior year. Emilie set up housekeeping with a flair and was an amazing manager for someone her age. Three years after they were married little Jenny was born. Then, a few months after Jenny's birth, Emilie's brother was left alone with three precious little children. His wife walked out the door as if she was going to the market and they never heard from her again. She had a recipe for stress. She was hassled by life's pressures, she was hustled by people's demands, and she was hurried by schedules and children. Her answer to stress was to check out, skip town, leave it all behind. Emilie's brother checked out too. He couldn't handle the recipe either and he escaped through alcohol and drugs. His motto was:

If you can't handle stress, you can try to blot it out.

Those little children were left to run life on their own. If a bottle was thrown into the crib, the baby drank; if not, she cried. If the little ones could find some food they ate; if not, they'd visit the lady next door. Early, one morning, they wandered over, totally naked, and asked for something to eat. The lady couldn't find their father so she called Emilie.

When Emilie found out the state of deprivation and neglect her brother's children were in, she asked him if she could take them until he could get himself pulled together. He gave over control and Supermom had to become Superwoman. For one month Emilie was fantastic, then she found out she was pregnant. Her energy level dropped and her stress level rose.

One afternoon she had all four little ones in bed and she collapsed for a nap herself. As she was sleeping soundly, she felt a little tap on her arm and she opened her eyes to see her niece Keri covered with red paint. Emilie jumped up and followed the footsteps to the neighbor's yard where she found an open paint can and a brush. She covered it up, took the child home, scolded her, and scrubbed her. When she had her all cleaned up, she put her back in bed and said, "Don't you dare get out of that bed again!"

Although Emilie was exhausted, the child was invigorated. Emilie fell instantly asleep and Keri toddled her way back to the paint. Suddenly Emilie awakened with that sixth sense a mother has, checked Keri's bed, and found her missing. By the time Emilie got to the yard, little Keri's fingers had pried open the lid and she was splashing happily in red paint.

Can you mothers feel how Emilie felt? Would you have grabbed this paint-spotted child, shaken her, spanked her, and wanted to strangle her? Might you have lost control? Are some of you so stressed out that you take your frustrations out on the first child who does something wrong? Mothers who abuse their children usually don't mean to and don't want to. They're just so overwhelmed and exhausted that when some trouble hits they thirst for the kill. They're like a rubber band stretched beyond its ability; one more pull and they'll snap.

Emilie says, "It's not because we don't love our children that we abuse them at times; it's because we're hustled or hassled or hurried. It's because that mixing bowl inside of us, with all of those ingredients, is festering up and we're filled with stress that we can't handle."

By the time Emilie gave birth to Brad, she had five children under five years old and she was only twenty-one. What does a young mother like that do? Does she throw in the towel? Emilie now teaches young mothers what to do from her own experience in her own *More Hours in My Day* seminars.

One woman came up to her and said, "Emilie, I want to tell you that if today doesn't work, I'm through. I am turning in my resignation. I'm not going to be a wife or a mother anymore." Another woman wrote, "I'm in a time in my life where I feel very frustrated. I'm a mother of five children; I just go around and around and around in circles. I get more discouraged every day. What would be your advice?" And at the bottom of the letter she printed, "Help!" Another wrote, "I'm a frustrated person. It seems I just can't get myself started. I'm a single parent working an almost full-time job. I just never seem to have time to get it all together. I've dated a wonderful godly man for the last three years and I'm sure that if I were a better homemaker he would have married me by now. My home is dirty and cluttered. Do you think you can help me?"

Emilie started her own coping behavior with a desperate prayer for divine help and God assured her, "I've given you this responsibility and I'm going to show you how to handle it." Emilie found Proverbs 16:3 where it says that we are to commit our works unto the Lord and our thoughts will be established. "God, that's fine," Emilie said, "but I have five little babies that are hanging on me all the time. I'm washing and ironing and pottying and diapering and I don't have time for myself."

God answered, "Emilie, you do have time. You could get up in the morning when the house is quiet; you could commit your day to me." Emilie began to get organized. In those frustrating days of five babies under five years old, she knew that if she didn't pull it all together that she wasn't going to be any different than her sister-in-law who copped out and ran away. Emilie recalls those impossible years:

I would force myself to set the alarm for ten minutes to five each morning. I would take my Bible, read some verses, and pray. I would practically throw myself across my daily scheduling of all the things that I had to do and I would say, "God, please help me to do those things which you would have me to do. Make me the mother today that you want me to be so that I can love, that I can touch, that I can hug those children. I can't do it on my own, I'm tired, I'm overwhelmed." God met my need every day that I committed my work to him.

After Emilie prayed for the ability to get organized, she started to do something about it. So many of us want to be organized, but not enough to do something about it. She made menu planners and let the children give suggestions. They loved the time when Emilie would call them to the table to decide what to eat for the week. The fact that they had a part in choosing made them more enthused when the meal was put before them. After a while they could plan the whole week in twelve minutes.

Next, Emilie typed up a marketing list and had it duplicated so she always had one on the refrigerator door to check off as she saw an item was running low. She used this list as she made her menus so that she could do her major marketing once a week and save time by not rushing to the store for emergencies. Emilie says, *As soon as children can read B-R-E-A-D, they can check off items they notice are needed.*

Even little children can do simple household jobs. So Emilie wrote duties on slips of paper and put them in a basket. Each day each child would draw one and when the job was completed the child got a star beside his name on the Work Chart.

Friday night was set aside as Family Fun Time when they would do something special together: go for a picnic supper in the park, play a favorite game, or pop a big bowl of popcorn.

The two sides stopped fighting. It was no longer mother against the world. They were now on the same team. Every day wasn't perfect, but the stress was reduced to a level with which Emilie could cope. After four years with five little ones, Emilie had organized her mind, her kitchen, her marriage, and her children. Her brother remarried at that point and took his three back. The woman he married had two children of her own, so *they* then had five!

If you are hurried, hassled, and hustled with two children, borrow three from your brother and keep them for a few years—or perhaps a few hours will do. When you can function well with them, send them back and life will seem so easy without them.

During the time Emilie was learning to manage five preschoolers, her mother had been under emotional stress caused by her son's problems and concern for her grandchildren. She was in her sixties and still trying to run her business. She was tired and lonely and by the time she called Emilie for help, she was bankrupt. She was unable to cope; she had no money and nowhere to go. Emilie and Bob moved her into their home and as Bob put her suitcases into the car, he said to his Jewish mother-in-law, "On Sunday we all go to church."

Emilie was surprised he'd made that statement and wondered what her mother would do. When Sunday came, Irene was dressed and ready and off they went to church. Irene was brokenhearted that she had lost her business and had to depend on Emilie and Bob. She was downcast, joyless, and depressed. She didn't want to go anywhere, but each Sunday she'd pull herself together and head for church. At the age of sixty-five Emilie's mother opened the door of her heart and asked her Messiah, the Lord Jesus, to come in. As he healed her broken heart, she was able to get a job in a department store and feel some self-worth again. When I first met her I was struck by the look of peace and joy on her face. The Lord took her home at seventy-eight years of age to join Abraham, Isaac, and Jacob.

By the time Emilie was in her mid-thirties both of her children were off to college. This fact is a fascinating contrast to my life in which I adopted a three-month-old baby when I was thirty-five! Emilie was ready to start a second life at the age when I was just starting with a new little one.

When I first met Emilie, I was so impressed because she had everything in her house organized. The garage was full of numbered boxes, cross-referenced into little files. She had made every chart imaginable and she had her home decorated to quaint and cozy perfection. Baskets hung off the ceiling, antique dolls sat on the stairs, and a huge scale weighed the plants on the coffee table. Emilie had organized everything there was to organize and decorated everything there was to decorate. Emilie had done it all and done it right!

When her second child went off to college, Emilie waved good-bye and reentered the house. It was empty. She went from room to room and no one was there. Suddenly she wasn't really a mother any more. From her teen years she had been majoring in motherhood. She'd never been a child; she'd always been a mother.

Emilie felt no one needed her any more and she threw herself on the floor and cried out to God:

They're gone. I'm not a Mom. I don't care any more. I don't even care to live. But God, I know you're there. I know you've brought me this far and I know that you have a plan for me, but I don't know what it is and I need it now.

Emilie didn't hear a word. She didn't hear God telling her where to go or what to do; she didn't get the answer she needed NOW! But on that floor with her face in the carpet she pledged:

God, make me the woman that you want me to be. I am here stripped of myself. Use me in any way that I can be used. I need to know that I am a woman again.

Emilie didn't sit depressed, waiting for God to get creative. She started a Bible study in her home for young mothers who needed HOPE. She attended a Christian class on self-identity. She and Bob started a couple's study that grew so fast it ultimately became a church.

From the time I met Emilie, I had always seen her as poised and put together. I surely didn't see her as a person in need. It wasn't until years later that she told me I had become her friend just when she needed someone to encourage her. It was my husband Fred who first suggested that we start a course together. "You two have so much to offer other women that you'd better write a seminar." Fred set up a time table for our writing and I distinctly remember our first FEMINAR because Fred had scheduled it for the week following our daughter Lauren's wedding. When other mothers would have been fluffing around in filmy frocks, I was proofreading copy and rushing it to the printers. Emilie and I met our deadline and that was the official start of our speaking ministries.

As I began writing books, I encouraged Emilie to put her organizational skills on paper so that women around the country could also have *more hours* in their day. One morning as Emilie had adjusted to her empty nest and was excited over her organization seminars, Bob walked into the house. Years before he had founded a mobile home business and had sold it to a large company who had retained him as general manager. As Emilie looked up, wondering why Bob was home, he stated calmly, "I am no longer employed."

What happens when a man in his fifties loses his job like Bob or has business problems as Fred has had? Does he automatically have a mid-life crisis? Does he run away from middle age? Buy a Corvette? Take scuba diving lessons? Run off with someone else's wife?

So many go through the same stages found in any loss situation as explained by Lauren in chapter thirteen.

- **Shock:** "I can't believe this is true after all I've put into this business."
- **Denial:** "It can't be true. There must be a mistake."
- **Anger:** "I'll kill the guys that did this to me."
- **Guilt:** "What did I do wrong? If only . . ."
- **Depression:** "It's over. I'm washed up. It's downhill from here."
- **Resolution:** (The hopeful acceptance of the facts as they are.) "I guess I'm going to make it."

One friend of mine was such a business success that he was featured on the front page of the *Wall Street Journal* (12 March 1982). Jerald Maxwell helped start Med General and his shares were worth $4 million. As chairman and chief executive officer he was over-confident and over-extended. Shortly after he was dismissed by his board the company went bankrupt. He was shocked that the group he called the "board of directed" had the power to fire him. He couldn't believe it for it was his company. He swung from anger to depression, secluded himself at home, and knew life was over. He was no longer respected in the business community and because of his volatile behavior, he lost what he had at home.

During two long difficult years when he openly talked of suicide, he turned in desperation to the Lord, even though he had previously scorned religion, and went through therapy "to get him to understand that he didn't have to be a rich and successful executive to be happy." Now Jerry spends much of his time speaking and counseling businessmen in mid-life crises and sharing his faith in Jesus.

What did Bob do when the business he had founded removed

him? Emilie was shocked and couldn't believe it. "They can't run that company without you." She was angry. "We won't have any retirement. What's going to happen to us?"

Bob picked her up in his arms and said, "Emilie, this is a celebration. God has something bigger and better for us." Emilie tried to be happy, but she couldn't understand why Bob was so calm and not out running around hunting for a job. Then a call came from a popular Christian radio show in Los Angeles asking Emilie to appear and talk with callers for thirty minutes. Bob went with her and so many desperate stressful women called in that they kept her on for three hours. Since her phone number was given out, calls started coming in for "More Hours in My Day" seminars. Bob took the calls and set up the schedules. Soon Bob was so busy managing Emilie's ministry that he had no time for another job. One day it dawned on Emilie, "I couldn't do all this without Bob. This must be God's plan and our celebration."

The stress wasn't totally eliminated for Emilie as she and Bob were together twenty-four hours a day. On the good days Emilie would serve Bob tea and cookies at 4:00 in the afternoon, but there were some bad days when Bob corrected Emilie on something she'd done perfectly well without him for five years. She knew she was to accept Bob's authority, but on her territory? In her ministry? God showed her it was *his* ministry, not hers or Bob's. He had given it and he could take it away. She had to learn to accept God's plan without knowing why. Emilie reminds us:

I have found that Satan's attacks come especially during physical, mental, and spiritual weakness. He uses family arguments, discouragements, and anxieties, the hassles, the hustles, and the hurriedness of life's stress, to weaken our faith. Again I went to the throne of God and I began to look up his promises. I realized that I cannot be anxious (Matt. 6:24). I learned that I needed to draw near to him and be confident in God that he knew what he was doing in our lives (Heb. 4:14–16). I saw that I must allow God's path to be known to me and I began to lift my heart and my head unto God who is my authority and unto my husband who is my next authority (Ps. 24). As I began to give over to Bob the major decisions of the ministry, I realized that my life was becoming what God wanted it to be. I now know that quality time with God is essential in resolving any kind of stress.

Many of us in mid-life are faced with defeats and disappointments, but Emilie and I are grateful that our men have the spiritual maturity to recognize the sovereignty of God and know he will provide. Be close enough to the Lord in the good times that when the troubles come you'll already have your "hand in the hand of the one who stills the waters."

All the women in this section have suffered some family stress or crisis. Bonnie lived for three years observing an adulterous relationship with no assurance that there would be a happy ending. Mona had the fairytale Christian life and was suddenly abandoned and divorced by her pastor-husband. Shelby, abused as a child, had determined to create a loving Christian home for her husband and children, only to have him leave for another woman. Emilie struggled with five babies when she was hardly more than a child herself and later faced the shock of her husband losing all job security when he was fifty.

Are you under some stress today? Is there a crisis in your life? In each of these case histories, different though they may be, these women all wanted to put their lives on the mend. They each did all that was humanly possible to help their situations and they each sought God's direction within their hearts and minds and souls.

Not one went running off, trying to solve her problems without God's help; not one sat despondent, waiting for God to wind her up and send her on her way. Bonnie did the right things for her husband when her heart wasn't in it because God told her so. She prayed for guidance and God showed her she was to obey him and provide the most warm and loving home possible for her husband, regardless of what he might be up to. As Johnny observed her ability to stay calm under the most stressful of situations, he took down his defenses. Her actions, not her words, became a living witness to him, and her consistent loving spirit caused him to change his ways and conclude, "A man would have to be a fool to walk away from such love."

Under stress Bonnie did the positive physical acts of gracious kindness and sought God's will in dedicated prayer and study. She now leads an ardent prayer group in her home each week and teaches others how to be loving wives before it's too late.

God does not solve every problem in the same manner, rather he deals separately with each heartbreak. When Mona found herself holding a church with no pastor and a family with no father, she was under instant shock and stress. As she cried out for direction, God caused those parishioners whom she had served so faithfully to respond to her needs, even to sleeping on the floor beside her. Mona had to leave the church she and her husband had built, move out of the parsonage that had become her dream house, and cease her "Transmitting Love" ministry which now had no ring of truth. She worked teaching school to support herself, but she never stopped believing God could redeem her life. Each verse was a love letter from God to Mona and she lost her stress to the peace of the Lord. After her humbling, yes humiliating experiences, God brought her a new husband, a new church, a new parsonage, and a new message of "Transmitting Love."

Not every Christian woman whose husband leaves her and who stays faithful to God gets a romantic Prince Charming, for Shelby is still a single parent who has been working hard to educate herself and two children. She had reason to stay depressed, to give up, to go on welfare, but as she called out to God, he told her to pull herself together and go get a job. He opened the way and she went to work. Being a single working mother while going to school could discourage the most stalwart of women, but Shelby met every challenge and now counsels other women in similar stressful situations from her own experience and the Lord's inspiration.

The result of Emilie's facing her family of five and developing organizational skills to minimize her stress is a ministry of teaching women all over the country simple practical steps to take the hassle out of life. God took Bob's loss of position and turned it into a plus. Bob was so spiritually in tune that he could see his crisis as a celebration.

Not one of us knows what tomorrow will bring so let's keep so close to God and his word that if we come apart at the seams, we'll know who's tending the mending.

Patching the Guilt Quilt

Showing how we can lift the guilt so common
in victims of abuse and attack.

So weary with disasters,
      tugg'd with fortune,
That I would set my life
      on any chance,
To mend it or be rid on't.

Macbeth
William Shakespeare

Attempted Murder and Damaged Designs

Victims come in all sizes, all colors, and all ages. Children are victims of sexual abuse, pornography, and incest. Women are victims of rape, attack, and exploitation. Anyone can be a victim of divorce, of disease, of disaster. Houses can fall victim to fire, flood, tornados, or earthquakes. Victimization comes when you haven't asked for it and you don't deserve it, but it falls upon you anyway.

In this section we'll look at the lives of three women: Jennifer, a rape victim; Jan, an incest victim; and first, Barbara, a victim of the vicissitudes of life.

Almost twenty years ago Fred and I taught our initial marriage class in a San Bernardino church. In the audience was an outstanding couple, Barbara and John Bueler. I first noticed Barbara because of her shining golden hair and her big brown eyes looking up in child-like innocence and perpetual surprise. John was her protector, ruggedly handsome, the Western macho male. He looked like the perfect Marlboro man, without the cigarette.

When we moved our marriage classes from the church to our home where we had up to ninety people in attendance every Friday evening, we trained small group leaders to meet with five couples and review the homework for the week. Barbara and John were in the first group that we trained, and they soon became gifted leaders and dear friends. The Buelers are good people who never

121

set out to get in trouble and surely didn't deserve it when it fell
upon them.

Barbara asks:

*How many of you can say that life has gone exactly the way
that you designed? You planned a conflict-free existence but somehow along the way you were disillusioned by people. You planned
a perfect design and somehow it became damaged. Some of you
carefully prepared a design for your life and now you find that it's
been destroyed and there's nothing left. There's no way to go back
and pick up the pieces. Some of you've lost hope that life has
any real shape or design at all. But I'm going to share with you
that God takes those disillusioned designs and restores them. He
takes damaged designs and reshapes them. He takes destroyed designs and renews them.*

Barbara's words sum up her life where her designs were disillusioned,
damaged, and utterly destroyed.

When she was thirteen, Barbara stared in disbelief as her father,
the Sunday school superintendent and the lead tenor in the church
choir, stood with his suitcase in his hand and his pillow under
his arm and announced, "I'm leaving you. I don't know if I will
ever return."

Barbara couldn't believe her fun-loving father meant what he
said, but he walked out the door never to return. Barbara stood,
disillusioned, beside her brain-damaged brother Dickie and her toddler brother Billy.

Barbara's mother, who already knew the father drank too much
and had another woman, threw herself on the bed and cried out
to God, "You've promised to be a father to the fatherless. I give
you Barbara who's thirteen, Dickie who's nine, and Billy who's
only three. Oh God, be their father."

Mrs. Ward remembered James 1:5—if you lack wisdom God
will give it to you. She prayed, begging for wisdom to know how
to raise these children on her own with no money. She had to
homestead the house and go on welfare. Even though she was
ashamed when the church sent baskets of food to them on Thanksgiving, she never sat around in self-pity. She took charge of the
family and determined they would all go to church each Sunday
even though she had to face people who'd ask how she was doing

since her scoundrel husband ran off and left her.

Even at this young age, Barbara knew people were gossiping and she didn't want to go to church, but her quiet mother held her head high and insisted Barbara do the same. Barbara sat with arms folded in defiance, looking straight ahead to avoid the inquisitive glances of the congregation. She said to herself, "I may sit here, but I won't listen."

Amazingly, even when we don't want to listen, God's words slip into our minds, take root, and grow.

One evening as Barbara sat alone in her little bedroom wondering why her father had left, she decided the only thing to do with her life was to run away from it. Wasn't that what her father had done? He hadn't liked his responsibilities and he'd run away. Barbara climbed out the window of her room and ran away. But where do you go when you run away? Who wants you? The lack of a good answer is depressing in itself and Barbara went home feeling worse than before. She pulled herself in through the window and got quietly into bed pretending she'd never left.

Out of the darkness came a voice, "Is that you, Barbara?"

"Yes."

"Where have you been?"

"I've been right here in bed."

"No you haven't. You were there when I went to bed, but in the middle of the night a voice woke me up saying, 'Barbara, Barbara.' I checked your room and you were gone. You see, Barbara, when I begged God to be the father to you children, I asked that he let me know when any one of you was in trouble before the neighbors would find out. He told me you'd run away and I've been praying all night for you to return unharmed."

Barbara learned from that experience that both God and her mother loved her and really cared for her. She also had to admit that they were both on the same team and she had better be on their side.

From that night on, Barbara and her mother were friends, and Barbara always dared tell her what was on her mind. One evening as they were doing the dishes together, Barbara threw a handful of silver into the sink, looked at her mother, and cried out, "I hate him!"

"Hate who?" her mother asked.

"I hate my father. He's left me, he's married that other woman.

She's got a little girl and that little girl has my daddy!"

How easy it would have been for the two of them to say every nasty thing they could conjure up about this irresponsible man, to chronicle his sins and commiserate together; but instead this woman who had asked for God's wisdom stated clearly, "Barbara Ann, you will never speak about your father like that again because he *is* your father and half of you is him. The organized part of you is from me, but your personality is from him. When you hate him, you hate half of yourself."

Barbara's design for her life had been disillusioned, but a godly mother was putting her back together again and God gave her a promise, "Someday I'll use your life to show forth the salvation of the Lord" (Ps. 71:15, NAS).

When Barbara was eighteen, she married John in that same church her mother had made her attend. There was no lingering rebellion as Barbara walked the center aisle, only memories of sitting with folded hands staring straight ahead, trying not to hear God's word. But now she was a bride and a Sunday school teacher herself.

Many years and two children later, Barbara was leading the junior high department and noticed a shy girl who sat alone in the back of the room. Remembering how lonely she'd felt as a teen, Barbara reached out to her in love. One Sunday the girl was missing and Barbara wrote her a note asking her to return. The following week, Sheila Smith waited until everyone had left and softly said, "Thank you for writing me. No one has ever written me before. I guess no one has ever cared."

Barbara had a real compassion for this sad and lonely girl and she made special efforts to include her in some family activities. As they became acquainted, Barbara learned that Sheila's mother was emotionally disturbed and had threatened to kill her. Barbara was stunned with this information and doubled her efforts to make the girl feel loved and accepted. Barbara even became friends with Mrs. Smith and brought her to the Bible studies I held in my home.

One day the mother flew into a rage and Sheila ran away. When she was found, she was taken to Juvenile Hall and put in with girls who were in all sorts of trouble. The authorities could see this quiet child did not belong in detention, yet Sheila was afraid to go home because her mother had threatened to kill her. They asked if there was any other adult whom she admired and she mentioned Barbara, her Sunday school teacher.

A probation officer called and asked if Barbara would be willing to come to Juvenile Hall and discuss this case. Barbara had just made two fresh apricot pies and she had dinner underway. Her children weren't due home from school for several hours, so she agreed to drive into town.

When Barbara arrived she was amazed to see that Mrs. Smith was already there and they were seated next to each other across the desk from the probation officer. As Mrs. Smith expressed her anger over her daughter's feelings, Barbara wondered what in the world she was doing in the midst of this uncomfortable situation. As she glanced around the small office trying to find a gracious way to get out of there, Barbara saw Mrs. Smith pull a small gun from her purse, point it straight at her, and pull the trigger. The first bullet hit her in the left cheekbone and lodged at the base of her skull. The second went through her neck, and as she fell to the floor, the third caught her in the back.

She tried to cry out, but her mouth wouldn't move, no words would come forth. She remembers thinking,

What's happened to me?" "I'm too young to die. I'm only thirty. I've got a good husband and two children. God, please let me live."

As these thoughts raced through Barbara's mind, the probation officer grabbed Mrs. Smith who didn't resist, but only asked, "Will my picture be in the paper?" She then looked down at Barbara and said, "Don't worry. She's a Sunday school teacher. If she dies, she'll go to heaven."

By now Barbara was covered with blood, her mouth wouldn't work and her eyes couldn't see. She was put on a stretcher, and amidst sirens and screams, she was pushed into an ambulance and rushed off to the hospital. A priest had heard the cries for help and had jumped in beside Barbara. He took her hand and whispered, "I'm a priest. It's my job in San Francisco to ride with emergency patients. I want to ask you one question even though I know you can't talk."

"Why can't I talk? Why can't I see?" Barbara thought.

"If you are a believing Christian, just squeeze my hand."

She squeezed his hand and he breathed, "Praise the Lord."

The priest prayed for her all the way to the hospital and she stayed conscious. When the doctors took her into surgery, they couldn't believe she was still alive. Barbara's mother was in a state of shock when she called me with the tragic news. Dickie had choked to death the year before and now Barbara had been shot.

My daughter Lauren and I raced to St. Bernadine's where we kept a vigil with the family. John was on the road with his construction business and even though we called the highway patrol to help find him, he didn't get our message until he arrived home at seven that evening.

During those critical days in intensive care, Barbara stayed conscious much of the time and couldn't believe what had happened.

Why me, God? Why me? I'm a Sunday school teacher. Why didn't you protect me? I never did anything to Mrs. Smith and I did not deserve this!

She remembered the promise God had given her years before, "I'm going to use your life to show forth the salvation of the Lord" (Ps. 71:15, NAS).

"Fat chance now," she thought.

Each day brought new surgery and pain. When the doctors removed the bullet from her back, they found it barely missed her heart. The one in her neck had missed her spine and the one through her face had lodged right against the main artery of her brain. The doctors brought the choice to John. "We've taken out two bullets, but we've left the one at the base of the skull. If we try to remove it, she may be paralyzed on that side for life. If we leave it in, an aneurysm may form around it and she could live for another ten years."

John chose ten years over paralysis and they left the bullet in where it is still resting today more than twelve years later.

As Barbara lay in that hospital bed, her mind was filled with bitterness and anger. She was an innocent victim. Her disillusioned design was now damaged beyond repair. How could she ever forgive a person who had shot her down and who was satisfied with her act when her picture appeared on the front page of the local paper?

One day in agony, Barbara prayed, "All right, God, I'll try to forgive if you'll show me where to start." That evening John brought her a tape recorder and the Book of Psalms on cassettes. "Since you can't read or write, I thought you might like to listen," he explained.

Barbara had a choice to make. She could listen to God's Word or turn on the TV where she could watch other people's problems and forget her own. Often she chose TV, but to show John she appreciated his gift, she also listened to the Psalms. Each day: Psalms or soaps?

As Barbara listened more often to the tapes, God used this avenue to heal her mind; and when she had to face Mrs. Smith in court she realized the bitterness had cleared and she was beginning to forgive. Mrs. Smith was sentenced to seven years but was out in two for good behavior.

During those two years Barbara was in constant pain and was unable to open her mouth because the scar tissue which had formed around the shattered hinge of her jaw sealed her mouth shut. Some of her teeth had been shot out and she sipped liquid through a straw placed in these empty sockets. She remembers one Christmas when she cried because she couldn't get a thin potato chip between her teeth.

The only help the doctors could offer was a suggestion that she try pushing popsicle sticks between her front teeth, forcing the scar tissue to split and rip. I can remember watching her, both of us in tears, as she would work to pry open her mouth.

One day she found a verse in Isaiah in which God promises to make Israel a new threshing instrument with teeth and she wondered, "Will I ever be a new threshing instrument with teeth?" (41:15, KJV).

The next time Barbara visited the doctor she asked what hope there was for improvement and he responded, "We've done all we can. You'll just have to accept that this is how you're going to live and get used to it. I do have one word of advice," he said in attempted humor, "Don't throw up or you'll choke to death!"

As Barbara turned to leave, the doctor added, "It's a shame we can't find you the right surgeon. There's only one man in the whole United States who could do anything for you."

"What's his name?" Barbara asked with a touch of hope.

"It doesn't matter. You could never find him, and even if you did you'd never be able to afford him."

"Well at least give me his name."

"Your chances are slim, but he's Dr. Phillip J. Boyne."

Barbara paid her bill and left, never to see that doctor again.

That weekend in an attempt to cheer Barbara up, John took her with him when he drove to the beach to meet with a client. At lunch, Barbara was grateful the restaurant was dark so people couldn't see how she was suctioning the soup through the spaces in her mouth. She had learned never to smile and if she ever did laugh she would automatically cover her mouth with her hand, a habit she is still trying to break.

After lunch the client's wife took Barbara with her while the men went to the bank. As the lady was driving her big blue Cadillac down Pacific Coast Highway, she said to Barbara, "Now I see why you're so skinny, you only eat soup. You could have had anything you wanted; we were paying for it. Maybe that's the kind of diet I should go on—just soup."

Barbara took a deep breath and for the first time in two years told her the whole story in less than two minutes. The lady gasped, "Why that's definitely worse than my hysterectomy!" Barbara explained further there was only one doctor who could help her, a Phillip J. Boyne, but no one knew where he was.

A few days later Barbara received a call from a doctor who was a friend of this lady. "I thought you'd like to know that I'm a colleague of Dr. Phillip J. Boyne and I can get him for you."

Dr. Boyne was an expert on such cases as he had operated on hundreds of Vietnam veterans and had learned that bullets stabilize after two years. He felt confident that Barbara's aneurysm of the carotoid artery would keep the bullet from moving while he operated on her jaw. He even volunteered to come to San Bernardino to perform the surgery so Barbara could be close to home.

Dr. Boyne did a coronoidectomy, removed the bone from the inside of her face, rebuilt the jaw, and removed the binding scar tissue. It still took eight months of painful therapy, some new teeth, and two years of braces before Barbara could proclaim, "God has made me a new threshing instrument with teeth."

Barbara still has constant headaches, there's a small scar on her cheekbone, the bullet is still at the base of her skull, and the left side of her face is numb. She still has occasional nightmares and she shrinks from a child who runs toward her with a gun, but Barbara is a new threshing machine with teeth and she speaks all over America today showing forth the salvation of the Lord.

As Barbara said, "Disillusioned designs can be restored and damaged designs can be reshaped." But what about destroyed designs?

In all the years I had known Barbara and John, they had been remodeling their old adobe home nestled on three acres in the foothills of San Bernardino Mountains.

During 1980 the family took a vote to complete this ten-year project. John added a huge family room with walls of glass for a stunning view of the city lights, a cozy breakfast area with a fireplace, and a loft for family and friends to play pool or relax with music.

Since John is a general contractor, he had access to specialty items at bargain prices. Imagine the fun of decorating around a shiny red brass claw-foot bathtub! Barbara tackled the challenge of decorating the master bedroom and bathroom around this unusual fixture.

John gutted the kitchen, Barbara cooked on a hot plate, and the family was excited as they undertook the last phase of remodeling.

I could hardly wait to see it, and each time I'd ask, she'd say, "As soon as we've finished, we'll have you over."

Throughout all the years of construction Barbara had kept her home open for Bible studies, pool parties, Mother-Daughter teas and other Christian activities. She was never too busy to teach or to listen and she developed open communication with her own teens.

I learned to take a cup of coffee in my hand and stuff a banana in my mouth so that I'd listen and not allow myself to over-react. I found out what was going on in their world and stopped being a dispenser of advice.

Three days before Thanksgiving in 1980 the Panorama Fire began to sweep through the San Bernardino Mountains. It hit the headquarters of Campus Crusade for Christ taking, among several buildings, Bungalow Two, next to Bungalow One where we had lived ten years before. As the winds carried the flames down toward the Bueler home, Barbara and her son John looked out those big glass windows and saw a huge fireball rolling toward their fireproof house. Barbara grabbed her purse and keys and ran out to turn the horse loose. As she opened the door, she was met with 90 miles per hour winds which caught her up as in a hurricane. Young John ran for the motorhome and the secretary came out of the office carrying the account books. By this time, smoke was choking them as they covered their faces and ran for the car.

Barbara recalls:

Tree limbs were flying through the air as flaming rockets ignited other branches and the tall grass. We drove the car and motorhome through walls of fire and wondered if we'd ever see that horse again as she whinnied and was lost in the smoke. At the end of the driveway we turned and looked just as a firestorm ate through the glass, swept into our newly finished home, and exploded, blowing the house in fiery darts to the sky.

Ten minutes before, I had a home I'd designed, now it was destroyed. As I drove away in tears passing the firetrucks that were coming too late, I said, "Barbara, let it go. If you don't let it go today you'll become a bitter old woman—mourning after sentimental things, material things, all the possessions you've gathered up in forty years of life. Let it go!

Barbara began to sing a familiar hymn:

Spirit of God
Descend upon my heart
Wean it from earth
Through all its forces move
Through my weakness
Mighty as thou art
And make me love thee
As I ought to love.

How does God bring out of our mouths words of praise and hope in times of utter disaster? He'd started with Barbara as a rebellious child, sitting in church next to a godly mother and trying not to hear a single word—but his word returns not void. He'd taken her disillusioned design and had restored it.

God had held Barbara, the innocent victim, in his arms and kept her from the clutch of death in that hospital, fed her with

Psalms, and promised to make her a new threshing instrument with teeth. He had taken her damaged design and reshaped it.

Could he save her one more time?

Yes, God can do it again, but he needs people to put legs and arms on his plans.

God sent a friend to take Barbara by the hand and lead her through J.C. Penney's to buy some simple basics of life, like underwear, when Barbara didn't even care if she had any. He inspired others to give her a "starting over shower" to make her feel like a new bride. People sent pictures of the children Barbara didn't know they had. Others brought favorite recipes, albums, paper, pens, stamps, and cards.

The emergency relief provided donated clothing and Barbara and her daughter Shara learned they could actually find suitable clothing in those Hefty bags. What do you give away to help those faceless unknown people in a time of tragedy? Is it anything like the items Barbara pulled forth from those bags? She and Shara temporarily relieved their pain by putting on a funny fashion show in her mother's tiny living room, modeling mini-skirts, outdated jeans, and blouses with the buttons missing. As they laughed and cried, they did piece together the start of a new wardrobe.

That Thanksgiving the family sat around Brother Billy's table with his wife and children and Barbara's mother. How could they be thankful? As Barbara looked around at those family members so precious to her, she realized she had lost her house, but she had not lost her home.

The following Sunday after church a group of friends went to visit with the Buelers as John carried the remains of his house off in a dump truck. Nothing was left standing but the stone chimney. Even the refrigerator had blown up and totally disappeared, but there in a pile of ashes was the red bathtub, the only item to survive.

I said to Barbara, "I never got to see this in your house so the Lord left it for me now." We stood beside the red tub, dulled with soot, and had our picture taken before John hauled it off to the dump.

Two days with a bulldozer and a dump truck and all that had been their home was gone.

When spring came Barbara went back one day to walk over the acres that had for so many years been her home. The horse had been found wandering miles away and she was nipping at some new grass that was sprouting up. Barbara looked at the empty garden where her roses had once grown and in the distance she saw one bright bud against the blackened wall. As Barbara ran to view this rose, she realized the roots had reached so deeply into the soil that even the firey furnace of life had not killed this plant. The vine had survived, the branch had pushed up, and one lonely rose showed forth the salvation of the Lord.

When our roots are deeply planted in God's word, he can bring forth "beauty for ashes, the oil of joy for mourning, the garment of praise for the spirit of heaviness" (Isa. 61:3, KJV).

JENNIFER BOTKIN-MAHER

Rape

At a luncheon for Christian leaders, I was asked what I was writing on at the moment. I explained the premise for this book, mentioning specifically incest and rape. "Why would Christians need a book like that?" one dignified gentleman asked. "There's none of that stuff in our church," a pastor added.

I explained that in our Christian Leaders and Speakers Seminars (CLASS) we found victims in every group of above average women, but most of them didn't know where to turn for help. As I tried to express the need for the church to provide answers for hurting women, I could tell these men felt I had been hanging around with a bad lot and hoped I'd come back into the mainstream with the other nice Christian ladies.

Before I left town, I was handed a letter from the one young woman, an executive with a Christian company, who had been at the table that noon.

Dear Florence,

I just wanted to write you a quick note to tell you how very much I enjoyed getting acquainted with you at lunch today, but of course, there is more I wanted to say or I wouldn't be writing this note!

Our meeting at lunch wasn't the time or place to tell you my reaction to what you were saying, but I would like for you to know what I was thinking. Five years ago, I found myself on the way to a hospital emergency room saying to myself, "I won't let something that only

lasted thirty minutes govern the rest of my life." A black man, drunk
or doped, had broken into my apartment that evening, wielding a hunting knife, with robbery as his first objective and rape his second. It
was my first year out of college and I was working as a reporter for
a local newspaper. He didn't get too far on the robbery (reporters
are notoriously underpaid), but he certainly accomplished his second
objective.

Despite my brave vow to myself that night, the rape has affected
my life and my relationship to God. I get so angry when I hear stories
about women who are attacked, and later tell of "claiming the name
of Jesus" and the attacker is converted. That type of "witness" implies
that those of us who weren't successful in our moment of violence
are somehow less favored in God's eyes. I really want to encourage
you to encourage the women of whom you spoke. The evangelical
community needs someone speaking to this issue—without the storybook ending—someone who is dealing with and has dealt with the
residual fear, suspicion, and the ongoing struggle with faith.

So . . . the purpose of this note: Please continue to pursue what
you were speaking of at noon. There is definitely a need.

Yes, there is definitely a need and it's time we opened our eyes
to the victims in our own congregations. According to Judge Sol
Wachtler, Court of Appeals, Albany, New York:

Rape is not simply a sexual act to which one party does not consent.
Rather, it is a degrading, violent act which violates the bodily integrity
of the victim and frequently causes severe, long-lasting physical and
psychic harm.[1]

Rape is the fastest-growing crime of violence in our country
and is also the most under-reported. Estimates are that one in
ten women will be raped and more than one-third of these will
be attacked within their own home or garage by men they know.

A friend of mine was raped by her husband's best friend while
her husband went to the store for ice cream. The police asked
her what she had done to lure him.

One young lady told us at CLASS she had left her two little
girls standing by the shopping cart full of groceries while she went
to get the car. A man she knew came by and helped her with
the key. As she sat down and turned to say thank you, he jumped
in and raped her while her girls waited at the curb.

Why do men do this? In the article "Why Men Abuse Women"
Dr. Joyce Brothers says:

These men are so insecure they have a psychological need to abuse women in order to restore their own egos . . . and reassure themselves of their manhood. The motive is not sex, but establishing power and humiliating the woman.[2]

A majority of these males were abused as children and often saw their fathers beat their mothers. Our staff member, Marilyn Murray, a victim herself, says in her ministry with young rapists in prison, over 80 percent were abused as children and don't feel they've hurt the victim. Some even feel they've done her a favor and some take the challenge of conquering an unwilling female as a natural part of the male ego.

Dr. Brothers says,

These men are frequently undersexed and have a deep fear of women. Most sex offenders have been emotionally and physically insecure and deprived in their childhood. They are apt to come from unstable homes with mothers who are strict, domineering and often cruel. . . . The boys grew up with the idea that women had to be taken by force. When a rapist marries, he will probably select a woman whose emotional problems are similar to those of his mother. . . . He may beat her up to show the little woman who's boss.[3]

The booklet *How to Protect Yourself Against Sexual Assault* points out: "Rape is not a crime motivated by sexual desire but one in which sex is used as a weapon to harm and humiliate the victim, who can be a child, wife, student, grandmother or another male."

The booklet also offers the following suggestions:

- If you find yourself alone and it's dark, get to a well-lighted area as quickly as possible. Walk close to the curb, on the side of the street that faces traffic. Walk confidently at a steady pace, avoiding doorways, greenery and alleys where a rapist could hide.
- If you think a car is trailing you, turn and walk in the opposite direction. If you feel danger is approaching, don't be afraid to scream and run. If you carry a whistle, blow it loudly. Attract help in any way possible. Yell "Fire!" or break a window in a store or well lit house.
- If you're walking and a driver asks for directions, never get close to the car. Call out your reply from a distance.

- If you live alone, install a peephole viewer in your door. Before opening the door to a salesman or repairman, ask him to slip his ID card under your door so you can check his office.
- Do not use your first name on your mailbox or in your phone listing—only initial and last name.
- Should a stranger ask to use your phone in an emergency, tell him to give you the number and wait outside while you make the call. Never open the door or give any indication that you are alone.
- Should your car break down, attach a white cloth to the radio antenna or raise the hood, then get back into the car and lock the door. If someone other than a uniformed policeman offers assistance, ask him to call the police or a garage.
- If you think you are being followed, drive to the nearest police station, gas station or public place.[4]

Does this ever happen to people we know? I first met Jennifer when she attended our CLASS at the Crystal Cathedral and shared her life story.

Jennifer grew up in Central California as a middle child. Her older brother teased her excessively, and she was often humiliated at family functions by being held down and tickled. When she would complain to her father about these actions, he would say, "Brothers are like that. They're just boys having fun." As a result, she grew up not trusting "boys having fun" and was afraid of men. But Jennifer's reputation as an easy mark had already been established. Consequently, she has suffered much emotional pain.

Experts tell us rapists look for vulnerable women who can be easily intimidated and overpowered.

Jennifer desired to help others, and she worked hard to become a nurse. She married, had three children, and lived in a beautiful Southern California home. Life was wonderful. But underneath, Jennifer was still frightened and her mind was often fragmented, flitting from thing to thing, seeming rattled and unsettled. One weekend she went to a retreat where the speaker gave her direction and she rededicated her life to the Lord Jesus. Prior to that weekend, Jennifer had desperately been searching for purpose and for a plan. In those three days God showed her she was to go home and be a godly wife and mother. She remembers the ride down the mountain. *I was glowing from the glory of God. I looked like Moses with a shining face.*

One evening Jennifer and her husband were watching a movie on TV about rape, starring Elizabeth Montgomery. The woman, an innocent victim, was treated as if she was the villain and had enticed her violator. Her friends and family couldn't handle the trauma, and they began to speculate: Had she brought this on herself? Had she invited the crime? Her husband also fell prey to this thinking and by the end of the movie he had deserted her.

Jennifer sat in shock at this turn of events and said to her husband "If that ever happened to me, I'd never recover."

Jennifer was not the only one touched by that movie. *Time* wrote about aftershocks throughout the country. Victims reported depression, guilt, broken relationships, obsessive fear, loss of trust, divorce, and suicide attempts. One victim from Southern California wrote, "There are bars on the windows, and floodlights on the house. I know there's no way anybody can get in, but I'm still scared."[5]

Jennifer read these reactions and tried to calm her fears by saying, *No need to worry. I'm a Christian. It'll never happen to me.*

One sunny Southern California afternoon Jennifer went out to work in her garden right after lunch. Her backyard was enclosed by high walls covered with ivy. Her husband was playing golf, her two girls were in school and her toddler was asleep in the nursery. Jennifer was happy to be alone and she started to sing a song from *The Sound of Music,* dancing around pretending to be Julie Andrews. Suddenly she stopped. She had a feeling someone was watching her, a hidden audience in the ivy. She looked around, but could see no one.

She said to herself: *There you go again. You're thirty-three years old, a grown woman. It's high time you stopped living in the past with these childhood feelings of fear and inferiority. Stop thinking of those times people scared you and made you the brunt of their jokes. Grow up, stop being afraid of your own shadow!*

After that little message, she forced herself to continue singing as she swayed across the yard carrying her potted plants. Before bringing a few inside, Jennifer decided to get some pie plates to put under the dripping plants. She went into the kitchen and bent over to reach for the pie plates in a far corner of the cabinet. She felt a tap on her shoulder. *That must be my imagination; there's no one here but me.*

Grabbing the plates, she felt another tap, stronger than the first. When she turned around, she faced a half-clothed man with a hood over his head, holding a knife pointed down at her. Jennifer jumped up screaming, clutched the edge of the kitchen counter for support, and hollered out the window for help. "Shut up!" he said as he pulled her body toward him. "Shut up!"

This must be a joke. This can't be happening to me.

As the knife touched her throat Jennifer screamed again.

"Shut up lady or I'll kill you!"

This isn't a joke. This is real. Where did he come from? How did he get in here? Oh, no! The open back door.

Suddenly Jennifer thought of her baby in the other room. *If she wakes up he'll kill her. I'd better not scream again. I'm trapped. Where are the neighbors? Didn't anyone hear me?*

As these thoughts raced through her head, Jennifer was being shoved down the hall to her bedroom, the one she and her husband had shared for thirteen and a half years. The intruder held the knife at her side and ordered her to undress. In humiliation and disgrace, Jennifer dropped her clothes to the floor. *My God, how can this be happening to me?*

As the man grabbed a scarf out of a dresser drawer and tied it around her head, the brightness of that afternoon turned black.

"I'm a Christian," Jennifer gasped as he pushed her down on the bed. "I belong to God. Don't touch me."

But he touched her, raped her, and abused her for about an hour as she silently cried, "I will fear no evil for thou art with me."

Rising to leave and wielding his knife over her, the intruder warned, "I'll be watching this house for a few days. If you call the police, I'll come back and kill you."

Jennifer lay there, crying with relief to be alive, yet devastated by the terror she felt.

I'm a victim like that lady on TV. There was nothing I could do. I was helpless, powerless, and alone. I was immobilized by fear. How could I resist? I could have been killed. I've been robbed of my dignity, of my worth. I'll never be the same again.

She crawled to the kitchen and dialed a friend who came right over. "We must call the police," her friend said.

Jennifer remembered that movie on TV where the victim sat in a cold lonely hallway at the police station with people gawking at her. *I can't go there. I've got rape written all over me. Everyone will know.*

Her friend rushed her to her private physician and by the time they returned home the police had arrived. Since the rapist had worn a hood, Jennifer couldn't describe the man. After only a brief questioning session the police departed saying there wasn't much evidence to be gathered.

Jennifer was left to pick up the shattered pieces of her life alone. By the time her children and husband arrived home Jennifer was numb. Jennifer's friend and husband began making decisions for her, while she sat on the living room couch. They concluded it would be best for Jennifer's safety if she left town. So the next morning she was packed up, taken to the airport, and sent home to Mother.

Though her family enveloped her with love and acceptance, Jennifer was too embarrassed to even talk about the incident. One day her mother slipped her a scrap of paper. On it was written the number for the local Rape Hotline.

Jennifer felt so guilty she quickly pushed the paper to the bottom of her purse so no one could ever find it. She couldn't sleep that night, and at 3:00 in the morning she finally got the courage to make that call. For over an hour she cried out her story to the sympathetic woman who had been a victim herself. It eased the pain to know someone out there understood.

A week later it was time for Jennifer to return home. What if Nick didn't love her anymore? Would he walk out on her like the husband on TV? Would he be able to accept a sexually abused and tainted woman? On the phone, Jennifer asked him all these questions and he assured her of his love and vowed to stand by her.

No sooner had she arrived home when he surprised her with arrangements for a vacation for the two of them at their favorite resort.

"Could we get married again?" Jennifer asked.

"We're already married," Nick replied.

"Yes, but I need to know you'd marry me again."

The two of them found a quaint little chapel on a bluff overlooking the ocean and were quietly remarried.

Jennifer decided to put the past behind her and she went back to her part-time job. Since the women's retreat, she'd been a vibrant witness in the office and she didn't want to change now. She couldn't let them know what had happened to her, she was too ashamed.

She told herself that if those worldly people knew she'd been raped and her God hadn't protected her, they'd never want to believe in him. *I've got to show them I'm still glowing with the glory of God.*

Jennifer spent the next year in a difficult time of denial, using every ounce of energy she could find to keep a happy Christian facade. Those few who knew about her trauma congratulated her on how spiritual she was. She memorized verses on forgetting the past and kept close to the church.

In spite of these signs of victory there were hints of defeat. Every afternoon at 1:00 a wave of fear would sweep over her. She told her mother how she felt and often this compassionate lady would call Jennifer at that time to talk until the fear passed.

Every time the dog barked Jennifer would jump up and run to the window, wondering who was approaching. She remembered the dog had made noises that fateful day, but she'd been too busy to pay any attention. Now, guilt was taking root.

She was afraid every minute her children were outside. Would he come back and kill them?

At night she'd awaken screaming in that same bed, seeing that man over her with the knife.

Jennifer had tried pushing aside her pain and pretending the rape had never happened. She wanted victory in Jesus, but her cross seemed too heavy to bear. One depressed afternoon she called a rape-trauma center and set up an appointment. After a few months of weekly sessions, the counselor suggested Jennifer come in twice a week. "I must really be bad," she concluded, "if I have to come in twice a week."

Since Jennifer had learned to be a people pleaser and was afraid of upsetting others, she went twice a week as suggested. After a few months the counselor took a pregnancy leave and Jennifer's counseling ended abruptly. Passivity ruled and she never asked for another counselor or checked on the staff's opinion for a replacement, and they never called her.

During the following years her depression returned. She couldn't do the things she'd done before, her mind was confused, her attention span shortened, guilt hovered over her, and she became irritated with her husband and children. She tried to repress her feelings of anxiety but one Saturday afternoon she found her daughter had used her hairbrush. That's not usually a problem a mother can't handle, but a rape victim often interprets a minor violation of property rights as another attack. Suddenly Jennifer couldn't hold herself together any longer. She screamed, exploded with years of pent up emotions—erupted like a volcano.

As the children flattened against the wall crying, "Stop, Mommy! Stop!" She threw a dish at them followed by a TV tray which just missed the little one's head. She stormed out, slamming the French doors behind her in such sudden strength that the glass shattered all over the room. She came back to see the children huddled in hysterics with splinters of glass all around them.

Oh God, that's my life in hundreds of shattered pieces. She sank to the floor amidst the splinters of glass and sobbed uncontrollably.

As she tried to pull herself together she thought, *It's over. I'll never be the same again. There's no hope.*

Jennifer's estimation of herself was not so far off as it might sound. Mental hospitals are full of people who have given up, tuned out, and know there is no HOPE. It was not easy to find a counselor who understood the potentially debilitating destruction of a sexual assault and who could help Jennifer rebuild her shattered life. As she shared her feelings of helplessness with her pastor, he encouraged her by saying, "This is a stepping stone to something greater. God wants you to trust him."

After several tries, Jennifer found a counselor who was able to show her clearly what had happened and teach her the seven stages victims go through to reach recovery.

1. **SHOCK.** Jennifer was clearly in a state of shock that day as she was attacked in her own home by a hooded naked man with a knife.

2. **DENIAL.** Jennifer had a double dose of denial. One, from natural preservation instinct that keeps one from admitting more than she can handle at any one time and two, from her Christian belief that she must be brave and keep on a happy face. This combination contributed to Jennifer's confusion and continued emotional suffering until God equipped her to face the truth.

3. **RATIONALIZATION.** As the impact of what had happened would seep through her wall of denial, Jennifer would push it

away and rationalize: you're still alive; you have no right to keep thinking about this; what's the matter with you? Back to denial and debasement.

4. **DEPRESSION.** After three years of deep denial and a forced facade, Jennifer was exhausted. It takes tremendous energy to keep your natural feelings under control, to suppress them each time they emerge. Jennifer was drained and depressed. She'd shut down her emotions completely and was wandering in a mental wilderness.

5. **RELEASE.** As with any volatile substance kept under constant pressure, there comes a day when it explodes. There may be no warning, the person may seem in control, but something as small as a borrowed hairbrush, suddenly brings the seething inside to the surface. Without proper understanding, the victim may sink into an emotional breakdown often assisted by weary friends who say, "Aren't you over this by now?" Such comments add to the guilt of the victim and fuel her feelings of hopelessness and powerlessness.

6. **ACCEPTANCE.** Although it wasn't easy, as Jennifer walked through these steps and discovered her reactions to her rape were normal, she began to stop living her life as a victim. There was HOPE.

Jennifer had to start with being totally honest with herself, perhaps for the first time in her dream-filled life. She had to admit she was angry over the rape but that she had felt as a Christian she must hide her hurts and march bravely onward. She had to face that she blamed herself and this was unjustified. She had not been in a bikini on a beach but in her own backyard watering plants. She was not responsible. Also, she began to see she had blamed her husband for not being home. If he hadn't played golf this wouldn't have happened. Since she was unable to express her feelings, even to herself, and since she desperately needed his assurance of love even to the point of a second wedding, she was sending out mixed signals to him of love and hate which neither one of them understood.

Jennifer also had to get honest with her two children. Three years had passed and her two oldest daughters, now teens, had never known what had happened to their mother. Jennifer recalls:

The energy that I used in trying to protect them and prevent them from knowing was killing me and I didn't even know it.

After the emotional explosion, the turning point, Jennifer sat down with her two daughters and told them the horror she had held from them for three years. They confessed they had known something was wrong and had believed she was dying of some strange illness. The truth caused them to be angry about the assault, yet relieved she was alive. Both were loving and supportive, and yet understandably mad.

For Jennifer this time of total honesty was painful, but when she finally accepted the truth and faced the facts, she was set free.

7. ASSIMILATION. Jennifer spent a weekend with three godly women who led her through a time of emotional healing. As they reviewed her background, they found her victimization began in childhood. Every time she had protested her brother's taunting her, she'd been told boys always tease their sisters. The lack of validation and affirmation contributed to her feelings of helplessness. Seeing she didn't make much of an impact and she couldn't change her circumstances, Jennifer passively accepted the way things were and denied her emotional pain. Growing up, she'd been called a dreamer by her parents: "You've got your head in the sand, you're on cloud nine, you're looking at life through rose-colored glasses." Little did they know they were right. She had pulled away from reality and was living in a dream of denial.

As Jennifer was exposed to the stifled emotions and fears of her childhood, she became determined to stem the tide. She had to learn to say NO—not to be defiant, but to assert a new feeling of self-worth. She didn't have to be held down any longer. She read Jo Berry's book *Can You Love Yourself?* and realized for the first time that God really loved her just as she was and had cleansed her from all unrighteousness.

As Jennifer was climbing up that big hill of restoration she had another experience that sent her back to square one. It happened six years after the rape. She received a call from an ex-friend of her husband's. He said, "I've missed seeing you. Is Nick at work?"

"Of course he's at work in the middle of the morning." As soon as she'd let those words out, she realized she'd violated the principle, "Never let a man know you're alone." As she gasped, he filled her ears with obscene words. Instantly she went through shock—this can't be real; denial—this friend can't be saying this to me! Abruptly, she slammed down the phone. She was a victim again, emotionally molested over the phone.

She called her husband who unexpectedly came home that afternoon to comfort her. He understood her feelings and knew why she couldn't eat for several days after. The next morning Jennifer met with her friends who worked with her on the Rape Crisis Hot Line and they encouraged her to confront the caller. "You need to call him up and tell him what you feel. You've got to stop being a victim!"

Jennifer could hardly bear the thought of calling the man, but she knew she had to do it for her emotional growth. She called information in surrounding towns and found his number. He answered and she said, "I was offended by what you told me yesterday. I will not listen to such filth and don't you *ever* call me again. If you want to know how we are you call my husband and talk with him."

Surprised at her own assertiveness and shaking all over, Jennifer knew she was on the road from victimization to victory. She knew she had made an impact, and she never received another call.

Because Jennifer believes God will use her experience and her growth to help others, she has claimed 2 Corinthians 1:3–4 as her verse: "Blessed be the God and Father of our Lord Jesus Christ, the Father of mercies and God of all comfort, who comforts us in our affliction, so that we may be able to comfort those who are in affliction with the comfort with which we ourselves are comforted by God" (rsv).

It is true that those who have suffered can intimately understand the emotion of the victim and can comfort them with the arms of the Lord Jesus. Jennifer has dedicated her life to giving HOPE to hurting women.

After an appearance on a Christian TV talk show in which she answered questions on rape, Jennifer got the following letter from a lady on the East Coast:

I'm a rape victim and I've kept it bottled up for over twenty-five years. I can hardly talk about it and listening to you opened up a Pandora's box. I'm scared and I'm having a hard time not feeling guilty. I'm afraid to let my anger come out. I still haven't told my family as I don't think they'd understand. I will never tell those in the church for I KNOW they would never understand. Please help me, someone help me make sense of what happened those many years ago.

Recently a distraught young girl named Dana pulled me aside at a Christian conference center and poured out her life to me in hopes I could help her. Her father had left her family when she was four and her mother later married again. The stepfather molested her, and she stayed away from home as much as possible. Church became her home and the people her family. When she was eleven, one of the elders she trusted took her into a back room of the church and raped her. At sixteen, while on a teen trip, she was accosted by the chaperone, a divinity student from her church, and in the same year she was attacked by the choir director.

When the young girl tried to tell the pastor, he accused her of lying. "These are all fine Christian men" he said. Because no one would believe her, Dana fell apart and had a nervous breakdown. While recovering, she vowed to make herself ugly and gained forty pounds in six months.

Later she tried to communicate her problems to another pastor who said, "You must have asked for it."

What's your opinion? Do you think Dana is some low-class girl who asked for it? She has a responsible position with a Christian organization and her boss, a top Christian leader, has been dropping sexual innuendos upon her. One day she was home recuperating from an accident and her boss called to find out how she was. She said she hurt too badly to move. Thirty minutes later the doorbell rang. She groped her way to the door and opened it to find her boss.

"I came for lunch," he said.

"I have no food," she replied.

"That's not the kind of food I'm after." She pushed him out and slammed the door.

When Dana reported this event to the president of the organization, his first comment was, "I hope you haven't told anyone else. We don't want to ruin his reputation."

This girl has attempted suicide twice and doesn't think she'll ever find any help.

Who knows how many ladies like these are sitting in your church knowing you'd never understand? The God of all comfort needs YOU to give HOPE and help patch the heavy quilt of guilt that weighs down so many victims like Jennifer and Dana. Don't leave them "so weary with disasters, tugged with fortune that I would set my life on any chance, to mend it or be rid on't." You *can* make that difference.

JAN FRANK

Incest

"Incest in our church? Surely not!" Five years ago I would have agreed with this all too common quote. I didn't think I knew anyone who would do such a thing. Seattle therapist Lucy Berliner says:

> We all think child molesters ought to be shot until we find out we know one. People cannot deal with the contradiction that men who look and act so normal do these terrible things.[1]

And FBI Agent Kenneth Lanning states, "The incest offender is often just a child molester who stays home."[2]

But could there be an incest offender in our church? Studies show, as reported in *LIFE,*

> a disproportionate number are outwardly religious; many are workaholics; and the majority manage to hide their deviant behavior from their wives, colleagues, and closest friends . . . some will even distort Bible passages to indicate to their kids that they should be having sexual contact or use the passage about "forgive and forget" when their daughters are angry.[3]

At one CLASS, a shy girl asked to see our counselor Marilyn Murray. Several church members sought me out at different times and suggested I tell Marilyn this girl was a psychopathic liar and not to believe anything she said. I weighed this information and decided not to pass it on. Surely Marilyn could tell the truth from a lie. Later I asked her if she knew any reason why these well-meaning ladies would call this girl a liar and she said:

Yes, because the girl's an incest victim and her father's very active in this church. He's passed this word around so that if she ever tells on him no one will believe it.

Incest is the ultimate taboo in the Christian community. In the past it was thought to be a rare occurrence, limited to a handful of isolated, uneducated, or irreligious families; yet it is today a real and devastating problem with which millions of Americans (yes, Christians too) must cope. Incest is a repellent yet misunderstood subject that needs to be talked about with compassion and sensitivity. And victims are becoming willing to share their experiences in order to offer HOPE and help for others.

The Catholic church, recognizing the problem, has added a sex offender program to its New Mexico alcoholism treatment center for its priests.[4]

One pastor's wife confessed to me in tears that she had been constantly molested by her pastor father. Her husband wouldn't let her seek counsel because he didn't want anyone to know about it. Plus he added, "If you were the Christian you ought to be, you'd be able to put this all behind you."

There *is* trouble right here in River City.

The dictionary defines incest as "ANY sexual contact between close relatives, or people who assume themselves to be related." (This includes stepfathers, stepbrothers, Mother's boyfriend, uncles, etc.) Some people think it is specifically sexual intercourse between father and daughter, however, this is not the case. The California State Penal Code explains incest as:

The crime of sexual relations or cohabitation between a man and woman who are related to each other within the degrees wherein marriage is prohibited by law.[5]

And a pamphlet put out by the Recovery Association of Dallas states:

Legally, incest is sexual contact with a child by a member of the family where if adults, the law would forbid their marriage. Psychologically, incest is the use of a child by any person serving in a caretaking capacity to meet their own sexual needs physically or just emotionally though no sexual contact was ever made.[6]

If we are going to be alert to possible victims of incest in our River City, we should know some of the symptoms. The victimized child may suddenly become fearful, pull away from the offender, become a bed-wetter, have nightmares, show signs of depression, or withdraw from others. One friend of mine knew a little girl who kept shutting herself in a closet to hide away. Another friend of ours checked to see why her child kept clutching her panties. Someone else wondered why their little girl screamed at the sight of a certain uncle.

As victims become teens, the symptoms may increase to acute depression, talk of suicide, sexual promiscuity, running away from home, and prostitution. One study quoted in *Christianity Today* said that 60 percent of young prostitutes are incest victims.[7]

As these victims mature they frequently make poor choices in husbands and often marry men who abuse them. Many have unexplained symptoms after marriage: migraine headaches, anger, self-hatred, frigidity, lack of any emotion, repeated victimization, and sexual problems.

Many serious difficulties often develop in the victim's handling of normal relationships. They have trouble learning to trust again, their emotions are severely injured, and their perspective of religious people is misshapen. Dealing with these devastating problems properly is necessary in order for the victim to have any productive growth. While they may grow up physically, their emotional development is often stopped at the time of the initial incident.

Betty Baye from *Essence Communications* states:

Women . . . because they were sexually abused as children, often grow up sexually confused, guilty and ashamed. These are women for whom intimacy with a man has a negative association with force and intimidation and pain and terror.[8]

We have found in CLASS that many victims are now women with pretty faces, but overweight bodies. Subconsciously the bulk, or physical unattractiveness is their protection from sexual abuse.

Do you know any victims? Perhaps a neighbor, a friend in Bible study, the shy child across the street?

Statistics indicate that one in ten women in the United States are victims of incest.[9] Reports of sexual abuse have increased 400 percent since 1977 when reporting began.[10] Shockingly, "Three-fourths of child molesters are friends, neighbors or relatives of the victim."[11] "A girl is three times more likely to be molested by her father or another trusted adult than by a stranger."[12] And contrary to what we might think,

> The most typical incest offender is seen by his children as rigid, stuffy and old-fashioned. He is likely to place a high value on the obedience of children and the subordination of women.[13]

And he is often found in the church.

Even though we don't like to believe it, every class, every family structure, and every religion has been touched by this betrayal of innocence.

One case that was brought to my attention involved a father who would "feel up" his shapely teenage daughter in order to excite himself and then go to his wife (her mother) and continue his sexual activity. This approach allowed him to use his daughter to arouse his feelings and desires to heighten his own sexual pleasure. During sexual intercourse with his wife, he fantasized love-making with his daughter. He rationalized that he hadn't really hurt the child. The used and abused feelings his daughter had were very traumatic. He told her not to inform her mother and she didn't know where to turn for help.

Another incident involved a father who used the "cover" of sex education as his means for molesting his daughter. The twelve-year-old child knew this was not right. Often the father used obscene language and masturbated in front of her, demonstrating his own pleasures and desires in touching her even after she expressed her revulsion. Under the guise of teaching, the father subjected her to seven years in which she was degraded and made to feel ashamed of her own body. She lived in ever-present fear of her father finding her alone, then fondling her breasts and telling her dirty jokes (which she didn't even understand). He encouraged her to respond to his manipulation and often would say, "I can tell you're really enjoying this." This feeling that she was happily participating encouraged his fantasy. Her constant fear of recurrence stunted her emotional growth in many areas and caused her to develop serious difficulties in maintaining normal relationships in life. She has now been married and divorced three times.

A child is not equipped to handle these devastating situations and cannot understand why a father who is supposed to love and protect could possibly inflict such deep and hidden pain. Incest is the biggest betrayal there is!

Is it any wonder that children abused in this manner have great difficulty in sexual relationships in marriage?

Jan was the youngest of three girls and was very small for her age, weighing only forty-nine pounds for three years in a row. Although she was tiny she had huge brown eyes with long fringed eye lashes that made anyone who saw her say, "Look at those eyes!"

When Jan was five years old, her parents divorced. She was very confused and didn't understand why she only saw her daddy on weekends. Since their mother was out earning a living and dating, the girls were left pretty much on their own. Jan's oldest sister married two years after their parents divorced and her mother remarried within three years.

The new stepfather was very different from Jan's natural father. He was a little distant and a strict disciplinarian. The family structure changed from little supervision to intense supervision virtually overnight. The girls were instructed to eat everything on their plates, a genuine obstacle for tiny Jan. Bedtime was precisely enforced and the entire household was compelled to absolute submission to the dictatorial decree. Jan and her sister continued to see their natural father during this time although it was difficult emotionally. Their mother and stepfather would often belittle their natural father and they didn't know what to believe. The girls were made to feel disloyal whenever they expressed their interest in seeing their natural father. During this intense emotional struggle, Jan remembers feeling "pulled between her parents." Eventually the sisters were pressured into not seeing their natural father anymore in order to keep peace at home.

When Jan was about ten years old her mother suffered an injury that caused her to have several hospital stays, and the girls had to take over many of the household responsibilities. Jan remembers this as a very difficult and lonely time without her mother. Jan and her sister began attending a Bible church, which helped her feel accepted and loved.

One night after going to this church for six months, Jan heard clearly that Jesus loved her and she walked down the aisle to commit her life to the Lord. She stayed after church to talk with the pastor and when she got to the car her stepfather reprimanded her for being late. She told him happily that she had asked Christ into her life and he replied, "Why didn't you wait until some night when your mother and I were there?" Little Jan was deflated and felt she could never please him no matter what she did.

Three weeks later he forced her to try to please him in an unforgettable manner way when he sexually molested her. This ten-year-old child was in shock. What should she do?

For those of you who are not victims, you can only imagine the fear, the horror, the devastation that a child experiences, especially when she has to face her aggressor daily wondering, "Is he going to approach me today?"

Jan's mother asked her a few months later if her stepfather had ever touched her. Jan said, "Yes!" After that, she never heard another word about it. She felt then that her mother was powerless in the shadow of her stepfather's dominance and if her mother was powerless, then surely she was also powerless!

Incest is a whole question of power, control, betrayal, and deceit going on within a family," comments Joyce N. Thomas, director of the child protective unit of the National Hospital Medical Center in Washington, D.C. It is a crime that by its very nature almost always occurs in the privacy of the home without witnesses—and when revealed often pits the word of a child against that of an adult, a situation in which the child is often the loser. Frequently the child who is a victim of incest feels not only guilt about what has been occurring between her and an adult male but also responsibility. She feels that she has somehow "caused" the sexual abuse and knows that a likely consequence of revealing what is going on will cause the breakup of her already troubled family.[14]

Jan remembers how she felt at ten years old when her stepfather took her and her sister to see a movie entitled *How to Murder Your Wife*. Intended to be a comedy, it wasn't humorous to Jan as she sat in the car at the drive-in, convinced her stepfather went to the movie to learn how to kill her mother. She fell asleep that night petrified, knowing she would have to live with him the rest of her life without her mother.

A small child does not have the power, the capability, or the defenses to survive what we as adults have manufactured. They live in panic and terror and often when they do cry out for help no one believes them. Mothers, fathers, if your child comes to you and tells you something has happened, believe them! They don't make these things up. They assume the guilt that becomes part of the damaging symptom that they carry for the rest of their lives. Many take on "false guilt" as adult women. Jan conveys her experience of a country picnic that was ruined when it rained. She was made to feel the whole thing was her fault because she had not read the weather report. Incest victims carry the guilt of the world upon them through life because it was given to them as a child.

When Jan was in high school, I met her for the first time. I was instantly fascinated with her gorgeous eyes and her waif-like innocence. She and Lauren were best friends and Jan quickly became part of our family. She waitressed in our restaurant with Lauren and the two of them made more tips than any of the other waitresses. Jan was a cheerleader, made straight A's, and was a compulsive perfectionist. I had no idea at the time of the depth of her problems, although she would frequently show up in the middle of the night because she'd had "some troubles at home."

Jan recalls:

I spent a lot of time in the Littauer home. It was the first time in my life that I had seen Christianity lived out twenty-four hours a day, seven days a week, not just on Sundays. They took me into their home, loved me as their own, and gave me a lot of biblical instruction, counsel, and discipline when I needed it. This caused some conflict at my house because my parents resented the fact that I spent so much time in their home.

In Jan's late adolescence she became rebellious, got involved in some very poor relationships, and dated some older men. We stayed close to her but she knew we disapproved of her choices. During her last year in college she began working at Juvenile Hall with abused and delinquent children. This was when Jan first realized that what her stepfather had done to her was a criminal act. Physical, sexual, and emotional abuses were apparent among these youth at the Hall. As she worked with them, they would look at Jan and say with anger, "But you don't know what it's like!"

Jan could truly respond, "Yes, I do!" She tried to encourage them and give them HOPE for the future even though she didn't have many answers at that time. Jan wishes she had known then what she knows now!

In her mid-twenties Jan rededicated her life to Christ and met her husband, Don, who is a committed Christian. They were married and Jan expected to live happily ever after.

About two years into their marriage, Jan became depressed. She felt burdened and full of anger and she didn't know where these feelings were coming from. After their first little girl was born she felt an inner rage seem to rise up inside of her at times. This scared Jan, causing her to feel out of control and to experience that same horrible helplessness she knew at ten years old. Jan attempted to cope with this very real struggle not knowing in which direction to proceed. Turning to the Lord she asked,

Why? Why? Everything should be together in my life now. I have a wonderful husband, a beautiful child. Everything should be right. Why can't I get away from these frightening memories?

Nightmares increased and migraine headaches became a pattern in her life. Jan prayed:

Lord, I don't have the answer to this but I need some help. I'm exhibiting some behaviors and some symptoms that I'm not happy with. I feel out of control.

It was at that point in Jan's life that she came to CLASS. She was intending to learn how to be a better speaker and to do *More Hours in My Day* seminars with Emilie Barnes, but when she got into her small group with a loving, caring atmosphere, she poured out the pains of the past. She sought me out and told me what had happened. I was shocked, as if it had been my own daughter. I felt instant guilt that I had not known enough during her teen years to have spotted her problem.

How many of you would have been alert to her symptoms? How important it is that we be aware of these possibilities and available to help.

Jan found a Christian counselor who was experienced in working with incest victims, and she began the long climb up to emotional health. Throughout this time, she developed her own steps to recovery and her analysis of the three types of victims.

First, there is the victim that is totally unaware that anything has ever happened to her. She has subconciously suppressed the trauma. She often exhibits inexplicable physical pains, burdened with torment and agonizing torture including migraine headaches. She may require hospitalization or exhibit suicidal tendencies. The only HOPE for this kind of incest victim is to get into therapy, get in touch with what happened to her, and begin to work through that experience. Marilyn Murray represents this type and now professionally councils trauma victims.

The second kind of victim is the one who knows something has happened to her. She has been a victim, but she has not realized the significance in her life today. She knows it happened but thinks it was a traumatic part of the past. Although she rationalizes that "life today is life today," she also is in error in her thinking and exhibits some of the typical symptoms that all victims share.

Third, there is the victim who, like Jan, thinks that this had been resolved for her. She knows it had been devastating in her past and had ramifications far beyond what she realized but she thinks that by forgiving the offender and going on with her life it is taken care of. This also is not true.

In order to communicate what she had learned to other victims, Jan put her "Ten Steps to Recovery" in an acrostic outline: FREE TO CARE

F ace the Problem
R ecount the Incident
E xperience the Feelings
E stablish Responsibility

T race Behavioral Difficulties and Symptoms
O bserve Others and Evaluate Self

C onfront the Aggressor
A cknowledge Forgiveness
R ebuild Self-Image and Relationships
E xpress Concern and Empathize with Others

Many of these steps were used in the same or similar ways by
Barbara Bueler, a victim of attempted murder, and Jennifer Botkin-
Maher, a victim of rape. When Jan first wrote them down she
had no real intention of founding a ministry but somehow women
began to call her—women who couldn't find anyone to help them,
women whose pastors had given them verses to forgive and forget,
women who had tried to share with someone and had been accused
of lying, women who weren't sure what their problem was but
had the symptoms.

Jan had a Bible study on the subject of self-worth with twelve
women. As she shared some of her own past and feelings of inferiority, four women in the group confessed that they were also incest
victims. As Jan ministered to them, they brought friends and soon
Jan had four support groups going. Some women drove sixty to
seventy miles to attend because there was no help for them in
their own area.

Jan volunteered to assist her church and helped form and co-
lead its first incest support group. She is currently assisting a local
psychologist in leading therapy groups for women. Jan has appeared
on Trinity Broadcasting Television, the 700 Club, and on a Los
Angeles radio talk show sharing her testimony of recovery and calls
have poured in.

Jan wants to break the chain of repeating victims that goes on
and on. Both Jan's parents were victims themselves and as it says
in Exodus 34, "The sins of the fathers will be visited upon their
children and upon their children's children unto the third and
fourth generation."

Jan has one sixty-six year old woman in one of her groups who
is still living with the symptoms of victimization. These problems
just don't disappear.

If you need help yourself or have a friend who does, consider
Jan's steps.

FACE THE PROBLEM. As I have personally worked with depressed women over the years I have found that admitting the

problem and wanting to do something about it is a difficult but necessary first step. Often in the incest case, the victim has denied the circumstances for such a long time that she hates to face the issue. Even though repressing her feelings has led to physical symptoms, she is often fearful of dealing with the past pain.

Jan had to face the fact that she had repressed anger when she flared up at her toddler and lost control of herself. She realized she was taking out on her child the rage she felt inside. Often victims seem fine until they get married and then everything breaks loose. They direct their misplaced anger toward husbands or children to the point that they are so overly critical that their husbands don't know what is happening.

Jan received a phone call one afternoon from a woman named Penny who hesitantly started the conversation by saying, "I'm not sure why I called. I was given your number by a local Christian radio station. They said you might be able to help. I'm not even sure what for."

"Penny," Jan said, "are you a victim of incest?"

"No," she emphatically replied.

Jan said, "Okay, let me just ask you about some symptoms you may be experiencing." She reviewed depression, anger, nightmares, migraines, eating disorders, critical spirit, overweight, sex problems, and gaps in memory and gave about a one-minute description of how each might manifest itself in her life. Jan then asked Penny if she could identify with any of them and she said, "I've got 'em all." Jan then defined incest, explaining that it could range from a one-time fondling incident to intercourse over a period of years.

"Penny," Jan said, "has anything like that ever happened to you?"

In a quiet, barely audible voice she simply said, "Yes." Jan spent the next forty-five minutes answering her questions, referring her to specialists in the area of victimization, and encouraging her. Penny had already begun the healing process because she was willing to face the problem and she had found someone who really understood.

RECOUNT THE INCIDENT. As a part of Jan's support group, at least one session is spent pairing the women up in order that they might share their own experience on an intimate level. There is usually a great deal of anxiety, nervousness, and apprehension. The result of their sharing, however, is overwhelmingly positive. Most victims report it allows them to release at least a portion of the burden. One woman in one of Jan's groups who had been through two of the ten-week sessions told the new members, "It's easier the second time." Most women say it's a validation, at least verbally, that they did not dream up their incident. It also allows them to bond with one another, knowing, even though their experiences may have been different, they have individually experienced similarities on the feeling level. Jan encourages getting into therapy with someone who specializes in this area or becoming involved with a knowledgeable support person. The victim has made a mental video tape of the incident and filed it away in a deep, dark closet. For the most part, it has never been verbalized. She can see it vividly, but she has never spoken the words. The healing process begins when the incident is verbalized and the experience is first shared.

Victims shouldn't run around telling every person they meet their problems, but they should find at least one supportive person who will let them recount the incident and later experience the feelings before those feelings blow up in their faces.

EXPERIENCE THE FEELINGS. Once the person involved has faced the fact that this pain of the past will not go away without being dealt with and has been willing to recount these problems to a supportive friend or counselor, the next step is to open up the hidden feelings that have been suppressed for so long. Many victims report they have experienced nothing on a feeling level since the time of their trauma. Their emotions and growth quit at that point and they are still like a little child inside. Jan remembers lying in bed one night really trying to assess how she felt at ten years old.

Without really knowing what I was doing, I began to sob and cry. I heard myself saying "I'm only ten years old. Leave me alone. I don't understand." It was necessary for me to get in touch with those feelings that I had as a child in order to work through them.

Some direct outbursts of anger toward a husband, child, or friend, when the internal cause really relates back to the aggressor.

Gina found herself physically abusing her seven-year-old daughter. She couldn't believe what she was doing to the child and was terrified that she might kill the girl when these uncontrollable rages came over her. By attending Jan's support group and finding others in the same situation, she was able to recount what had happened to her when she was seven. By allowing herself to work through the feelings she had suppressed and never told anyone about, she was able to eliminate her misplaced anger.

Some become repeat victims and always seem to be at the wrong place at the wrong time. They marry abusive men, accept beatings as a way of life, or get taken advantage of in job situations. They somehow feel they don't deserve to be well-treated.

The chronic underachiever in school and also the other extreme, a person who is driven to do better than everyone else (like Jan), may well be an incest or abuse victim.

Because of a hidden fear that the "inner child" will get out, this type of person often becomes compulsively in control of others. She may be a confident overachiever who is subconsciously working her way to heaven to make up for the bad feelings she has about her victimization. Often this kind of person goes into self-sacrificing work especially in some type of Christian ministry.

Marilyn Murray, director of Restoration Therapy Center and a member of our CLASS staff, surveyed the female staff of a large Christian organization and found an above-average percentage of incest victims. Marilyn says that these girls are trying to make up to God for the guilt they feel over their abuse. Some who are not interested in any religion become social workers as Jan had done during and after college. By using her own incident of child-rape as an example, Marilyn who daily deals with trauma victims describes the conflicting emotions within these girls. She says there are three emotional levels the child experiences. Each one of us starts with an "original feeling child," who left in a normal pattern of growth will become a mature adult. When abused this inner being becomes a "sobbing, hurting child." At this point the child makes a decision whether to stay hurting, to die, or to bury the sobbing child and become the "controlling child." Marilyn, after she was gang raped at age eight, buried her hurting child so deeply that she blanked it totally out of her mind. She went on to be an outstanding achiever, a Christian leader in her community, and the founder of *More than Friends*, a national support group for women.

Throughout her overachieving life Marilyn suffered from migraines, leg and body pains, digestive problems, and asthma. When she was in such pain that she wanted to die, she went to Dr. Peter Danlychuk, who is now her partner, and by Christian regressive therapy he uncovered her trauma.

She not only found the cause for her pain, but she had to relive the incident until the pool of pain had been poured down the drain. By the end of her intensive therapy, her pains and problems had disappeared. She now lectures and counsels in the area of childhood trauma and abuse.

When the time comes for the victim to experience the feelings, there are several ways to do it. If these emotions are close to the surface, she can share them with a supportive, nonjudgmental person who will keep her thoughts confidential until she wishes to talk about them openly. She can locate a group such as Philippian Ministries who provide intercessory prayer counseling to release the pains of the past.

She can join—or start—a support group where there are others who have experienced similar hurts. As in Alcoholics Anonymous, receiving help from someone who's been there gives a person HOPE.

She can find a Christian counselor or pastor who understands abuse problems and can lead her through and out of her dark tunnel.

She can go to a professional like Marilyn who has been victimized, who has been through intensive regressive therapy, and who has an excellent record in leading others to emotional restoration.

Whichever way she chooses, it is important that the victim works through her feelings of the past so that she can wipe the slate clean.

ESTABLISH RESPONSIBILITY. Those of us who have not been through abuse or traumas, often assume the child would have known it was not her fault, but somehow the victim ends up with the feeling that she's to blame. "If I hadn't worn those panties Daddy liked." "If I'd gone to church instead of staying home." "If I hadn't sat on his lap." "If I'd only been a good girl."

This thinking is often enforced by the victim's mother: "You must have asked for it"; by the pastor: "I'm sure your father wouldn't have done that"; by siblings: "You shouldn't let him do that to you."

Even if the child seems to grow up "normally," underneath she has the guilt of "it must have been my fault." She also absorbs guilt for other problems that are not her responsibility and often becomes a target for those who are looking for someone to pick on or to blame.

Elaine was a woman who felt guilty about everything and whose complex kept her from making any decisions for herself. She was in a job that she hated where a co-worker constantly abused her verbally. Elaine couldn't stand up for herself because underneath she figured her co-worker's accusations must be right. After being in Jan's support group for several months, Elaine realized she had a pattern of carrying everyone else's load. She had assumed total responsibility for the success of her marriage, for the lives of her children, and for anything else someone might dump upon her. Through counseling she's discovered this pattern in her life stems from her assuming responsibility for the incest perpetrated by her uncle. After working through this step of establishing the blame where it belongs, Elaine is learning to balance this issue and get a realistic view of those things in life that are her responsibility. She is now aware when she starts to apologize for things she hasn't done and is no longer an automatic guilt-absorber.

Jan had felt guilty all her life for what had been done to her and she learned through her counseling to put the responsibility for her victimization where it belonged. She says:

Realize that the child trusted the perpetrator, the person in authority, and that person came and violated this trust. He took something away from that child that can never be given back. The victim needs to understand that she is 100 percent innocent and place that burden she's been bearing on the back of the abuser where it belongs.

A child who has been taken advantage of grows up not trusting anyone, especially anyone who may be similar to the aggressor. About a year after Jan and Don were married, he asked, "You don't really trust me, do you?"

Jan answered, "No, I guess I really don't. Every man I've known has done me dirty and I don't expect anything different from you."

After she had verbalized her feelings, she realized what an unloving statement she had made and how much she needed counsel. As she received help she was shown for the first time that she was not responsible and that she must place the blame where it belonged 100 percent. She told me the relief was unbelievable; it was like laying down a sack of potatoes she'd been carrying around for a lifetime.

TRACE BEHAVIORAL DIFFICULTIES AND SYMPTOMS. Those of us who have women coming to us with problems can learn to recognize symptoms that clue us in to a person's difficulties. When we find migraines, body pains, eating disorders, asthma, fear attacks, or nightmares, we should direct our questioning to the possibility of child abuse. If there are gaps in the memory and the person is unable to recall big chunks of time, this is an added sign.

Marilyn Murray has developed a way to spot trauma victims by looking in their eyes and I have learned some clues from her. If there is a look of pain deep in the eyes, the person probably grew up with a deprivation of love, approval, or the basic necessities. If when you are conversing you notice a darting of the eyes around the room as if in fear someone will find her, or see a "frightened rabbit" look in the back of the eyes, you should question in the area of abuse, incest, or rape. Some victims will have a dead look in the eyes—you see no life or sparkle. This may mean a victim experienced a trauma which caused emotional death.

Not everyone will have a feel for this sensitive observation but as I have employed this method, I have come up with more accurate appraisals and saved time in getting to the cause of the abnormal behavior patterns.

When women complain of a disinterest in or fear of normal sexual relationships the root of this may be from childhood abuse. Dr. Dennis Bull of Dallas, a professional counselor, says:

As would obviously be expected, poor sexual adjustment as an adult is a primary symptom of incest. It can take two extreme forms. For some, the sexual feeling side is shut down. They find it difficult to even be casually touched by a friend. If married, they literally endure sex and are seldom aroused, or may even permanently refuse sex with their partner. On the other side, sex has been the primary way some former victims have learned to relate to men. It is a way to get attention and hold affection even if in an empty form. So many find themselves acting out by being very promiscuous. It is not unusual to also swing back and forth between the two extremes because neither is very satisfying.[15]

It's no wonder victims cannot relate normally to their spouses. These girls were never allowed to develop the natural trusting feelings for father, uncle, or other male figure that lead to the intimate relationships involved in a healthy marriage. Their emotions were replaced with misshapen ideas, confusion, and a guilt-ridden unnatural awareness of sexual activity.

When a destructive and damaging introduction to what is meant to be a wonderful and trusting intimacy shared between husband and wife is experienced, the effects are devastating and debilitating. The reason many victims go for long periods of time without having intimate relations with their husbands is because it just becomes too difficult for them, too much of a reminder of the past. I've heard numerous stories from victims with tremendously painful problems in this area who have blamed their apparent frigidity on everything from an overweight husband to the color of the sheets. Jan says:

One night when my husband and I were being intimate I remember feeling frozen. All of a sudden I just froze and I didn't know why. As I began to think about it I realized my husband had on the same aftershave lotion that my stepfather had always worn.

Flashbacks, much like those experienced by Vietnam veterans, give vivid nightmarish conditions which constantly curse victims' lives. Many times these flashbacks are so real they prevent them from normal functioning in their day-to-day activities and prohibit any further emotional growth.

The foundational problem for any victim is low self-esteem or poor self-image. This major difficulty will demand continuous attention to encourage and improve the victims' self-respect through the rest of her life. She was shown by her aggressor, in essence, that she was no good, had no rights as a person, and would never have any worth to herself or anyone else. Many times, due to a poor self-image, a teenage victim will run away from home and become promiscuous.

In *Christianity Today*, Dr. Mimi Silbert is quoted as saying that most incest victims were "first molested at the average age of ten, and that physical force or emotional or physical threats were used. Their typical responses were 'I felt disgusted by sex'; 'I felt dirty'; 'I felt terrible.' "[16]

This victimization "lays the foundation for prostitution. A lifestyle of learned helplessness ensues. Through incest and other abuse, girls feel sexually spoiled, their feelings of inferiority are compounded by other degrading experiences which lead them into prostitution as their only choice."[17]

Tracing is an exercise that allows the victim to see the source and challenges them to break the negative patterns of behavior. The victim should be able to say, "Now that I see where my behaviors come from, I can begin to make better choices."

OBSERVE OTHERS AND EVALUATE SELF. One consistent step we all need to take if we are to help victims is to know what's really going on in life. It is so easy, especially in the Christian community, to think these people with problems are somewhere else. We need to be observant and notice hurting people, and we need to be able to educate ourselves about symptoms, solutions, and support groups. Local agencies often have material we can easily acquire and study so that we can be more aware and helpful.

Often victims think they are the only ones who have ever been molested and are afraid to tell anyone for fear they'll be looked down upon or ridiculed. Support groups consisting of people with similar problems provide a freeing feeling for the victim. Jan says,

It's been such an experience for me to see women come in to our groups and in ten weeks observe a great change. The familiarity of being with someone else who has gone through a similar experience is so comforting for them.

It is also important for us all to know that the aggressor is not just a weird man hiding behind doors and lurking in dark alleys. He is often intelligent, middle to upperclass, and of high moral standing in the community. When these perpetrators are exposed we are usually shocked.

We also should understand that there are co-contributors, others who knew what was going on and did nothing about it. This is most often the mother who looks the other way rather than get in trouble herself or risk having to support herself. In fact, *Newsweek* says that "the father's tendency is to tyrannize the family and the mother's fear of questioning his absolute authority prevents her from acting in their behalf."[18]

Sometimes the co-conspirator is another family member. Jan had one girl tell her that her uncle once molested her. Her brother walked into the room, saw what was happening, turned around, and walked out. The victim was as angry with her brother as she was with her uncle.

CONFRONT THE AGGRESSOR. This step is not for everyone and should never be entered into without prayerful preparation and godly counsel. When Jan is asked about this sensitive step by one of her support group members she explains that the Lord Jesus heals in many different ways according to the individual and they will have to evaluate the possible outcome of their particular confrontation. Unless you are spiritually led to confrontation it can be deathly, for even God-ordained it is difficult.

When Jan came to Fred and me suffering physical problems because she had to keep a social relationship with her stepfather, we suggested a "cooling-off period" where she would have no contact with him for awhile. Each holiday gave her a headache and she described her visits as opening her old wounds again and again. She couldn't continue to torture herself with these reminders, so she called her mother and made an appointment to see her.

Jan started by telling her mother she was not going to see her stepfather for an indefinite period of time and she asked for her cooperation and understanding. Her mother was astounded. She knew what had happened, but she assumed Jan had dealt with the incest and put it all behind her. Jan explained that she had always discussed the subject from a point of weakness and she needed some peaceful time to rebuild her own self-image and gain strength.

During what became a year of separation, Jan did an in-depth study of God's word on self-worth. She began to seek God in a new way and tried to find who he was in her life. She realized that she and many other victims tend to see God with the face of their aggressor on him. They believe God is vengeful, and there is no hope for victory.

As Jan studied what God said about himself, she was able to erase the false picture she had of him and allow him to become the warm and loving Father she had never known. When Jan got to know her Father, she was able to see herself as a child of worth, slightly lower than the angels.

In preparation for her confrontation Jan not only filled herself with God's word but prayed for the proper place and timing. She says: *It is always necessary for the victim to go into confrontation from a position of strength.* Jan also prepared her mother by sending her a book on incest. After her mother had read it they met together and Jan had to tell her how angry she had been at her for not stepping in and protecting her. As they reconciled their past feelings, Jan explained she had to confront her stepfather and needed her mother's help.

At first he refused but as Jan asked him over the phone, "Are you telling me that what you have to do is more important than meeting with me?" He finally agreed to meet with her, but he added, "I thought you were a good enough Christian to have forgiven and forgotten by now."

She realized the aggressor was again attempting to make the victim carry the responsibility. She knew it was important that she respond to his accusation. She asked God to show her how to reply. She knew confrontation was necessary to resolve the problems of the past, put the responsibility where it belonged, and *offer* to reconcile the family together again. Once she saw her outline clearly, she went with the strength of the Lord beside her.

Jan laid the whole story out before her stepfather, clearly explaining the long term effects his actions had on her. She gave a detailed list of her symptoms of low self-esteem, bad relationships, migraines, sexual problems, bursts of anger at her child, perfectionism, and a critical spirit.

Jan complimented him on taking her to church and challenging her to go to college. She confessed that she had not handled herself well at home and had not been the perfect daughter he had wanted her to be. But she told him he must accept full responsibility for the molestation in order for there to be a reconciliation of the relationship. She was unwilling to carry the guilt she had been bearing for twenty years. Because of the strength of her position, he looked at her and said, "I am totally responsible. Will you forgive me for what I did?"

"Yes, Dad I will." She gave him a big hug and they both cried. Then she added, "Dad, God could have healed me instantly twenty years ago, but he allowed me to carry this burden so that you might experience God's forgiveness at the same time I extend to you my forgiveness."

The father-daughter relationship is not perfect, but Jan is free from the burden that held her captive. They can now spend time together without feeling uncomfortable. Jan has resolved the past, put the responsibility where it belongs, and reconciled the family.

For Barbara Bueler confronting her aggressor was not a healthy option and would not have promoted a rational response; however, when she went through her day of inner healing with Lana she faced this woman in prayer. Visualizing the Lord by her side, Barbara was able to confront the perpetrator, see her through his eyes, and forgive the act that had almost stripped her of her life. The results for Barbara gave her a new sense of peace, a freedom from debilitating nightmares (see chapter 8).

Lana says, "What I see in Barbara is a growing ability to control her reactions and responses to stressful situations enabling her to choose victory over victimization."

ACKNOWLEDGE FORGIVENESS.   Once a victim has confronted the aggressor personally or in prayer she must be willing to acknowledge forgiveness and appropriate this release for her life. It is a slow process working through this devastation, for emotional brokenness takes time to be repaired and rebuilt. A distorted life seen only through the shattered view of a child's injured emotions needs to see the HOPE that forgiveness can supply. It does not happen overnight. It takes time to work through. A victim may have been told "You should be over this by now. If you would only forgive him you would be healed." This mending of broken emotions may be compared to a compound fracture of the leg. Would you tell the person with the broken leg, who has been run over by a truck, that if he would only forgive the truck driver his leg would be healed? Both physical and emotional breaks take time to mend, and forgiveness is the healing balm. "There is a balm in Gilead that heals the sin-sick soul." Oh, how we need to acknowledge forgiveness.

REBUILD SELF-IMAGE AND RELATIONSHIPS.   As Jan dedicated that one year separation from her parents to rebuilding her self-image, so must each victim seek to lift her worth through the Word. Jan gathered others around her with similar needs and together they found Christian material to study. She led them in heart-felt search and prayer to reach for the hem of his garment. Knowing as that woman, "If I may but touch his garment I shall be whole" (Matt. 9:21, KJV).

Only as the victim can become whole can she begin to accept others as they are and rebuild relationships. Often the husband has suffered, his masculinity has been questioned, and he may feel of little worth himself. Jan's husband, Don, has been willing to put himself on the line and open up to the husbands of incest victims. He can say in reality, "I know how you feel."

A pastor's wife in one of Jan's support groups was so discouraged over trying to deal with her low self-image and constant depression that she decided to leave her husband. As Jan worked with her and showed her how God valued her, she began to see some HOPE for her future. She stopped pushing her husband away and assuming he didn't love her and began to put her marriage back together. She found his self-worth had been beaten down first by a domineering mother and then by her self-negation. He thought, "If she's that bad and I'm married to her, I can't be worth much myself."

The victim so needs to rebuild herself and her relationships.

EXPRESS CONCERN AND EMPATHIZE WITH OTHERS. Although it is difficult for victims pulling out of the pain of their own problems to reach out and touch others, this act is one of the most rewarding. No matter what we have been victims of, when we see some HOPE for our own situation we should be open to helping others. Some are able to step out quickly and some need more time for the healing process. But when God gives us the green light, we should be willing to express concern for others. No one can empathize with a victim as well as a person who's been there.

In CLASS we aim to prepare people to speak and counsel on the subjects with which they have had personal experience. What a load it would be off the pastor's shoulders if women like Jan would offer to empathize with other victims in the church, to let them know they're not alone, and to set up support groups.

One girl whom Jan has trained and encouraged has made herself available to help children in her church and community who have been victimized. She's been able to support the children through ugly court procedures and help the parents receive professional counsel.

Yes, there is trouble in our River City and we must be willing to help. "God is always at work in us to make us willing and able to obey his good purpose" (Phil. 2:13, TEV). Jan is willing and God has made her able to give HOPE to hundreds of victims and their husbands and to start their lives on the mend.

Sewing Up the Sorrows

Showing how we can relieve, and not add to, the sorrows of depression and death.

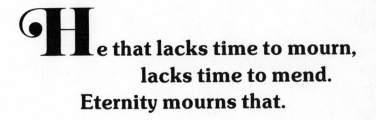

He that lacks time to mourn,
lacks time to mend.
Eternity mourns that.

Philip Van Artevelde
Sir Henry Taylor

FLORENCE LITTAUER

Teen Depression
and Suicide

As I sat alone in a coffee shop in Tulsa, an adorable bright-eyed waitress came along to take my order. Throughout the meal we conversed and she asked what I was doing in the hotel. "I'm writing a book to give hope to women."

"In what areas?" she asked.

I listed a few and then added, "Today I'm beginning the chapter on teenage depression and suicide."

Her smiling face changed and she said sadly, "I spent my teen years deeply depressed and I tried to commit suicide three times."

"What caused your depression?" I asked.

"I guess it started when I was three and my father died. I thought he left because he didn't like me. My mother remarried and I *knew* my stepfather didn't like me. We moved a lot and I never felt I stayed anywhere long enough to have any worthwhile relationships. I guess I grew up thinking nobody really cared."

"What made you try suicide?"

"Now that I think about it, I guess I was calling for help. I wanted someone to say it made a difference if I was alive, but no one did so later I tried again."

"What method did you use?" I asked as I worked to enjoy my dinner.

"I slit my wrist with razor blades, but as soon as I saw blood I stopped."

"What kept you from finding another way and finishing the job?"

"I was afraid I'd go to hell. You see I'm a Christian."

"I'm a Christian too," I added. "Are you happy now?"

"Well, I've been married a year and it's been difficult because underneath I'm afraid he won't really like me and he'll leave. I don't know what I'd do then!"

The busboy came along and he wanted to add some material to my book. "Are you depressed?" I asked.

"No, I'm pretty good. It's my roommate. He used to be a straight guy like me, but he started smoking pot. Later he turned to acid and quit school because he couldn't study and he didn't care. The drugs cost so much he started selling them to pay for his own. Even that didn't give him enough and one night he held up a liquor store. As he sped away he cracked up and the police got him. Now he's in jail waiting for his trial on armed robbery and possession of cocaine. Is he depressed!"

"I assume you've learned a lesson from this," I stated.

"You bet!" he said.

Within fifteen minutes I had acquired two fresh case histories from young people who were not only willing but eager to have some unknown lady listen to what was in their hearts. From these two we can quickly learn some basic principles on teen depression.

It often starts in the early years with a feeling—right or wrong— that the child is abandoned by a parent and isn't loved. Remarriage often reinforces the left-out assumption and frequent moving prevents long-term peer support. By the teen years when self-image is at its lowest, these fears that no one cares lead into depression and often suicide attempts as a cry for attention and help. When the act itself does not produce new floods of love, the teen believes he was right in the first place and tries again.

The other case is more drastic but there are no degrees in death. Once dead it's all over. So many teens think smoking pot is not harmful and until recent years many supposed experts agreed. Although scientific evidence now shows slowed reactions, brain damage, and possible lung cancer, teens don't read the results of these studies. Using marijuana, the largest cash crop in California, leads in most cases to hard drugs. Because of cost, no young person's salary can supply the needs and they either stop, sell, or steal.

When not on a high they become deeply depressed. Fifty percent of teen suicides are drug related.[1]

Were these just two isolated stories I happened to find in a coffee shop in Tulsa or is teen depression and suicide a problem everywhere? Do we as mature and moral adults need to know about this unappealing subject? Is there, in fact, a danger in our section of town? In our church? If there is, what can we do about it?

One youth director in a church where I spoke recently told me he had, in one week, two of his young people attempt suicide, one arrested for stealing auto parts and selling them for drugs, and one boy whose mother brought him to the church, handed him over to the pastor and said, "Here, you take him. The church can have him. I can't stand him any more!" She walked out and slammed the door.

Is there trouble right here in River City? Statistics in this country show that a thousand teens a week try to kill themselves and a hundred succeed. But the true figure is probably closer to 24,000 in one year since so many suicides look like accidents and families try to avoid reporting their child's death as a suicide. The total is up 300 percent in the last twenty years and suicide is the fastest growing cause of death in this country. Recent studies show that more than two million high school students attempted suicide last year.[2] Twelve percent of our teens are on both drugs and alcohol (polybuse) and in England heroin addiction has tripled in the last two years.[3]

"Aren't these just kids from bad families?" you might ask. The answer is that they come from all strata in life but primarily from the middle and upper class. Plano, Texas, is a model community where every leisure-time activity ever invented has been installed. *Texas Monthly* wrote that this city is "a sprawling enclave of corporate achievers and their families. About twenty miles north of Dallas, Plano is one of those pop-up communities that began to dot the Sun Belt in the '70s as upwardly mobile young executives in search of the good life moved in from the floundering cities of the East."[4] The article tells about how perfect this city is and yet it has the dubious honor of having the highest teenage suicide rate in the entire United States. "An idyllic Dallas suburb is discovering the sorrows of ruthlessness and isolation."[5]

Another recent increase of teenage suicides was seen in an area twenty miles south of downtown Houston, Texas, Clear Lake City. "This affluent development of 25,000 people, is a 20-year wonder where everything is sleek and clean and the air is fresh and unpolluted. This is home to the astronauts and the engineers and to others whose jobs revolve around NASA's Johnson Space Center."[6]

Affluent Ridgewood, New Jersey, experienced a real rash of teenage suicides. The high school administrators put up a sign on the bulletin board to announce to teenagers who were contemplating suicide that they were going to bring in suicide counselors. Nearly half of the 1,600 high school students immediately signed up for help. The pressures to succeed are high in this community, the parents are trying to make their children achieve, and 80 percent of the graduates of the school go to first-ranking universities.[7] *Time* says, "When you add pressure to a high divorce rate and a high number of dead marriages, you see a lot of youngsters in isolation, not relating to their parents."[8]

Yes, there is trouble in River City. Why? "Why?" is the big question. One article I read was titled "Federal Help Is Needed to Reduce Teenage Suicide." It gave many statistics but no answers and concluded it would take a five-million-dollar grant to find out "why."[9]

Teens don't decide to kill themselves on a whim nor does this thought come suddenly. Many have been unhappy since childhood and some are quietly depressed. The actual impetus to suicide may appear to be over a trivial circumstance but one that happened to be, for that youth, "the last straw."

Picture in your mind a foam rubber pillow. Now push your figurative fist into it and hold it there. You have depressed the pillow; you have pressed it down. It no longer has any spring to it in the area you are holding. If you don't press down too long, the foam will bounce back when you remove your hand. But if you were to put bricks on it and continue to keep it under pressure, it might never spring back to its original shape again. That's what depression is like. The spirit is held down. If the depression is short the person can bounce back, but if it's prolonged that person's nature becomes so pessimistic that he sees no HOPE and a minor spark may cause a major catastrophe.

Some teens commit suicide when a girl friend jilts them or they flunk a course, but this trivial cause is usually the result of a deep depression.

In my book *Blow Away the Black Clouds*, I have dealt at length with the symptoms of depression, the types of people who get depressed, and many steps in overcoming this problem. The material in that book will be very useful for anyone who wishes to pursue this subject beyond what can be done in this one chapter.[10]

What does this subject have to do with me personally? Why am I writing on teen suicide? Did I have a child who tried to kill himself? Gratefully no, but because I have studied, written, and spoken on depression for years, I have been aware of the symptoms. This awareness has helped me deal with my teen son through some trying times. It has made me alert to his needs and able to prevent what could have led to deep depression.

Because I believe prevention is the best cure, in fact the only cure, for suicide, I want to share with other parents how to be aware of the needs of teens so that they might circumvent this current crisis.

As I have studied this problem I have found that the depressed teen gets his seeds for suicide early in life. While we can't possibly review them all, let me mention some of the vicissitudes that lead to the valleys of the shadow of death.

EARLY REJECTION. Children with a melancholy temperament easily feel rejected even when there is no obvious problem. As parents we must realize that a perceived rejection is as valid as a real one to a child. When one parent departs either in death or divorce, the child perceives this as rejection. "He didn't love me; he didn't care." Often this abandoned feeling makes the child work harder to keep the attention of the parent who is still available. If the child becomes either a clinger who won't leave his mother's side or a child who gets into constant trouble, sooner or later the parent pushes him aside for a gasp of air. The child reads his parent's behavior as another rejection. Unfortunately, this over-zealous bid for attention causes repeated rejections, which lead to depression and possible suicide.

One young lady who picked me up at an airport had told me a history of eight major rejections before we got to the motel. She was constantly doing extremely generous deeds for others, giving extravagant gifts to those she chose for friends—binding them to her by guilt. Sooner or later her friends would feel suffocated by the inordinate attention and would have to push her away. She would take this as rejection—"after all I've done for her"—and sink into depression. Several times she attempted suicide.

She had established a pattern in childhood that she continued into adulthood. She didn't see that she set herself up for repeated rejections.

Adopted children often have a feeling of rejection even if they don't understand their situation. They need special affirmation coupled with loving discipline if they are to grow up emotionally stable. We adopted Freddie when he was three months old and told him when he was still little that he was special, that we chose him on our own free will. Out of all the little babies in the world, he was God's selection for our son.

No matter how positively a parent paints this picture, the day comes when the adopted child is suddenly swept with the reality that he was illegitimate and that his "real" parents didn't want him. Add to this the fact, for our son, that we made him a second Freddie, named after our first son who had died. He soon gathered that he was a replacement for both of our lost boys and no matter how much love we gave him, underneath he felt rejected.

FAMILY TENSION.   Since home is the world for little ones, family fights, quiet animosity, or physical abuse, either suffered or observed, can cause emotional damage to a child that can lead to depression. As our little Freddie grew up, I was trying to get over my own depression from losing my sons, my husband threw himself into his work to keep from facing reality at home, and we kept our marriage together "for the sake of the children." Surely there were family tensions.

FREQUENT MOVES.   The more times a family moves, the more insecure the children may feel. A positive attitude from both parents can prevent this insecurity. My brother Jim, as a chaplain in the Air Force, moved his family all over the world with no negative effects because each move was enthusiastically heralded by both Jim and Katie as one more exciting adventure.

For many wives each move is a negative, foreboding event plotted by their husbands to thwart their social life and throw them into depression. The child senses the mother's feelings and is fearful of where he may end up next.

When Freddie was three we moved from Connecticut to California, from a new twelve-room home to an old five-room bungalow, from affluence to full-time Christian service. I was in shock and I'm sure the children felt the vibrations. Gratefully, our sincere dedication to the Lord and our daily family prayer time provided the needed peace.

SIBLING RIVALRY. Often one child will not do as well as his brothers and sisters in school, in sports, in music, or whatever feature seems to be important to the family. Even if this deficiency is not pointed out, he feels that he's not up to par. Lauren and Marita excelled in everything they touched and they moved fast. Freddie just got by in school and sports and he moved slowly. When Marita left for college and Freddie was twelve, he said to me, "It'll be lonesome for you with Marita gone. There will be no one to laugh with any more."

Even though I'd never verbalized this thought, Freddie had noticed that Marita was my fun, that she had a sense of humor. I set out to affirm every touch of lightness he came up with and let him know that he too had a sense of humor.

HIGH STANDARDS. While the idea of lofty goals is a positive one, these aims must be within the range of the child's ability. Because Lauren and Marita quickly climbed to the top of each chart, we urged Freddie to follow in their footsteps. We didn't take into account his different personality and achievement level. I am so grateful that he sat down with Fred and me in his teens and said, "I want to tell you two that I am not like Lauren and Marita. I am not of your blood and I did not inherit your love for fast action. I am myself and I would appreciate it if you would consider that fact as you set my standards."

Gratefully the Lord kept our mouths shut long enough for us to swallow and say, "Thank you for sharing that with us and for being honest about your feelings. We'll surely try to keep what you've said in mind."

Those young people in Clear Lake had not been able to communicate that point. They felt they'd never achieve what their intellectual parents expected of them.

RIGID RULES. Recent studies have shown that parents whose rules are inflexible, who are considered authoritarian, produce teens who are as troublesome as those with permissive parents. Rules were always very important in our home and when they were disobeyed the children felt we would never forgive them. As Fred and I grew in the Lord, we saw how rigid some of our rules had been and we relaxed our standards on those things that didn't affect the children's morals.

Some of you really strict parents might discuss with your children where they think you are too harsh and allow for some flexibility on minor matters. Not everything has to be done our way now! I remember the day last year when I stood in the garage by the washing machine admiring the rack of shirts I had hanging there for young Fred. As I stood proudly looking at the product of my labors, he drove in the garage right beside me. As he got out of the car, I said to him, "Fred, look what Mother has done." He glanced at me and said what my children all say when I do any household task, "Noble Mother." I thought "noble mother" wasn't really enough. So as he headed off, I called, "Fred, come back here. I want you to take these shirts in to your room with you." He turned to me and replied, "That is not on my schedule right now." It went through my head to say, "I didn't ask about your schedule. I don't care what you are thinking. I want the shirts taken in now." Gratefully, I was able to keep my mouth shut. I swallowed a couple of times and said, "That's fine, Fred, whenever you have time." As I stood alone in the garage I thought, "Do I need to pressure that boy to carry his shirts in the house right now? Does it matter if his shirts are in his closet? Would it matter if they hung in the garage for a week? Would it matter if Fred lived in the garage with his shirts? Would it really make any difference?"

LACK OF LOVE. Even though we parents know we love our children, their perception of love is not always what we expect. When Marita was in sixth grade I asked her one day, "Do you know Mother loves you?"

She replied, "I know you would if I got better marks."

I had never verbally tied her marks and love together, but that's how she saw it. By Fred's sixth grade he had already reasoned that his "real mother" couldn't have loved him and that he wasn't too sure of me. When I'd say, "I love you," he'd shrug or grunt. Because I like response, I could have easily given up, but I kept hugging him and affirming him and after five years of this, one day he said, "I love you too."

LEARNING DISABILITIES. Children that have any problem that keeps them from progressing normally tend to misbehave as a cover-up or get depressed, depending on their temperament. Freddie tried to do well in school, but in certain areas he just couldn't achieve. In his high school years we had some tests done and found that he had a learning disability that made math and foreign languages extremely difficult. I'll never forget Dr. Spitz as he looked at young Fred and said, "You must have a pretty stable home life, because most boys with this problem would be juvenile delinquents by now!" I'm sure the doctor meant well, but our son was so crushed he vowed he would never take another test like that again.

We had to work with him to build up his strengths and understand why he couldn't do well in math. My husband began to teach Fred his business and literally poured his life into his son with patience and love. At twenty-one young Fred now runs the business with his father. Recently he visited with some of his high school buddies and reported, "They haven't grown up at all. They're right back there where I left them."

FEAR OF NUCLEAR WAR. One day when Fred was a senior in high school he came home and said, "My friends and I were discussing committing suicide today." My first thoughts were, "What would make you want to commit suicide? This nice house, your own room, me for a mother? Fortunately I said none of the above but asked, 'Why?' "

"We're all eighteen. We're going to be drafted and we'll be sent to war. We'll all be blown up by nuclear bombs so we might as well end it now."

These boys were not alone in their fears. In England 87 percent of the teenage boys expect to be involved in nuclear war in their lifetime. In this country it's 58 percent.[11] One page in *USA Today* was filled with articles on the fears teens have of being victims. Brown University was the first of several colleges to pass a student referendum asking the pharmacy to stock cyanide pills so they could quickly kill themselves before the nukes landed.

By patiently waiting for Fred to express his feelings, I was able to lead him into a discussion of God's plan for his life and encourage him to give HOPE to his fellow students.

POOR COMMUNICATIONS. How easy it is to give up on even trying to communicate with our teens as they seem to be so disinterested in us and our opinions. In the last few years as I've been traveling so much, father and son have had many dinners together. My husband never knows what mood young Fred will be in and some nights he says absolutely nothing. It takes patience and restraint to sit quietly until the day young Fred is ready to pour out everything he's been mulling over for weeks, but it's worth the wait.

I took him to Europe on a speaking trip and I knew this would be a test for my Christian maturity. Would I be patient when he didn't respond? Could I sit for hours on a bus and let him stare out the window? Could I allow him to be bored with the thought of one more cathedral? Yes, I could and I did. I sometimes thought of how excited Marita and Lauren would be if they were with me, but the Lord would say, "They're not here; see Europe Fred's way."

On the last night as we stood on the balcony of the Jerusalem Hilton quietly impressed with the Holy City, Fred opened up with, "During these three weeks I've been thinking and I've come up with my philosophy of life." For forty-five minutes he poured out deep and beautiful principles and precepts and I learned that my patience had paid off.

POOR EATING HABITS. Young Fred has a low energy level and my nutritionist, Dr. Starr, has kept him on a proper diet with the correct food supplements for his needs. While friends had colas, Fred drank apple juice. One night before I first spoke on teen suicide, I took him out for dinner and explained my topic. He'd had two friends who had killed themselves and I asked his opinion on why teens get so depressed.

His first answer surprised me, "They don't eat right."

He then explained that none of his friends had mothers who cooked dinner every night. I asked if he could give me a sample day's menu for a typical teen. I took notes on the placemat as he said, "Yes, let's take Don. He starts out the morning with two cups of coffee, a cigarette, and a bowl of sugared cereal. In the middle of the morning he has coffee and doughnuts and another cigarette. A little while after that he has a candy bar. For lunch he has a Big Mac, an apple turnover, and a large coffee. In the afternoon he has candy, ice cream, cigarettes, and cola. When he went out with me the other night for dinner he ate a burrito, cinnamon crisp, and another cola. Mother, they are depressed because they don't eat right."

Other factors contributing to teen depression that I have not had to face personally are drug and alcohol abuse, homosexuality, and lack of faith in God. That night in the restaurant my son said, "Mother, for most of the boys my age, there is just no light at the end of the tunnel. Most of them don't believe in God and when they don't believe in God, they don't think there is a future life after death."

I asked, "Do you have any advice for mothers?"

He said, "Teach them about God and tell them not to make their boys feel that they are worthless bums. I heard one of my friend's mothers say, 'You are a disgrace to the family.' After that the boy didn't care what he did. If he was a disgrace to the family, why bother living?"

I am so grateful I have weathered these teen years and have, by the Grace of God, raised three normal children to be productive adults. With God all things are possible!

What can our churches do to stem the tide of suicide?

RECOGNIZE THE PROBLEM. We have to realize that there is trouble in teen city and the church needs to be ready with a plan. Watch for the symptoms of depression and reach out a helping hand before it's too late.

RESTORE THE FAMILY. In these troubled times of loneliness and lack of love, our churches must work to enforce and enhance the supportive structure of the family. The reason the Mormon church is growing so rapidly is because of their emphasis on loving family life and their clear instructions on how to achieve it. We must realize that as the family falters so too does the church.

REVITALIZE THE COMMUNITY. Support groups, instruction, and hotlines are some simple starts on solving the problems in our Christian community. We should not leave our hurting people out in the cold forcing them to turn to worldly groups for help. There must be a sense of caring for our young people. Bowling and pizza parties are no longer enough.

REVIVE GOD. Since *Time* proclaimed, "God Is Dead" on its cover (8 April 1966), our country has buried him a little more deeply each year. So few teens believe in God or an afterlife that they see no reason to live. Many equate death with a perpetual drug high, floating serenely forever. We in the church have failed to communicate in a clear and convincing way that God so loved each young person that he sent his only son so that if we would believe in him we would not perish but have everlasting life. We must preach not only salvation, but also the Bible's reassurance of eternal life for each believer.

It's not easy; it takes time and talent but we can:

> *Recognize* the problem
> *Restore* the family
> *Revitalize* the community and
> *Revive* God!

It is possible to raise emotionally stable young people in today's unstable world when we show them eternal HOPE and wrap them in God's arms of love.

MARILYN HEAVILIN

Death of a Child

As Christians we like to assume that no one in our church, in our group of friends, or certainly in our family would ever get drunk. And if they did, they would be rational enough not to drive. Unfortunately, today's statistics prove both of those assumptions to be wrong.

You may not be able to change the church or your friends but you can influence your own family, first by making them aware of the facts. We assume that ignoring problems means we are avoiding them, but in the area of drinking, no matter how virtuous we feel our teens are, we must wisely present them with the truth.

Since 75 percent of American youths are drinking alcoholic beverages when they get their licenses at age 16, it is no wonder that 59 percent of the high school males and 42 percent of the females have had drinking and driving difficulties. Each year eight thousand teens and young adults are killed and forty thousand are injured in drunk driving incidents. Of those who die in single car wrecks, 65 percent are drunk.[1]

How drunk is drunk? The legal measure is .10 percent blood alcohol level in most states, but since arriving at this varies according to weight and frequency of drinking, we must let our young people know that "just a few beers" can make them legally drunk. They may feel fine, but if they're stopped and checked they may be booked as intoxicated.

Traffic officer Carl Becker with the California Highway Patrol has an intuitive sense when a driver is drunk and says the defense he hears most often is, "But officer, I only had two beers."[2]

In October 1984, 50 percent of all crashes handled by the East Los Angeles police were somehow alcohol related. The California Highway Patrol tackled this problem with a massive publicity campaign in December 1984. Taking out full-page ads in newspapers, they put in headlines, "If you drink and drive in California we'll introduce you to some new bars." Walter Pudinski, Commissioner with the California Highway Patrol, stated publicly, "We are arresting every drunk driver in sight. The Patrol's standing orders are: Find them, arrest them, jail them, and prosecute them." Lloyd G. Turner, Chief Officer of Traffic Safety warned, "An appalling waste of the California economy will be eliminated, along with the tragedy of innocent suffering and needless dying, with continued enforcement and firm prosecution. The drunk driver cannot be tolerated."[3]

Large groups of concerned merchants donated money for these startling ads which included a Blood Alcohol Content chart as shown below.[4]

NUMBER OF DRINKS IN ONE HOUR
APPROXIMATE BLOOD ALCOHOL
CONTENT (BAC)

DRINKS	BODY WEIGHT IN POUNDS								
	100	120	140	160	180	200	220	240	
1	.04	.03	.03	.02	.02	.02	.02	.02	
2	.08	.06	.05	.05	.04	.04	.03	.03	
3	.11	.09	.08	.07	.06	.06	.05	.05	
4	.15	.12	.11	.09	.08	.08	.07	.06	HAZARDOUS
5	.19	.16	.13	.12	.11	.09	.09	.08	(may be illegal)
6	.23	.19	.16	.13	.13	.11	.10	.09	
7	.26	.22	.19	.16	.15	.13	.12	.11	
8	.30	.25	.21	.19	.17	.15	.14	.13	ILLEGAL
9	.34	.28	.24	.21	.19	.17	.15	.14	
10	.38	.31	.27	.23	.21	.19	.17	.16	

One drink = 1 oz. of 100 proof liquor or one 12 oz. beer.

Don't assume your teen or your mate who only has "a few beers" is aware that he could be caught and convicted of drunk driving. Don't preach and moralize, just show them the facts!

About 140 Americans will be killed today. Nearly 548 will be maimed or disfigured. Half of them because someone had too much to drink.

Nearly 25,000 Americans are killed each year in alcohol related accidents.

In fact, the number one killer of Americans is Americans.

Someone like you.

Someone, who just this once, had too much wine, beer or mixed drinks.

Someone who, just this once, drank one more than they should have and got behind the wheel of a car.

Either way, someone alive is suddenly dead.

An individual driving under the influence is the greatest single threat you face.[5]

Although you may not know who Stevie Wonder is, it might impress your teens that this Academy Award winning singer-composer has written a song against drunk driving. A victim of an inebriated teen, Stevie said in an interview, "I want to remind people, you can have a good time—no one says you can't—but you just have to remember that, yes, you do have a responsibility to life."[6]

A study compiled by the National Institute of Alcohol Abuse Fatal Accident Reporting System indicates that there was a distinct pattern in 1983 involving young drunk drivers. It states, "January had the fewest fatalities and the number of deaths rose steadily month by month through February, March, April, and May, dipped slightly in July and August. The number of fatal accidents declined during the last three months of the year. Thus, the pattern generally follows a pattern of the warmer the month, the more deaths young drunk drivers cause. Holidays during the warmer months were inordinately dangerous . . . with Labor Day the worst (168 mishaps caused by young drunk drivers). The Fourth of July was almost as bad (150 deaths), and Memorial Day third (133)."[7]

How important it is to educate your family and yourself about these dangers and how much better it is to risk their thinking you're old-fashioned than to have them, through ignorance, drink, drive, and end up dead or end up causing an innocent person's death.

Do these tragedies happen to people we know?

I first met Glen and Marilyn Heavilin when we were "new staff" together at Campus Crusade for Christ Headquarters at Arrowhead Springs in California a number of years ago. As we became acquainted, we found that we had both lost two sons, ours to irreversible brain damage and theirs to crib death and pneumonia.

One Thursday in February of his junior year, Nate, the Heavilin's youngest living son, returned from a field trip and stopped by Marilyn's office to check in before leaving for the evening's basketball game. As he bounced invisible balls and trotted backwards out the door, Marilyn asked, "What time will you be home?"

"Oh, I don't know. The game might run late and if it does, I'll give you a call." As he dashed off to his locker, he called back, "Don't worry, Mom; I'll see you later!"

Marilyn spent that evening alone while Glen was at a college class. Her mind wandered often to thoughts of Nate: "How's his game going? Is he scoring points? When will he be home?" She even remembered him saying, "Don't worry, Mom; I'll see you later."

She went to sleep early but woke up with a jolt at exactly 11:44 P.M., according to the digital clock. Glen wasn't in bed. She found Glen alone in the living room and asked, "Isn't Nate home yet?" Glen, who never wasted words, just shook his head.

"Something must be wrong. He said he'd call if he was going to be late. Oh Glen, what if something's wrong!" Marilyn tried to keep calm on the outside, but inside she cried, "Please Lord, bring him home. Please bring him home." Glen called the coach who said he last saw Nate at McDonald's; then he dialed a friend who always rode with Nate, but there was no answer. A sick feeling flooded over Marilyn when there was no one home at midnight.

She thought, "His family never stays out late; they must have heard something. Why haven't we?"

They called another friend. As Marilyn stood dazed she heard Glen say, "What hospital is he in?"

While Glen dialed the hospital, he told Marilyn that there had been a terrible head-on collision. The nurse in the emergency room told Glen they had received a young male, listed as John Doe. "Does that mean that he is dead?"

The hospital attendant said, "He's alive, but he's unconscious and unable to identify himself."

Then she added, "Mr. Heavilin, come quickly."

They wanted to rush but they seemed to move in slow motion. Marilyn needed desperately to get to him, and she kept telling herself everything would be all right once she got there. Mothers always know they can fix anything if only they can get there. If she could touch him and speak to him, he would wake up. All the while she was dressing, Marilyn kept whispering, "Hang on, Nate. I'm coming; I'm coming. Just hang on."

Even though their minds were in a muddle, they still functioned in an organized manner. Their other son Matt remembered to take rolls of coins for phone calls, and Marilyn grabbed her address book, thinking, "We've got to call everybody and tell them to pray." Then she thought of the grandparents: "How could we tell them Nate might be dying? Grandchildren aren't supposed to die."

As Glen drove, Marilyn prayed. "God, is it happening again?" Glen and Marilyn had already buried two of their children. Jimmy died at seven weeks, the victim of Sudden Infant Death Syndrome. Nathan's twin, Ethan, born on Christmas day 1965, had died of pneumonia ten days later. The Heavilins knew what it was like to lose a child; they didn't deserve to bear that pain again. Marilyn continued praying out loud, "Lord, please don't let it be Nate's fault. Please heal all of the kids if it's your will. Lord," she hesitated and began again. "Lord, we want your will in Nate's life, and Lord, we're giving you power of attorney over Nate."

At the hospital, the mystery began to unfold. Glen talked with a police officer who verified the car involved in the crash was Nate's—that meant he'd been driving. Was it his fault? The accident occurred at 11:44, the exact time Marilyn had awakened so suddenly! How often God gives mothers special intuition about their children.

A security guard appeared and called out "Clear the halls, we're bringing a patient through." Glen and Marilyn flattened against the wall as a stretcher was pushed quickly past them.

Several people huddled over the person on the cart, so nothing could be seen but a touseled head of brown hair, a pair of blue jeans, and a big foot wearing a white sock. Just as the cart was rushing out of sight, Marilyn realized it was Nate. She wanted to run after him, but the door swung shut behind him. She could hear his voice again, "I'll see you later, Mom."

"Oh God, please help him; please help us," she sighed.

As they stood in shock, a nurse called them into a small, cluttered office, and in a warm, but very concerned voice, she said, "We have just taken your son to surgery. His leg has been crushed; he has brain damage and extensive damage to his heart and lungs. His heart stopped once already, and we opened his chest to massage his heart and start it again."

Marilyn felt sick as she envisioned someone's bare hands on her son's heart. As the nurse continued, Marilyn wondered, "What is God's will for Nate?"

She asked the nurse, "Do you think he's going to make it?"

Her eyes dropped, and she shook her head, "No." At that point their daughter Mellyn and husband Mike arrived. They hugged each other tightly, prayed, cried, and waited. They soon learned the three students in Nate's car were seriously injured, but the doctors said they would survive. One prayer was answered. The next report revealed that the man who hit Nate had been arrested for drunk driving. Marilyn experienced anger and relief all at the same time. It wasn't Nate's fault! Another prayer answered, but their son was dying because someone had been foolish enough to drink and drive. Their son, who never drank and was from a family who didn't drink, was the victim of a drunk driver. How unfair!

The words "drunk driver" were still spinning in their minds as Marilyn received a phone call from a friend who asked, "How's Nate doing?" Marilyn replied, "He's dying." Instead of the expected sympathy the lady scolded, "Don't you talk like that. Don't you know death comes from Satan and if you admit he's dying you are giving in to Satan? If Nathan dies, it will be because you gave up!"

Marilyn hung up the phone and all strength drained from her as she added guilt to her shock and grief. At that moment the nurse came around the corner and when the family looked in her face, they knew. Marilyn asked, "Is he gone?"

She nodded, "Yes."

As Marilyn fell into Glen's arms she told him of the phone call. "I gave up and that's why Nathan's dead."

Glen, grief stricken himself, comforted her by saying, "You didn't give *up*, you gave *over* to God. You gave him power of attorney and he chose to take Nate home with him. Remember, you didn't give up, you gave over."

By the time the family returned home at 3:00 A.M., forty friends had arrived. They prayed and cried together and some stayed throughout the night. The next morning Vonette Bright of Campus Crusade for Christ spoke at a scheduled prayer breakfast. She shared emotionally and compassionately about Nate's tragic death.

After the message, a young couple came up to her and said, "Vonette, we have a verse we would like you to take to your friend." When Vonette arrived at the Heavilin home, excited even though her heart was broken, she read them the verse: "The good men perish; the godly die before their time. . . . No one seems to realize that God is taking them away from evil days ahead. For the godly who die shall rest in peace" (Isa. 57:1–2, TLB).

By noon that day five people had brought that same verse to the family. Perhaps the reason was because J. Vernon McGee had preached on that passage that same morning on the radio. What timing!

Through that verse, God said, "Marilyn, it wasn't an accident. I wasn't on vacation the night Nate died. I knew about it before it happened. Marilyn, I'm taking him away from something worse. He's with me, and he's doing fine."

Over a thousand people attended Nate's funeral. Marilyn was impressed with the fact that Nathan had touched so many lives in his short seventeen years when many of us don't impact that many in seventy. As she looked over the congregation filled with young people, she thanked the Lord that what they were hearing that day would count for many years to come.

During that next week six-hundred people went through the Heavilin's home, many of them teenagers. Gratefully, food was provided by many of the friends who came to call. One friend arrived with a sack full of groceries: cheese, crackers, bread, cinnamon rolls, snack foods, napkins, and paper plates. How useful these all were.

Some brought pictures of Nate, taken at different times in his life. Some laminated the newspaper articles and pictures of the accident and the funeral. Two of Nate's classmates came and cleaned the house and continued to come weekly at no charge for the rest of the year. More than six hundred cards arrived and Marilyn especially appreciated those with personal notes telling of their love and memories of Nate. Plants that were sent to the house provided a living memory of Nate, a living extension of his existence. At the next band concert in which Nate was to have played the trumpet, a mother of another teen borrowed Nate's instrument and played in his place.

Although no one thought to bring a guest book for all those people who dropped by to sign, their friend Nancy did something special. Not only did she come over each day for several weeks, making needed phone calls and helping with meals, but she kept records of what went on and later gave Marilyn a legal pad full of notes plus a cassette tape. She said to Marilyn, "Here is the start of your book if you ever decide to write about this. I have been taking notes ever since Nathan died. I have been writing down everything that has happened at this house: your comments and your reactions, your feelings about certain people that came, all of the details that were in the paper. I have written them all down and then I also made a tape just of my own impressions of what has happened because it has touched me so much. Now here it is; you can read it or listen to it whenever you are ready."

It took Marilyn six months before she was ready. She recalls:

I couldn't even touch it for a while. I never thought I would forget some of the things that happened during that special two weeks, but when I started to listen to Nancy's tape I discovered there was a lot I had already forgotten that would have been lost, but it is there now so that whenever I do write, I'll know how to get going.

The teenagers in one family suggested their whole family have a two-week moratorium on TV watching in memory of Nate and the agony the Heavilins were suffering. One of the girls from the school wrote:

One of the things that I continue to be thankful for is the precious memories I have of Nate. I miss walking through the halls and singing with Nate. He always had a song that he would share. He often asked me how he could help. When no one else knew I was down, he carried my burdens. He was and is a dear friend. I just wanted you to share my thankfulness. Love, Sue

The pastor not only came that first night, but for weeks he would call the Heavilins between nine and ten at night to lovingly check in with them. He would ask them how they really felt, and they were free to express their feelings, sorrow, anger, or guilt without fear of being judged or chastised.

In the midst of positive assistance from friends, the Heavilins had to face two trials. One was the expected proceedings of the offender and the other was a surprise. Marilyn recounts her feelings at that time.

Because all of the teenagers in Nathan's car came from Christian families, I hoped we would be able to work together in harmony. I was wrong. We had difficulty finding anything we could agree on. We wanted to settle everything quickly. The other families were slowing it down. Their attorney advised they prolong the settlement to make sure they had discovered all of their children's possible injuries. Because of this, the insurance settlement which we had hoped would come in sixty to ninety days finally came after fifteen months of problems and hurt feelings. My bitterness began to build.

I knew God could help me overcome these feelings, but I didn't want his help. I preferred to sit and stew. Why couldn't the other families understand we needed to get all of the legal matters finished? It was as though we were waiting for the benediction at the funeral. We couldn't make decisions on our own or set a calendar, and every time I thought I was learning to handle things, we would get a call from our attorney, or the insurance company would call, and it would start all over again. I was angry at the situation and at the people who were causing everything to drag on so long.

When I saw the other families, my hands would start to shake, and when they called, I would start to cry. Through my anger, I was allowing other people to dictate my reactions to everything and everyone around me.

One day when the anger was boiling inside of me, I received a note from a friend. She stated, "Marilyn, I don't understand everything that you're going through, but I have one thought I would like to share with you, 'Keep the wound clean.'"

What timing! I burst into tears as I cried out to God for help. I had not kept the wound clean but had allowed it to fester with bitterness and anger. As I confessed to the Lord, I asked him to forgive me and help me clean out the wound of anything that would keep it from healing properly: the anger, the bitterness, the frustration, the impatience. The desire for these wrong attitudes to leave came immediately, but it took, and it still takes, lots of work and determination to keep the roots from taking hold.

Later, Marilyn read Joni Eareckson Tada's book *A Step Further* and was blessed by the following explanation.

It's a kind of scale, I finally reasoned. Every person alive fits somewhere onto a scale of suffering that ranges from little to much. And it's true. Wherever we happen to be on that scale, that is, however much suffering we have to endure, there are always those below us who suffer less, and those above who suffer more. The problem is we usually like to compare ourselves only with those who suffer less. That way we can pity ourselves and pretend we're at the top of the scale. But when we face reality and stand beside those who suffer more, our purple-heart medals don't shine so brightly.[8]

God let Marilyn see she had become pious about her suffering. After all, how many people do you know who have lost three children? She placed herself rather high on the scale of suffering; surely no one had suffered more than she had. She finally admitted that she didn't know what it was like to be a Joni Eareckson, to be confined to a wheelchair for the rest of her life or to suffer through a divorce or to sit by the bed of a child who is in a coma. Many people were experiencing a grief greater than hers.

As she evaluated where she was on the scale of suffering, God began to give her a greater understanding and feeling of compassion toward those with whom she had been angry. From their perch on the scale of suffering, possibly they also were having a hard time realizing that someone else could be suffering more than they were. As Marilyn began to pray for them daily that God would supply their needs and give them peace and understanding, she prayed the same prayer for herself. In God's time, one of the families had a change of heart and asked forgiveness for their lack of understanding and compassion.

The legal case was a constant and irritating reminder of Glen's and Marilyn's tragedy! Eleven different times they went to court to face the offender only to find the case postponed again. Marilyn felt that each postponement was like a hammer driving her lower and lower into the depths of despair.

Before the twelfth trial date, the District Attorney told them it would probably be cancelled again and so they might as well stay home. They did and that was the day the offender pled guilty and was sentenced but was put on probation without a single day in jail. They were not there to say a word, one more frustration in the long line of bewildering legal proceedings.

Marilyn still looks back and wonders why there appears to be no justice, why life isn't fair, why Nate had to die. She hopes some day she won't cry when she sees a basketball or flinch when someone asks, "How many children do you have?"

The first Christmas after any death is a difficult one, but because Nathan and Ethan had been born on Christmas, Marilyn especially dreaded December. She says:

I admit I had considered asking God to cancel December, because I didn't want any part of Christmas. The thought of gifts, Christmas carols, and Christmas programs seemed incongruous with what we were facing.

One day Marilyn found a poster of a big, beautiful red rose. The flower had opened and dew drops were visible on the petals. At the bottom there was a quote that contained a message from God to Marilyn: "GOD GIVES US MEMORIES SO WE MIGHT HAVE ROSES IN DECEMBER."

God heard her cry and comforted her, "Marilyn, I'm not going to cancel December, but I'm going to give you roses in December. I've given you many, many wonderful memories and through the special things I'm going to do for you this year and every year, you're going to have bouquets of roses, even in December."

That poster is now framed and hanging on her bedroom wall so that each morning she is reminded of what God promises to do for her. Marilyn states:

God is continually keeping his promise by providing roses, sometimes in the form of actual flowers, sometimes through friends, and often in the form of memories as his reminder he is caring for me, and he hurts when I hurt.

Marilyn's favorite rose and her memory with a promise is Nate's last sentence, "Don't worry, Mom. I'll see you later."

LAUREN LITTAUER BRIGGS

Grief and Loss

How many times have you wanted to comfort a suffering person, but you didn't know what to say? How many times have you felt compelled to go to a funeral, but you were afraid you'd have to talk to the widow and you didn't know what to say?

Would you have known how to help Marilyn when her teenage son was unnecessarily killed by a drunk driver? Would you have been understanding of Mona as she suddenly found herself alone? Would you have been accepting of Georgia once you knew she'd been "on drugs"?

So many of us in the Christian community just don't know what to do or say when another member of the body is hurting. Too often we quote a verse which may inflict added guilt or totally ignore the fact that the person has a problem.

We would all like to function in fairyland where everyone is happy and there are no bad endings, but reality strikes even Christians. We should be the most loving, supportive, and comforting people in town, but so often we don't know what to say.

My daughter Lauren has been a deeply sensitive girl from the time she was a little child. She always wanted to be a mother and she loved playing with dolls. One year her only request for Christmas was a pathetic doll named "Pitiful Pearl." Pitiful was somewhat of a forerunner of the current Cabbage Patch kids. She was a sad-looking waif with long stringy hair and a babushka. Her baggy cotton stockings were red and white striped, there were real patches on her dress, and she looked as if she'd just gotten off a train from a concentration camp. I could not imagine anyone finding little Pitiful appealing, but Lauren had such a soft and compassionate heart that she did what the manufacturer had planned and took pity on poor Pearl.

When Lauren was four, I presented her with a real live doll who didn't in any way resemble Pitiful Pearl. As Lauren took her first glimpse at tiny six-pound Marita, she dedicated her young life to caring for her new baby sister. Being a very serious and responsible child, Lauren was able to heat bottles and change diapers, even at the tender age of four. She thrived on responsibility and let me know from the beginning she was able to raise this child without me.

By the time Marita was one and a half years old and beginning to buck Lauren's authority, I brought home another doll, Frederick Jerome Littauer III. Little Freddie was a rare and beautiful china doll. He had platinum blond hair, huge blue eyes, a turned up nose, and dimples. Lauren was in heaven with her new toy and she again dedicated herself to this new life. When he cried in the night, Lauren would beat me to the nursery. As he got to be six months old, he cried often in the night, and Lauren and I would meet at the crib taking turns trying to calm him down. He would throw his head back, stiffen up his back, and cause his little fingers to go rigid. We didn't know how to comfort him.

One day Lauren and I took him to our family pediatrician. Because Lauren felt she was a real mother to little Freddie, she was in the office with me when Dr. Richard Granger looked at me and said, "Florence, I don't know how to tell you this, but your baby is hopelessly brain-damaged. You'd better think about putting him away, forgetting him, and maybe having another one."

Neither of us could believe what we'd heard. Since we were both practical and couldn't accept defeat, we wanted to believe some doctor could fix him up somehow. We took him to others but the diagnosis was the same.

I did decide to have another baby and during that pregnancy Lauren and I took turns holding and comforting little Freddie as he suffered through ten to twelve convulsions a day. I remember the Christmas card we had made that year. My husband always seemed to take too long to get the children posed for the annual picture and by the time he took it, Freddie was stiffened up and screaming, Marita was tired of smiling and had started to cry, and Lauren was so depressed over the scene that she was also in tears. I can't imagine that we ever printed this photo and sent it out, but we did, with the caption "Have a Merry Christmas and a Howling New Year!" I must have been trying to put a light touch on a tragic situation.

The next August 14th I gave birth to a new son and named him after Lauren: Laurence Chapman Littauer. While I was in the hospital with him, Fred put little Freddie away in a private children's hospital and Lauren and I never saw him again. Fred felt he was saving us heartbreak by not letting us say good-bye, but Lauren grieved deeply in her heart for her missing brother.

We both tried to cheer ourselves up by hovering over little Larry and we both determined we would bring him up to be a perfect boy. Friends and even relatives had verbalized that Freddie's problems had come from neglect and that perhaps he had not had proper care. These comments hurt Lauren deeply because she felt personally responsible for his welfare. She decided she wouldn't let anyone say that again and so she doubled her maternal efforts.

Larry was a duplicate of Freddie in his looks, and he was a joy to care for and play with. His presence did seem to relieve our loss of Freddie who died of pneumonia when Larry was six months old. We did not openly grieve over Freddie and tried to forget we'd ever had him. We did not encourage Lauren to mourn his death; we didn't take her to the private funeral, and we felt that the less said the better. I realize now how necessary it is to grieve appropriately and work through a loss, but at that time we tried not to look at negative circumstances. "What you don't know won't hurt you," but it did.

Shortly after Freddie's death I went in to pick up Larry from his nap. His room was all done in aqua and pink and the crib sheet had tiny aqua giraffes and pink pigs all over it. As Lauren and I looked down at him, he didn't seem to respond. I passed my hand over his eyes, but they didn't move. He had a blank look. We dressed him quickly and Lauren held him as I drove to the doctor's office. A brief examination caused the doctor to look up in disbelief and say, "Florence, I'm afraid it's the same thing."

An operation at Johns Hopkins Hospital revealed that there was no real functioning brain and we had to put little Larry into the same hospital where his brother had died. Lauren recalls:

One afternoon as I was playing at my friend's house, I glanced out the window to see Mom and Dad backing out of the driveway. I ran outside in time to find out that they were taking Larry away to the same children's hospital where Freddie had died just one year before. I never saw him again.[1]

In those days no one talked about grieving. There were no books on the stages of grief and no speakers giving helpful advice. We'd been taught to grin and bear it and most of all, as my mother said, "Don't air your dirty wash in public."

I didn't realize that not talking about our losses would have a long-range effect on all of our emotions.

When Lauren entered the second grade, she began a life-long study on the human embryo and genetics. She did a huge project and was able to understand and explain how a little baby developed. During high school she often did research on brain damage and continued her quest for answers to what had happened to her brothers. She majored in psychology in college and desired to help others who had retarded or handicapped babies.

After Lauren was married and was deciding whether to have a baby she had tests done on Larry, who had lived in that hospital for nineteen years. Lauren also sought the advice of a neonatologist and geneticist.

During those early years of Lauren's marriage, her mother-in-law, Mary, was suffering from the effects of multiple sclerosis. Her last walk had been down the aisle at Lauren's wedding. Lauren helped her as much as possible and prepared meals for her but it was heartbreaking for Lauren to watch a beautiful, vivacious woman decline with this debilitating disease. After her death people said things like, "She's so much better off." "At least she's not suffering." "It will be easier for all of you." These are all well-meaning comments, but they miss the point of sharing meaningful memories of the deceased with the family. Lauren lost not only a mother-in-law, but also a potential grandmother for her future children. One year after Mary died, Lauren gave birth to her first child, James Randall Briggs, Jr. He was a beautiful, healthy child but when he was around six months old, he started crying for no reason. I remember driving with Lauren to the doctor's that day and thinking to myself, "What will you do if there's something wrong? Could you take this all over again?" Somehow these traumas are even more unbearable when it's your daughter facing them instead of you. I remember the look of relief that flooded Lauren's face as the doctor said, "He's fine. He just needs some more food."

Two years later Lauren decided to try again, but this time she was not to be so fortunate. One day while Fred and I were away teaching a marriage seminar, Lauren lost that baby mid-term and the results of tests showed "severe abnormality and brain damage."

When we arrived at the hospital that night, Lauren was devastated. She, who wanted so much to be a mother, who had lost her two little brothers, was in the maternity ward with no baby.

What do you say when tragedy strikes? What do you feel when you've lost your own babies and then your much-wanted grandchild?

Some people tried to comfort her by saying, "Well you're young; you can always have another one." "Be grateful you've got little Randy." "It wasn't full term so you never got to know it." "She's better off with the Lord." "Remember all things work together for good!" But somehow these comments were not blessings.

One nurse came in and asked if Lauren was going to breastfeed her baby and another brightly asked, "Did you have a boy or a girl?" One hospital in Texas has come up with a method to prevent these unintended hurts by putting a teardrop on the door of mothers who have lost their babies.

No one but the grieving mother knows how hard it is to hear those other babies cry and know you don't have one, to go home from the hospital empty-handed. Lauren recalls:

People tried to help but they didn't know what to say. They didn't know what they could do to comfort me. I really couldn't understand why this loss was so traumatic to me. I didn't understand why it hurt so much. Why did I cry when a McDonald's commercial came on TV with a little girl trying to eat a huge hamburger and her big brother teaching her how? Why did I cry? I didn't understand why I could not walk down the baby food aisle in the supermarket. I talked to my genetic counselor and I found out that there were other women who were facing the same situation. Because of this need I was instrumental in starting a support group for moms who had lost pregnancies mid-term. We found out that the community around us couldn't understand why it hurt so much. They couldn't see why in two weeks or by the time we had our post-partum check up we weren't fine. Why couldn't we forget it, put it aside, and go on to other things? No one could believe that we had already grown to love that child inside us. We found that we were all the recipients of these well-meaning but hurtful comments. People didn't know what to do and they didn't know what to say.

Lauren dared to try again and one year later she gave birth to an adorable little boy, Jonathan Laurence Briggs. She calls Randy her Pride and Jonathan her Joy.

Shortly after Jonathan's birth, Lauren took my mother into her home to live. Oh, how Grammie Chapman loved those little boys, replacements for my two she'd never been able to nurture, read stories to, and watch grow up. Unfortunately, she had cancer, and she lost weight and grew weak. The boys couldn't understand why she wouldn't play with them as much as she had done before. She was their Grammie who lived with them and I was "Other Grammie," the one who lived on an airplane.

It was so difficult for Lauren to watch again the process of death take its grip on Grammie. One night she had a stroke and was taken to the hospital where she never regained consciousness. Lauren explained to Randy, Jr. that Grammie was in the hospital, was unconscious, and would probably die. She asked, "Would you like to go and see Grammie? She's asleep and won't know you are there, but I'd like to take you if you'd like to go."

Six-year-old Randy said wisely, "I just saw her yesterday and we had a good talk."

Grammie passed quietly away the next day and a few weeks later Lauren heard Randy telling a playmate, "I'm not going to see Grammie ever again." There was a little pause and he said, "Well, that is, until I go to heaven." He then proceeded to relay detail by detail to his six-year-old friend what had happened to Grammie Chapman but that he would see her when he got to heaven. He looked at his friend and thoughtfully asked, "Do you think they will have a store that sells He-Man action figures in heaven?"

Just a few months ago when I had little three-year-old Jonathan in a bakery choosing cupcakes, he looked up to the clerk and said brightly, "Grammie Chapman went to heaven, but (pointing to me) I've still got this one."

"I'm so glad he's 'still got this one.' "

Because Lauren has been through so many times of grieving in her life, she has a compassionate heart. Not only is she the leader of a support group, but she spends hours a week on the phone and in person comforting hurting women. Lauren feels God has called all of us to be comforters. In Isaiah 40:1 he said, "Comfort ye, comfort ye my people."

"As a mother comforts her child, so will I comfort you," saith the Lord (Isa. 66:13, NIV).

Who needs comfort? Anyone who has suffered a loss.

What is a loss? Anything that doesn't meet your realistic expectations.

- You expected a normal marriage, but he's gone.
- You expected a perfect baby, but she's developmentally disabled.
- You expected all A's, but you got two B's.
- You expected to enjoy your husband's retirement, but he's dying.
- You expected your best friend to live next door forever, but she's moved away.
- You expected your business to prosper, but you're going bankrupt.
- You expected your body to stay whole and healthy, but you've had a mastectomy.

These are all realistic expectations, but they've fallen short. Any loss causes grief. Do you know a friend who's in any of these or similar situations? Can you be understanding and compassionate whether or not you think this loss is worthy of note?

Lauren has three steps that will help you show concern for others.

1. ACKNOWLEDGE THE LOSS. In even a seemingly petty loss, let your friend know that you care, that you know she is hurting. As soon as you hear of a loss acknowledge it.

How?

Call the person up. Let them know you've heard and you're sorry. One girl said to Lauren, "It's been five weeks since I lost my baby and not one person has acknowledged it. They talk about all kinds of cheerful things, but they don't even mention my loss." Ask the person how she feels, what you can do specifically for her. Could you bring a casserole tonight at six? Could you pick up her child in the morning for school? Could you do an errand or make a call? Be specific in your offer.

Go. Be the arms of Jesus and go enfold this hurting person. So many assume someone else will do it. Don't assume, go! When you get there, listen. Don't feel compelled to drop a verse which might lead to guilt or to tell of other people with this same problem who died instantly. As a child I remember when my mother had phlebitis and a friend looked at her leg and said, "When my sister's leg was swollen like that she died within two hours." Mother watched the clock waiting for death to appear.

Some hurting people don't want to talk, so respect their feelings. One of my most valued friends was one who accompanied me with my babies to doctors' offices and just sat quietly beside me in the waiting room.

Romans 12:15 says, "Rejoice with those who rejoice, weep with those who weep" (RSV). So whatever your friend is feeling, share those emotions with her. One mother said to Lauren after she had lost her child in mid-pregnancy and was still hospitalized, "Lauren, I would give anything if just one employee would walk in my room and say, 'Mary Ann, we know why you are here. We know you lost your baby and we are so sorry. I want you to know that we are going to do everything we can to help you while you are here.' " But she said instead, "No one paid any attention to me. They treated me as if I had some bad disease. My medical needs were taken care of but nobody reached out to me emotionally. No one even acknowledged why I was here in this hospital."

One mother had a developmentally disabled child. The baby died at one month old. Shortly after her death the church family was very supportive and cared for them. But after a month or two they figured she should be over it. The lady wrote Lauren:

> Most people said the usual things. "All things work together for good." "She's better off in glory with our Lord." "Be thankful you still have Sarah." "Can you imagine having to take care of her the rest of your life?" "She would never have been perfect anyway." The other hurtful things were the friends that disappeared from sight and the friends and strangers who told me I should be over this by now. People would corner me at church and give me scriptures rebuking me to cheer up.

Don't try to cheer up people artificially. You don't know how they are feeling. You don't know what they are going through. Lauren notes:

When I lost my second pregnancy mid-term it seemed like such a minor loss to most of the people around me. But they didn't have any idea of the hurts that were buried inside. They didn't realize that this was just one more loss added to a string of devastation.

There is a loving album entitled *For Those Who Hurt* written by Christine Wyrtzen. She has one song that addresses the issue of loneliness and depression. It says:

My family has come with words to console and friends have been calling on the telephone.
In spite of the well-meaning words they've all given, I can't help but feel that I'm standing alone.
Lord, I do have some feelings I want to confide.
I feel so alone though my friends offer smiles.
It's only Your love that can carry the hurt.
May I ask You to hold me for a few painful miles.
Carry me, carry me, won't You carry me now.
I'm too weak and fragile to walk on my own.
I'll rest in Your love till once more I can stand
to journey beside You and follow You home.[2]

Send a card. If you can't call or go, get an appropriate card. Read it over and try to picture yourself receiving that card at a similar time. Would it help you? Lauren has made a study of cards and has found three greeting card lines that she finds particularly helpful: Heart to Heart, Blue Mountain Arts, and Flavia. The following inscriptions can be found in cards put out by Heart to Heart. One reads, "I would like to wrap you up in love, and take the hurt away." What does this card do? It acknowledges that a person is hurting and it gives permission to hurt. By sending this kind of card, you are allowing the person to grieve. This is the first step in comforting someone. Another card says, "When you hurt, I hurt too."[3]

God wants us to share our brother's and sister's burdens. He wants us to be there with compassion and a desire to alleviate the sorrow in their lives. We need to reach out. Other cards in this line say, "I know you are going through a rough time," and "It must be hard to understand. I don't understand either, but I love you."[4]

How many times have you heard people offer suggestions as to why a tragedy has happened in someone's life? It's usually better to say something like, "I don't understand, but I love you." Job 16:2 says, "I have heard many such things; miserable comforters are you all" (RSV). Why did Job say that? Because all those well-meaning, sanctimonious, pious, religious people were coming to Job and telling him why he was in this mess. "God must have chosen you for mighty things that he has brought this into your life." "There must be sin in your life." "God is trying to teach you something." "You must not have enough faith." "You need to trust in the Lord more, that is why these things are happening." Job said, "I have heard many such things; miserable comforters are you all."

I caution you not to be a "miserable comforter." Try to avoid making explanations for why your friend is going through the hurt she is experiencing. Could any of you look Job in the eye and tell him why he had to face the traumas he had to face? Could you look at Lauren and tell her why her brothers were brain damaged? Why Grammie had to get a terrible cancer? Why her child had to be disabled? Can you tell her why her mother-in-law had MS? Be cautious not to tell your friends why they are facing the things that they are facing. If the Lord has a revelation for them, he can offer it himself.

2. **ALLOW THE PERSON TO GRIEVE.** Grief is a God-given natural reaction to the traumas that we face in life. Hurting people need to do their grief work. Yes, it is work. It does take effort. It takes time. Don't try to jolly them up and rush them to the other side too quickly. Let them work through all the feelings and emotions they are experiencing; tell them it's all right to be upset. Weep with those who weep. In Chuck Swindoll's book, *For Those Who Hurt,* he addresses a very beautiful and important topic, tears.

> When words fail, tears flow. Tears have a language all their own, a tongue that needs no interpreter. In some mysterious way, our complex inner communication system knows when to admit its verbal limitations and the tears come.
> Did you know God takes special notice of those tears? In Psalms 56:8 he tells us that he puts them in his bottle and enters them into the record he keeps of our lives. David said, "The Lord has heard my weeping" (Ps. 6:8, TLB). A tear drop on earth summons the king of heaven. Rather than being ashamed or disappointed the Lord takes note of our inner friction when hard times are oiled by tears. He turns

the situations into moments of tenderness; he never forgets those crises in our lives when tears were shed.[5]

If those moments are important enough for God to take notice of, they are important enough for us to care about.

In the book *It Hurts to Lose a Special Person,* Amy Ross Mumford says, "When death takes your special person it hurts. It hurts in the middle of the day, in the middle of the night, and in the middle of your stomach. When death takes your special person, it hurts, but it hurts a little less with time and still less with more time."[6]

3. SEEK A HEALTHY RESOLUTION.   As you work with grieving persons know there will be shock, denial, anger, bitterness, guilt, loneliness, and depression, but as you are there walking through all those emotions, you can help them resolve that grief so that ultimately they can accept the trauma and find that life is worth living once again. They will see that their pain does diminish with time. It doesn't mean that they will ever forget what happened to them or that life will ever be exactly the same. Lauren says:

I will never forget the two brothers that I had, the two brothers whose childhood I was denied. I will never forget the beautiful mother-in-law we lost to MS. I will never forget the daughter that I did not get to raise. I will never forget Grammie Chapman, but the pain does diminish in time.

Lauren remembers leaving the hospital after losing her daughter. Her genetic counselor said, "Now, Lauren, realize you will have some good days and some bad days." Lauren thought, "Good days? I would be thankful to have one good hour when I wasn't thinking about my loss." I remember that it was years before the first thing I thought of in the morning was not the two sons I had lost. Lauren adds:

Some months went by and suddenly I realized I didn't think about my baby that day. As more months went on I realized it had been a couple of days, maybe even a week since I had thought about that loss. I will never forget, but the pain does diminish and our focus can shift.

When it seems we may never laugh again, God's love eases the pain. It's not easy to comfort another in grief, but God will reward your effort.

Don't offer cliches or vain optimisms to cover up your insecurities about reaching out to a friend, but do indicate your love by saying, "I really feel awkward because I am not sure what to say or what you need, but I want you to know that I love you, I am praying for you, and I am available.

Dr. Ward Swarner who was with Lauren through her loss told her of an experience he had with another patient of his. There was a young mother who had a difficult premature delivery. Two days later the baby died. Dr. Swarner went in to see her in the hospital room to explain the medical circumstances surrounding the child's death. After they had completed their conversation he said, "Nancy, do you have any other questions?"

She said, "I have one. Why won't anyone talk to me?" He was on the hospital staff, so he asked, "What's the matter? Isn't the medical staff being receptive?"

She answered sadly, "No one will talk to me. The nurse comes in, she takes my blood pressure, she leaves. The doctor comes in, he checks my bleeding, he leaves. My parents come in, they tell me what is happening in the world outside, and they leave. No one talks to me."

The concerned doctor took a deep breath and explained, "Nancy, I will be honest with you. When I leave that intensive care nursery, I have a choice. I can turn left and get on the elevator and go home to my family where I can relax and have a fun time with my kids, or I can turn right and go down the hall to your room. I can walk in to you and risk sharing your pain, risk feeling your hurt. Quite frankly, it is easier to go home."

In your comforting, remember those Nancys lying in the hospital bed asking, "Why won't any one talk to me?" Why? Because it is easier to turn and go home; it takes effort to be a comforter.

Situations may arise in your life and in the lives of your friends that are so traumatic you don't know what you can do. You don't know how to comfort them despite all of the sensitivity, the compassion, and the well meaning that is in your heart. If that is the case, the best thing that you can do is go over to your friend, put your arms around her, give her a big hug, and say, "I don't know what to say."

Repairing the Tearing

Showing how God is able to mend lives that have been torn apart and to repair both physical and emotional pain.

Better to hunt in fields,
for health unbought,
Than fee the doctor
for a nauseous draught.
The wise, for cure,
on exercise depend;
God never made his work
for men to mend.

Epistle
John Dryden

EVELYN DAVISON

Physical Pain

The pursuit of pain has never been a popular pastime. We find a pill for whatever part of us hurts. We take Anacin for arthritis, Bufferin for bad backs, Tylenol at the first twinge of a toothache, and aspirin just in case. We do not see suffering as a glory road and no one wants to play the role of Job even in a Sunday school pageant.

According to the National Center for Health Statistics nine out of ten Americans suffer from headaches, up to 25 million are victims of migraines and 42 million each year have such pain they seek a doctor's help for it.[1] In the article "It's All in Your Head," Michael Woods says, "Most headache researchers today agree that prolonged anxiety, stress, frustration, depression and internalized anger are the major causes of muscle-contraction headaches." Once the tension has triggered the pain, "the vast majority of headaches result from dilation, stretching, or irritation of veins and arteries that lie inside and outside the skull, or from sustained contraction of muscles in the head, face and neck."[2]

Dr. Paul Brand, an expert on leprosy, was asked whether people who had undergone tremendous suffering turned toward or away from God. He concluded that there was no common response. Some grew closer to God, some bitterly drifted from him.

The difference, Brand said, was in their attitude toward the cause. Those hung up with the questions ("What did I do to deserve this? What is God trying to tell me? Am I being punished?") often bitterly turned against God or else resigned themselves to a fatalistic despair. The most triumphant sufferers were those who sought the best response for Christians and trusted God fully despite their painful conditions.[3]

Last summer I met Dr. W. M. Buchholz who interviewed me for a book he is writing on the effect of HOPE on suffering. He teaches cancer prevention workshops and is finding when there is a supportive structure around the patients that provides HOPE, they do not have such debilitating pain.

What would you do if you reached for your pills in a fit of pain and they were gone? Or if you become allergic to any medication? Or if your body totally rejected any antibiotic, anesthesia or painkiller?

When Evelyn Davison begins her talks on "Living Above Physical Pain," she starts by asking the audience, "How many of you had a headache this morning?" Many hands go up. "How many took an aspirin or a Tylenol today? This week? This month?" By then the large majority of the audience have their hands in the air. She has their attention!

She tells them she grew up believing that an apple a day kept the doctor away, but she never quite had enough apples. Evelyn inherited a family blood disease that precludes taking any known medication. She also became a stammerer and a stutterer. From frequent hemorrhaging she developed aphasia, a loss of ability to use speech. Although it was not diagnosed in childhood, she also had the learning disability called dyslexia, which results from a biological defect in the brain.

Doesn't that sound as if Evelyn needed more than apples? If you had those disabilities would you perhaps check yourself into the local morgue and wait for your turn?

Because she couldn't talk easily, Evelyn's father called her Dago and others made fun of her. David Gaw of the Gaw School for dyslexic boys in South Wales, New York, says:

Dyslexia can produce emotional and psychological problems as well as educational deficits. A fourth-grader who doesn't know left from right, pin from pen, or spells *blow* as if it were *dlow* is the certain target of humiliating taunts and classmate jokes.

The dyslexic is an intelligent person who often has been treated as a dullard. These children are often ridiculed by other children because they don't learn as fast.[4]

The word dyslexia had not ever been heard of in Cut 'N Shoot, Texas, where Evelyn began life. But when her family moved to Cleveland, Texas, there was a teacher who took a special interest in Evelyn. Up until that point Evelyn was an enigma to the teachers. She appeared bright but she couldn't do her work correctly or speak clearly. There were no programs for those with learning disabilities and they were just considered dumb. In fact, the only spanking Evelyn ever got in school was in fourth grade when an insensitive teacher insisted she say "refrigerator" and she couldn't do it.

Evelyn had a determination to overcome her handicaps and when this one compassionate English teacher saw her value as a person and began to help her, Evelyn was ready. The teacher coached her to improve her stuttering, showed her how to read with her disability, and even encouraged her to be in the school plays. Evelyn says now, *I didn't know enough to know I couldn't be in a play so I went on and did it.*

There was no little theatre group in her town, so the young people performed, using the backs of big lumber trucks as their stage with the audience sitting on the ground around them. Shakespeare would have called these people "groundlings" had he dropped by the truck shows in Texas.

One day the teacher asked the group to perform at her church. Evelyn's family didn't go to church, but they could see no harm in letting her go. There was something different about the people there and two weeks after her first visit, Evelyn went back to Sunday school. The youth director stood up and shared these simple words, "Jesus loves you. He loves you just as you are. You don't have to be perfect for him to love you."

Evelyn listened, amazed. All her life she had been striving against realistic odds to become perfect enough that her alcoholic father would love her and people would accept her. She asked the young man, "Is that true? Does Jesus love us just as we are? We don't have to be perfect?" The very thought of this truth so overwhelmed Evelyn that she started to cry and pour out her heart to the Lord.

That morning Evelyn invited Christ into her life and asked him to make her into the woman he wanted her to be.

She ran home and told her mother what she had done and that she needed a Bible. Her mother gave her a quarter and she ran to the dime store where she got both the book and some change from the quarter.

She took her flimsy little Bible and tried to read it. Because of her dyslexia she couldn't really understand the words so she would hold the Bible in her hand and say, "God you know I can't read this and make any sense of it, but I trust you to teach me the things I need to know."

Oh, for the faith of a little child! God did instruct Evelyn and people could see the difference in her life. As she grew up she was determined that she could show others what Jesus Christ could do in a life totally dedicated to him.

Evelyn had many physical problems besides her speech difficulties. In her early teens she had an operation to correct some female problems. After years of pain that prevented participation in sports, Evelyn, at nineteen, was rushed to the hospital for emergency surgery. Doctors removed an ovarian cyst the size of a grapefruit. At twenty-three she had the first of six surgeries to remove fibroid tumors in her breasts. And during these years she developed migraine headaches.

Evelyn had a childhood crush on a Van Davison, but her shyness and insecurities held her back from even daring to approach him. Fortunately, she didn't have to because he noticed her big bright hazel eyes and her love of life.

After their marriage, Evelyn settled in to being the best wife and homemaker she could be although she was frequently in pain. She gave birth to two little boys, followed by surgery for endometriosis, a displacement of tissue on the ovaries and bladder, causing up to 7 million women a year to suffer, 85 percent of whom are undiagnosed.[5] Evelyn became very active in church and she remembers:

I was sincerely interested in changing my world and letting people know about the love of Christ, so any time there was a job to do, whether I was sick or well, I did it. I wasn't watching out for my own health as I was so busy helping others. Suddenly this came to a screeching halt.

Evelyn had surgery twice in one year: a hysterectomy and removal of a tumor in the colon. She had to stop serving others as she desperately needed help for herself. Van sent for his mother and told her how critical the situation was. When she arrived she stood by Evelyn's bed and told her what she'd done. "When I heard how bad you were, I dropped down on my knees in my bedroom and begged God for your life. I asked him to let you live to raise those precious boys and to take my life instead of yours." They wept together as Evelyn realized the depth of her mother-in-law's love for her. "Greater love hath no man than this, that a man lay down his life for his friends" (John 15:13, kjv).

Evelyn made a remarkable recovery, knowing this godly lady loved her just as she was. She didn't have to be perfect. Six months later when her mother-in-law died, Evelyn grieved but she had the assurance God would keep *her* alive to raise her boys.

But, he didn't promise a pain free life and a few months later she had to undergo major surgery on her throat that was so serious she could only whisper for three months. As she was recuperating and trying to keep very calm to speed up her recovery, she got a phone call at 4:00 in the morning from the Houston police. "Your brother has been murdered. We just found his body on Mt. Houston Road and we'd like you to go and tell your parents."

Evelyn remembers that as the blackest day of her life. When she told her father, he went into a rage against God. He ran to the front door, opened it up, and hollered, "God where are you? Where are you?" He turned and ran to the back door. "God where are you?" For the first time Evelyn didn't know where God was. She couldn't answer her father, for she wondered herself.

I could not tell him where God was so I dug a hole for myself. I used a shovel of anger and a hoe of defeat. It was a four-sided hole: disillusionment with God's plan, discouragement with my response to the question, depression over the death of my brother, and despair over my health.

In her forties, Evelyn had bleeding ulcers added to her migraines, a massive abdominal hemorrhage, and both kidney and bladder surgery.

On her fiftieth birthday, pains in her chest became so severe she went to the hospital. The results came in the form of a double mastectomy, followed later by reconstructive surgery.

Evelyn had sufficient reasons to be discouraged and to stay in her hole, but instead she began a search, like the sages of old, into the mystery of physical pain and suffering. She began by asking in church, and she got typical religious answers. "If you had enough faith you'd be healed." So she set out to find faith. "There's no doubt some hidden sin in your life." So she started searching her life for sin. "You need to live a crucified life." She was already close to crucified. "It's God's will for everyone to be well so you must be out of his will." Where was she going to find his will?

One day in desperation she got down on her knees and cried out to God, "You are a liar. Jesus said he came to give me abundant life and I'm sick and in pain. I don't have an abundant life."

As she wept, God impressioned upon her to read the book of Galatians. She found Paul's words, "I am crucified with Christ, nevertheless I live . . . and the life which I now live in the flesh I live by the faith of the Son of God" (2:20, KJV).

That day Evelyn gave up trying to live in her own power. She prayed, *Lord I'm dead. If I ever move again it will be under your power, the power of the resurrected Christ.*

Evelyn realized that God hadn't given her a healthy body and that healing would not come until she received her glorious resurrected body and became like him. Until then, perfect health was not part of the package.

So Evelyn started a journey of learning how to live above physical pain and suffering. Once she had ceased pleading for a healing, God gave her ways to come to grips with her pain and rise above it.

For the first year I knew Evelyn and worked with her I had no idea she had these problems, for she is able to smile and radiate the power of her resurrected Lord for all to see in spite of her constant pain.

In Evelyn's search for answers, she asked God where to start and he said, "Start in the beginning with Eve." When she was confined to her bed, Evelyn pictured Eve. She let her mind wander out to the garden and she strolled down the path with her new friend. Eve and Evelyn, hand in hand. She pictured God walking in the cool of the day. "And He walks with me, and He talks with me, and He tells me I am His own; And the joy we share as we tarry there, None other has ever known."[6]

As Evelyn would lie in a bed of pain, she would visualize her fellowship in the garden with her God, and he would cover her pain with peace. One day as she pictured Eve, she saw her reach for God's hand, but before she could touch her living Lord, Satan offered her a substitute, an apple. Evelyn thought, "She's just like me. She needed God's love and she took a substitute instead."

Day after day, Evelyn asked God to give her the real thing, not a replica, and he taught her some lessons. At that time she didn't think she'd ever be strong enough to teach or articulate enough to be a speaker, but she let God give her a message from Eve's apple.

She knew from childhood that an apple a day keeps the doctor away and that she was the apple of God's eye. Now, while in pain, she was to put her thoughts together to use later in helping others accept their suffering. She called out to God:

Oh Lord, how often I weep. I feel today an inexorable tide and rolling waves of great stress. I have waited and waited for you to answer, and I know I have washed the world clean with my tears. Tears from resentment, tears of hope, tears in darkness which seem to stretch as far as this silent universe. I have looked everywhere for a message from you. You have not written it anywhere I can find, not on the mirror in my bath, not on the wall in my den, not on the sink in my kitchen, not on the sand in the yard. Oh Lord, where do you hide your message?

When Evelyn cried to God, he gave the apple of his eye a lesson of love sliced in five sections:

A pply the promises
P ray believing
P raise in all circumstances
L love through pain
E xemplify Jesus

APPLY THE PROMISES. As Evelyn studied God's word and prayed for direction, he began to show her his multitude of promises to help her live above physical pain and suffering. Someone told her God made 7,487 promises in his word, and though she didn't count them, she estimated that if she studied one a day she could keep going for twenty years. *One a day was all I could handle!* Evelyn recalls. She started keeping a devotional diary and each morning she would jot down her feelings—such as this paragraph on fear.

Fear holds terrible power when it is fed. It has blinded me, shackled me, filled me with anxiety and weakness and has given torment to both my day and night. Fear has given birth in my life for a request of God to reveal the reality of his love, power and the limit I can go. I ask though, How long? Do I hear an answer?

Evelyn would then search the scriptures for a promise. "My grace is sufficient for thee: for my strength is made perfect in weakness. Most gladly therefore will I rather glory in my infirmities, that the power of Christ may rest upon me" (2 Cor. 12:9, KJV). She would write down the verse and soon she developed a system.

1. **Memorize the promise.** She would read and review until she had the promises in her heart. The concentration on the verse often eased her pain.

2. **Meditate on the principle.** With each promise she found a principle or condition that would assure God's results. For example, John 15:7 says, "If you abide in me . . . ask whatever you will, and it shall be done for you (RSV). Jesus promises to stay with us if we stay close to him. Because Evelyn has built a library of Christian books, she often reads supplimentary material to further explain God's promise.

3. **Pray that promise.** She would memorize and meditate, then claim that promise and ask God to make it real in her life. She would pray over and over. God doesn't mind repetition.

4. **Take authority over the enemy.** God's word tells us to "Submit yourselves therefore to God. Resist the devil, and he will flee from you" (James 4:7, KJV). Here is another promise. When we submit to God and resist the devil, he will flee. As we accept promises we must say, "I bind you Satan in the power of the Lord Jesus Christ."

   We must "Put on the whole armor of God, that you may be able to stand against the wiles, [tricks and deceits] of the devil" (Eph. 6:11, RSV).

   We must not "give place to the devil" (Eph. 4:27, KJV). and we must remember he is not a passive spirit, but our adversary, "as a roaring lion, walketh about, seeking whom he may devour" (1 Pet. 5:8, KJV).

As Evelyn wrote: "Fear is Satan's scarecrow to keep me in this rut of pain, to keep me out of the field to gather the harvest."

5. **Apply the promise.** Evelyn found as she applied the promises in her life, God let her know she was in his will. He comforted her by saying, "Beloved, think it not strange concerning the fiery trial which is to try you . . . but rejoice, inasmuch as you are partakers of Christ's suffering" (1 Pet. 4:12–13, KJV).

Evelyn says:

As I began to apply God's word I discovered some things: I discovered that as I believe the promises, they bring love into my life. I discovered that as I practice them, they make me holy and whole. I discovered that as I lived them, they made me joyful even in adverse circumstances.

PRAY BELIEVING.   Evelyn's second slice of her APPLE is the prayer that she keeps giving to the Lord each minute of every day. If I ever knew a person who prayed without ceasing, it is Evelyn. When others cry *out* in pain, Evelyn cries *up.* She has studied Matthew 6–9 so thoroughly she has worn out three Bibles, and yet she has not been healed in a miraculous way. Well-meaning Christians have said, "If you had enough faith, you'd be healed." How often we play God with our sick friends and put a pronouncement upon them that causes more grief and pain. Evelyn wrote in her journal:

During my years of persistent pain, good-hearted Christians pressured me by pinning my pain on lack of faith. So, I set out to find faith. Which leads to the next question, "Where do you find faith?"
God says we are brought to him by grace through faith and it is a gift. Grace is an unmeasured gift, and faith is a workable gift. It has to be a gift; otherwise, we would work for it, earn it, trade for it, or build it without God."

Others asked, "If healing is in the atonement then why aren't you healed?" In days and nights of anguish, Evelyn sought the answer.

This question battered, badgered and bruised me more than any other. It was the hardest one of all for me to reconcile. The turmoil has followed me from illness to illness.

I believe today that perfect health is a promise of God, but Jesus also promises we would live with suffering. I believe the promise of perfect health will be delivered when Jesus returns to give me a glorified body. Jesus was thirty-three when his body went to heaven, and he has promised to prepare a place for ours as we are given a new body like his. Perfect healing is like perfect salvation. Jesus purchased it at Calvary; however, I do not now in this body have, nor will I receive, all God has for me (Matt. 8:17). At his second coming, I will be delivered from sin and the limitations of this body and will receive all Christ purchased for me at Calvary. Absolute sinless perfection is in the atonement, but none of us has yet received it or attained it in this body. Romans 8:18– 23 tells us that we are adopted, physically and spiritually, and that we will not be perfect until the bride is united with the groom.

Evelyn prays believing in God's will, not in the doubts of others. She has learned to accept pain and not be crushed when people say, "If you were really a Christian this wouldn't have happened. There must be sin in your life." Evelyn writes touchingly of the lessons she has learned.

Jesus at the Garden gave us the example of surrender to God's plan which includes suffering and pain. Matthew 26:39 gives us the direction for asking for God's will: "Not as I will, but as Thou wilt." This eliminated our privilege of demanding, or taking healing, if it is not in God's plan. We must be like Jesus, surrendered, ready to have suffering continue or death to come if that is God's will. He never wants me to suffer unless it is for his glory, just as it was with our Saviour. Disease like all other pain or suffering follows a sinful race as determined by the choice Adam made. Still God uses it for my preparation for sacrifice, service and his glory. This example is given to us by Paul, who tells of his thorn in the flesh and how he "besought the Lord thrice, that it might depart" (2 Cor. 12:7–8, KJV).

And he said unto me, My grace is sufficient for thee: for my strength is made perfect in weakness. Most gladly therefore will I rather glory in my infirmities, that the power of Christ may rest upon me. Therefore

I take pleasure in infirmities, in reproaches, in necessities, in persecutions, in distresses for Christ's sake: for when I am weak, then am I strong (2 Cor. 12:9–10, KJV).

Paul prayed for good health and God declined. Paul repeated and repeated and yet God refused. Instead he taught Paul a great lesson: how to be humble, broken, and dependent on God. He discovered his strength was made perfect in his weakness. Paul gave us a great example, even as Jesus, when he changed his prayer and instead of mourning and being depressed because he did not get his way, asked for the revealed will of God. The lesson Paul learned is one God has taught me over and over: sometimes sickness is better than health, as Jesus is honored. It is not fun, but often it is fellowship in his suffering and that is JOY.

Paul tells us in Philippians 3:10, "All I want is to know Christ and feel the power of His resurrection; to share in His sufferings and become like Him" (TEV).

Evelyn knows Christ so well he radiates from her face, and she knows his power as he has lifted her from her sick bed so many times and given her the strength to get moving even when her prognosis was discouraging. Surely she has shared in his suffering and each day she becomes more and more like him.

Evelyn prays, believing in God's perfect will for her for this day. During those long nights when pain kept her awake, Evelyn developed a prayer plan. She prays through the whole alphabet in praise.

Jesus I Adore you
       Believe in you
       Cherish you . . .

When she gets through she tries again with her requests.

Jesus I need Affirmation of your love
           Blessings from above
           Confidence in your strength . . .

If she is still awake, Evelyn tells God there must be a "communication blockage" on her part. She then goes through the alphabet again in confession.

Jesus I confess I am Annoying to my family
                     Bothered by judgmental Christians
                     Critical of others . . .

Once a friend asked Evelyn what sin she had that began with a "Z" and she answered quickly, "Lack of zeal!"

Evelyn really does not lack zeal as she is able to work the plan of salvation into any conversation. She tried for years to convert her alcoholic father and considered him "the bruise on my apple." Many nights she would intercede over and over for her father, praying and believing without seeing results.

During one of her many hospital stays, Evelyn hemorrhaged for over two weeks. Since she can't tolerate pain killers or anesthesia, they had her packed in ice. Her veins had collapsed and the blood transfusion was going into her foot. Her father came and sat beside her for three days while her mother cared for the children. Through her pain, Evelyn kept saying, "Father, I need you; Lord Jesus, I love you."

As she repeated these words his heart seemed to soften. Months later, Papa asked, "Baby, how do you know when you die if you're going to heaven?" Evelyn replied, "It is by accepting Jesus Christ and the atonement he made at calvary for my sins, allowing him to become Lord of my life." She then asked, "Have you ever done that?"

He said, "Yes, I have. I was listening to Richard DeHaan on the television."

The exciting thing about that decision made by this seventy-year-old man was that Evelyn personally had nothing to do with it, apart from the ministering of God in her life and her goal to so live that Jesus Christ would be seen in her.

Even though she has not been relieved of suffering, Evelyn has prayed believing and God has answered by changing her father's life. From that time on her papa stopped drinking and came often for Evelyn to teach him the Bible.

One day he said, "Nobody loves the Lord Jesus more than I do. And nobody believes more than I do and I don't know how you can tell people that but I want you to tell them." Two weeks later he died and Evelyn shared that story at the funeral.

God answers prayer. The response may not be what we expected, but when we pray believing, he shows his will for our lives.

PRAISE IN ALL CIRCUMSTANCES. Evelyn calls this part of her APPLE her bitter slice because she can't humanly understand why a loving and caring God who allows her to be visited with pain and suffering expects her to thank him for it. She studied 1 Thessalonians 5:18, "In everything give thanks: for this is the will of God in Christ Jesus concerning you" (KJV). She labored over Colossians 2: 6–7, "As ye have therefore received Christ Jesus the Lord, so walk ye in him: Rooted and built up in him, and stablished in the faith, as ye have been taught, abounding therein with thanksgiving" (KJV). She memorized Psalm 26:7, "That I may publish with the voice of thanksgiving, and tell of all thy wondrous works" (KJV).

As Evelyn prayed and praised she concluded that God wanted her to thank him for who he was and what he could do in her life. He didn't expect her to cry out all day, "Praise the Lord! Praise the Lord!" but to have a genuine desire to look to God for his best.

Evelyn calls this her "attitude of gratitude." She starts each day by praying, "Lord Jesus, thank you for this day. Just as you give it to me, so I give it back to you. You plan my day Lord, you give me the strength and power, and we will live it together."

Evelyn had a severe testing of her ability to praise when she had to go for breast surgery. The mammograms showed a 90 percent chance of malignancy on both sides and she was thanking God for one more chance to trust him. The next day the doctor said it was only an abcess on each side. What a relief! Evelyn and Van really praised the Lord, but the next day the doctor returned to say they had made a mistake and Evelyn needed bi-lateral mastectomies. How can you say thanks for such bad news?

Van kept repeating, "God help us. God help us."

Evelyn was quiet and after a while she said:

Lord Jesus your word says that in everything I am to say thank you. Now I don't feel very thankful but by the act of my will I say thank you because I know that you are a big enough God that I can trust you with the circumstance. Amen.

Looking back upon that time, Evelyn recalls:

Circumstances are God's way of changing us, of establishing an attitude of gratitude, of touching and healing and mending. As you begin to think about praising God in everything, first take Authority over whatever the circumstance is, then Believe God for the better, and then Confirm it by your walk. These are my ABC's of praise. As I learned to thank him, I discovered that thanksgiving brings thanks-living. It does create an attitude of gratitude.

LOVE THROUGH PAIN.   It's easy to be loving when we're happy, when things are going our way, but how much our love to others is appreciated when they can see we are giving more than we've got to give.

As a child Evelyn's aim was to become perfect so people would love her and she committed her life to Jesus when she heard he would love her just as she was.

Evelyn has a ministry of love and when she is in pain she calls someone on the phone who needs love more than she does. Evelyn works with International Students in Austin, Texas, and so many desperately need help. She introduced me to a Cambodian lady who once was so hungry when she escaped her country that she and her family ate the bodies of those who died on their boat. When Evelyn feels overcome with pain, she calls this lady who knows what suffering is beyond anything we have ever experienced and she prays with her.

Evelyn writes encouraging messages to those in trouble and sends gifts of love. Just this week I received three pairs of pantyhose in a color I had been unable to find. Evelyn had known my quest, had found the color, and had sent them to me. Evelyn's life of pain has made her sensitive to the simple or deep needs of others. Evelyn agrees with Paul, "Love suffers long and is kind" (1 Cor. 13:4, NKJV).

As Evelyn records her thoughts each day, she talks to Jesus.

I feel today like I have been rubbed hard on the washboard of life and hung out to dry my tears of loneliness. Where are the faces to fill the spaces in these vacant rooms of my mind?

She then fills those empty rooms with people who need her love. She pictures Jesus standing with them and she prays for them, or she writes to them, or she calls them, or she sends them little gifts.

Through loving others, Evelyn "beareth all things, believeth all things, hopeth all things. Love never fails."[20]

EXEMPLIFY JESUS CHRIST. The last slice of Evelyn's APPLE is to exemplify Christ and become like him. As she prayed about how she could best do this, God showed her she must take care of her body in the best way she possibly could.

She went to an allergist and found many foods that had contributed to her poor health. By eliminating those, she has less pain. She went to a nutritionist and found some new patterns of eating and some appropriate food supplements. She has eliminated sugar and caffeine and has added energy giving foods in their place. When we were doing a CLASS in Temple, Texas, the staff went into Grandy's for breakfast. They had huge cinnamon rolls pictured up on the menu board. Evelyn looked up to the sign and said to us, "When I see cinnamon, I see SINAMON!"

She got Stormie O'Martian's book and exercise tape, *Greater Health God's Way,* and began to follow Stormie's suggestions.

She asked her surgeon what she could eat to prevent colon cancer and he gave her a recipe. "Mix 3 cups of Miller's bran, 2 cups of raisin bran, and 1 cup of bran buds. Add 1 package of cut up dried fruit and 1 package of slivered almonds." Several of us on staff carry little plastic bags of this mix with us and use it for breakfast while on the road.

Evelyn realizes she cannot run as fast or go as long as the others on staff, and she knows when to quit. She restores her body with rest and her spirit with God's word. "Thy words were found and I did eat them; and thy word was unto me the joy and rejoicing of mine heart" (Jer. 15:16, KJV).

Evelyn also charges us to abide in the positive. When we go to bed knowing we won't sleep, we don't. When we know there's no hope, there isn't. She is a living example of a person who, despite constant pain, thinks health, prays health, talks health, believes health, and lives health. When Evelyn stands before our CLASS and shares her testimony, no one can understand how she's still alive. She says:

I have my own ERA amendment: Eat, Rest, and Abide. I have a sky-high view of brokenness and wholeness, defeat and victory because of the pain Jesus endured at the cross. It is my aim to exemplify Christ to a world of hurting people.

Because Evelyn has been able to produce her own apples on her own tree of life, she has planted many seeds in the hearts of others. Seeds of growth in her children, of joy in her husband, of faith in her friends, of hope in the hearts of all who hear her speak.

What could have been a depressing life for her melancholy husband, Evelyn has turned into one of living positively above her physical pain. When he has been discouraged, she has lifted him up. When he's tried to keep her calm and in bed, she's found the strength to go out and minister to others. One day after Van gave Evelyn over to the Lord he said, "I have decided that if you are going to die, I want you to die happy."

By Evelyn's example, Van has developed a sense of humor over her frequent ailments. One day when asked how Evelyn stayed so slim and trim, Van quipped, "Oh it's easy, she checks into the hospital every year and gets rid of her unnecessary parts!"

Some of us wonder if there are any parts left to remove, but Evelyn keeps growing and glowing for she knows who's repairing the tearing.

LANA BATEMAN

Emotional Pains
of the Past

Do you have some lingering pains of the past that pop up at
the most unexpected times? Some of us have so many unforgiven
and unforgotten moments that they bounce around us like balls
in a pool. We push one under water only to have another emerge
in its place. As we shove that one down, up pops a bigger one.
We wear ourselves out trying to keep the past problems under
water. Often we think if we can hide them they won't hurt us,
but is that really true? Don't these unresolved hurts still harm
us? Don't they keep us from the emotional freedom God wants
us to have?

As Christians we want to put aside the pains of the past and
forgive all who have harmed us. The majority of us assume we
have accomplished this worthy goal. From the time we were children
we have prayed, perhaps too routinely, "forgive us our trespasses
as we forgive those who trespass against us." Because we are told
being angry is wrong and forgiving is right, we try to be spiritual,
suppressing ill-will and mouthing forgiveness. While our intentions
are genuine, often putting our feelings behind us is really putting
them inside us.

We think we have forgotten only to have a similar situation
bring forth a collective issue of anger from the past. Why did we
get so upset over such a small matter? Because it reminded us of

a resentment we had not fully released; a ripple turned into a roar! Where did that come from?

Psychologists tell us that in our minds we have a record of every incident we've ever experienced, whether good or bad. We have all these thoughts filed away in our mental cabinet, although not necessarily in alphabetical order for easy recall. Sometimes when we want to remember a certain Christmas, a certain childhood caper, we reach for the file folder and it's not full. Some of the facts have faded and we fashion it into fiction. But what about those times when someone hurt us, embarrassed us or ridiculed us? Somehow those moments are up front in our folders. We may have filed them away but the emotional impact of the time kept them fresh. We don't have to fish for those facts for they've never been forgotten.

I clearly remember the lady who, during the depths of the Depression, stood in our store and looked at us three children and said to my mother, "It's a shame there's no hope for those children for they seem so bright!"

I remember another lady, a distant relative, who appraised us three and enthused over my brothers, "Aren't they adorable?" She then looked me over and sighed to Mother, "She must be smart." It was that day I made a conscious decision to "be smart" as I was obviously not going to make it on my looks.

I remember the pink sweater I wore the day in college when the geology professor caught me talking to the boy next to me. I wasn't the only one ignoring his lecture but he chose me to be an example and he made me stand up in the middle of the classroom. "Miss Chapman likes to talk. We will let her recite ten times the definition of a mountain." Gratefully, I knew it and I stood humiliated as I repeated, "A mountain is an extreme example of diastrophism."

Today upon the mere mention of a mountain, my mind, and sometimes my mouth, reviews, "an extreme example of diastrophism."

The delightful may drift away but the humbling hurts hover over our hearts and memories.

Shakespeare said, "The evil that men do lives after them; the good is oft interred with their bones."[1]

In Hebrews 12:1-2 we find good advice, "Let us lay aside every weight, and the sin which doth so easily beset us, and let us run with patience the race that is set before us, looking unto Jesus the author and finisher of our faith" (KJV).

In these verses God says to me, "Florence, I have put you in a big race of life. Jesus has led the way; he is the author of the plot I have prepared for you. He will lead you to the finish line. You must run with patience the course I have set before you."

As I accept the position of Christian leadership God has put upon me, I must consider Jesus as he was insulted, hurt, even betrayed, by his friends. I must realize he endured far more personal pain than I have known.

Verse 3 tells me that if I don't put out of my heart those past hurts, if I don't lay aside these weights, these grudges, these unforgiven people, I will be "weary and faint in my mind." How many times I have been emotionally drained, fatigued, weary in well-doing, and "faint in my mind!" Why? Because I've still got some people I haven't forgiven and something a woman said to me today about her problems triggered a memory of mine that I haven't dealt with properly. Suddenly from her review of her husband I remember some things Fred said fifteen years ago that I haven't yet forgiven. From another story of a pastor who didn't understand her, I recall the day I told our pastor that Fred and I were leaving to go into full-time Christian service and he threw a Bible at me!

As soon as these memories bounce up, I push them under, I reprimand myself for these unforgiving thoughts, for these records of wrongs, and feel guilty as I become "faint in my mind."

God tells me to lay aside these weights, not push them under. He tells me to "lift up my hands which hang down" and to strengthen my "feeble knees" (v. 12). He doesn't want me limping through life and he says, "Make straight paths for your feet, lest that which is lame be turned out of the way; but let it rather be healed" (v. 13).

How Lord? How? "Follow peace with all men" (v. 14) and let no "root of bitterness" spring up to trouble you (v. 15).

Let's assume that we all accept peace, forgiveness, and lack of bitterness as goals in running the race of life. Let's say we can even recite verses on these subjects and we mean well. How can we weed out bitterness and bound ahead to peace?

In the Christian world today there are different methods of healing hurts. Some say the reading of the word of God is sufficient; we need no counseling, personal help, and certainly no emotional experiences. Others say those with the gift of healing can change lives with or without a scriptural knowledge in the victim's mind. I've seen results in both areas and know with God all things are possible, but I can only write with conviction of what happened to me and of what I have learned personally.

The concept of emotional healing appeared in the early 1900s as Agnes Sanford, daughter of missionaries to China, cried out to God for a way to minister to the deep emotional hurts and needs of believers. Her prayers were answered as our Lord began the process of teaching her a new way to pray for these suffering Christians. This new form of visual prayer required that the individual picture Christ walking with him through every painful circumstance of life, thereby giving meaning and healing to debilitating memories. Generally, these prayer steps are taken in a one-on-one or small group framework and involve praying through a lifetime of hurt.

An explanation of what inner healing seeks to accomplish in each individual is given in the *SCP Journal:*

> The phenomenon known as inner healing has two goals. Its primary and spiritual objective is to extend the Lordship and healing power of Christ into our past history, affecting even our preconversion experience. Its secondary and psychological goal is thereby to release us from whatever emotional and psychological bondage our past experience has produced.[2]

Those involved in emotional or inner healing ministries state:

> That emotional blocks and habitual behavior patterns (with their negative fruits of frustration, defeat, and poor self-image) prevent us from moving into the abundant life that Jesus promised. Therefore, they conclude, a special effort should be made to heal these inner wounds, so that we may be free from the many ways in which they constrict and impoverish our lives."[3]

There is little question that an unloved child or one who has experienced severe trauma or abuse is often crippled in the area of emotions. Is this always true?

We know the mind never forgets a single experience or perception. While most memories are neatly packed away in inactive files, some thoughts, by virtue of the pain or fear that surrounds them, are held in a radioactive center. This box contains those circumstances and responses, whether conscious or subconscious, that can have a deforming effect on the human personality. As Lana Bateman speaks on pains of the past, people often ask how a child who was brought up in a "normal home" becomes emotionally disturbed. She answers:

There are only two ways that a child from birth to eight years old can perceive or receive love. While there are many sophisticated means of expressing parental love, such as a roof over the head, food on the table, clothes in the closet, an automobile, or a private school, there are only two that a young child can grasp as love.

The first is a tremendous amount of healthy physical affection— especially from the parent of the opposite sex.

The second is having a parent or parents who want to know a child and who take the time to draw out his thoughts and feelings. This eye-to-eye communication prevents the child from harboring suppressed sentences which may become twisted and distorted in his mind. If real love is not felt then the results of these scars and buried memories can deeply hinder a person's ability to relate to God and will ultimately sabotage any attempt to obey Jesus' commandments which require man to love God and to love his neighbor as he loves himself. Symptoms of this emotional pain can include chronic depression, neurotic perfectionism, self-deprecation, intense insecurity, and an incapacity to accept forgiveness and the redeeming love of Christ.

Many of these symptoms have been expressed in the lives of those we've already examined throughout this book. Paulette, Patsy, Barbara, Jan, and I have already experienced emotional healing prayer with Lana, "forgetting what lies behind and straining forward to what lies ahead" (Phil. 3:13, RSV).

Perhaps you are wondering if you have some suppressed problems of the past or how you can identify others who have hurting hearts. Let's look at one example of God's emotionally crippled children.

When I first saw Lana Bateman at our CLASS in Fort Worth, Texas, she stood out like a beacon. Her striking beauty of black hair, green eyes, ivory skin, and exquisite bone structure caught my attention, but it was not long before I saw a radiance about her countenance that reminded me of the description of Moses when he came down the mountain from his communion with God.

I couldn't keep my eyes off her glowing face and as I spoke it was as though the Lord had lit a neon arrow pointing down at Lana's head blinking the words, "She's special."

At the first break I spoke with her and found she had a ministry in helping people overcome the hurts of the past. God made it clear to our staff very quickly that Lana was his hand-picked choice to bring a healing touch to each of us personally and to provide a gift of discernment that our ministry needed.

On the second day of CLASS Lana gave me the manuscript of her book, *God's Crippled Children,* and I sat down to read it, unprepared for the life I was going to have spread out before me.

In the preface she has included a poem written when she was twenty-eight describing the feelings of the little girl within her that controlled her emotions:

A CHILD'S SONG

I can remember the sound of my feet
    As I shuffled along the walk,

And the look on my mother's face
When she never had time to talk.

I can almost hear the sound of my voice
    Singing alone in that tree,

And I often recall my father's "good-night"
    As he passed, never touching me.

    Sing a child-alone song
      Sing a dusty rhyme,
    Sing a childhood-blue song
    Sing of long lost time.

I can remember the day that she died
    It was quiet and I was alone,

And I still recall the thoughts that I had
    Of a mother I'd never known.

No, we never quite reached for each other
    So few were the things we shared.

      Where in the world
  could those lost years have gone
      And why hadn't anyone cared?

Sing an all-alone song
Eyes are filled with tears,
Sing a sad-but-true song
And weep for wasted years.

Some of us may look back on a childhood of emotionally wasted years where we did not receive these two nurturing necessities: our parents' loving touch and genuine communication.

Lana was raised in Big Spring, Texas, where nothing grows but mesquite trees and nothing blows but sand and tumble weeds. Her parents had lived through the Depression and were determined to provide well for their family. They worked hard building a successful chain of dime stores and were determined to give their children what they had never had. Because they were so busy, Lana's parents didn't have the time to sit and listen to the child's thoughts or to give her the physical affection she longed for. Without realizing why she was doing it, Lana began to lie and steal to get attention.

When she was five, Lana had a friend who had boxes of doll clothes that she wanted. The day before the girl moved away, Lana stole some of the clothes, put them in a shoe box and buried them in her backyard. After the girl moved, Lana dug them up and claimed them as her own.

When her mother told her she could not take a favorite doll to school for show-and-tell, she sneaked out at night and hid the doll under some bushes. The next morning on the way to school, she retrieved the doll and got her own way without her mother knowing what she'd done.

Lana took things from her father's stores and one day stole money from her father's wallet and bought every child in the first grade a box of cough drops. The teacher, somewhat suspicious of Lana's sudden generosity, called her parents and she was spanked soundly. Lana remembers this event in a positive way because she received concentrated attention from both parents.

Lana, a child who was crying for approval, was hurt when she heard her father tell her mother to take her out of her dancing lessons because she was too clumsy to waste money on and surely had no future in ballet.

Lana remembers her early childhood as a constant and futile search for a lap she could crawl into.

Every time I found one it would get up and walk away. I was screaming, "Love me, please love me," and they all kept walking away. I was emotionally bankrupt and to fight my feelings I became loud, demanding, selfish, and obnoxious.

Lana was the type of child all teachers hoped they didn't get the next year and when they did, they would often reprimand her in front of the whole class. One teacher unjustly accused thirteen-year-old Lana of leading the older boys astray and humiliated her before her classmates. A biology teacher decided one day to give predictions for each student. When he got to Lana, he proclaimed, "You will become an alcoholic." Lana had never even had a drink and she was held up to ridicule again for something that had no foundation in truth.

When Lana was twelve her mother, who had always wanted to be a blond, took her to the beauty shop and had her black hair bleached. To keep it light, Lana had to go each week for a touch-up. She begged her mother to let her have her natural color, but her mother was determined she'd be blond. One day Lana went alone to the shop and had her hair dyed back to her natural color. She went home proud and excited, but her mother flew into a rage, dragged her back to the shop and had the color stripped off.

Lana got the message: "I'll only love you if you look the way I want you to look."

During high school Lana was the lonely misfit, always on the fringes of the action looking in. By the time she went off to college she was so emotionally depleted that she could not make the simplest of decisions. She recalls:

I couldn't decide to get up in the morning and if I did, I couldn't decide what to put on. If I did dress, I couldn't make myself go to class.

One day when her mother came to college to visit, Lana asked, "Why didn't you teach me to make decisions?"

The answer was, "Well that's a ridiculous question and it is not a subject for further discussion." There was still no meaningful communication between them.

At this time Lana was dating the first young man she'd ever

met who seemed to accept her and love her as she was. She was crazy about him and looked forward to living happily ever after. One week after her mother's visit, this young man broke off their relationship without explanation and Lana was devastated. She swallowed forty Librium and twelve Bufferin in an effort to end it all. For the first time she had dared to believe someone loved her and she'd been rejected. As she was recovering in the school infirmary after sleeping for three days, she received word that her strong healthy mother had dropped dead of a cerebral hemorrhage. Lana went home for the funeral and the next day dyed her hair black. She could finally be herself.

Because her father was in a state of shock, Lana did not return to college but stayed to help him. A few months later her father tried to commit suicide and then had a complete nervous breakdown for which he required lengthy hospitalization. Lana's brother had joined the army and her little sister had been taken by an aunt, so Lana was completely alone in the house in Big Springs and also alone in the accountant's office when he announced, "Your father is bankrupt."

At eighteen Lana had been stripped of any support or self-worth. *It was a time of emotional horror in my life and I sank deeper and deeper into depression.*

Her spirits were brightened by the sight of a dashing Air Force cadet, fresh out of West Point, who came to Big Springs for pilot training and was the most strikingly handsome man Lana had ever seen: 6'7", black glossy hair, brilliant blue eyes, Hollywood gorgeous. He was the son of an Air Force General and walked as if he owned the world.

Lana longed for love and acceptance and when he responded, she fell in love. They were married by a justice of the peace after the General had refused to attend the wedding they had planned because he did not approve of Lana.

As she says:

It was a tragedy from the very beginning. We were both from homes where there was a great deal of hurt. As marriage partners we were like caged animals. Neither of us had anything to give, neither of us knew how to take, neither of us understood healthy love. After Rob and Brett were born and four years of marriage had gone by, Bob left. I found myself with no money, no car, no food, no job, no nothing, and in a tremendous deep depression. I had a three-month-old baby and a three-year-old little boy and I was frantic.

Lana was virtually abandoned in Dallas by her handsome playboy husband who no longer felt marriage and children were fun. Months of misery went by before Lana got a job at American Airlines from a kindly gentleman who took pity on her. During the eight years she worked there, Lana went through many phases. Because she was so bitter and angry she turned to drinking to blot out the agony of her life. This diversion ended when she fell asleep at the reservation desk in the midst of a conversation, and the boss, who had been monitoring the call, shook her awake and threatened to fire her. Looking desperately for a husband, she went the rounds of singles' bars and night clubs always attracting irresponsible men who had as many problems as she had.

The frustrations and anger, the sheer weight of her problems drove her one day in November to pray. It wasn't that she even believed in God; it was a prayer "to relieve the steam on the top of the pressure cooker." Lana shook her fist at God and said:

There's a few things we need around here. If you're there and if you care, I need $300. I've got bills to pay and you know I can't stand it when I owe people money. Don't you think we need a car around here? I'm sick of driving that 1956 DeSoto and putting bricks under the wheels at night and losing the foot brake as well. We need a house around here. What kind of boys do you think these will grow up to be if all they know for a lifetime is living in an apartment house? They need trees to climb, a yard to mow, and a dog. They need a normal life. Don't you think it's about time we had a husband and father in this house? What hope do these boys have without a father?

Once Lana had poured out her problems to an unknown God, she forgot the whole outburst. A few days later a man from the Dallas Big Brothers Association came by to pick up Rob and take him to a meeting. He greeted Lana by handing her $300 and saying, "I know it's near Christmas and I thought you might need a little help." Lana paid off the bills.

In December her father called and offered some help. He had married a woman with four children who would not let him associate with Lana so she was shocked when he said, "I'm sick to death of worrying about you in that old jalopy. I'm going to take you out and make the down payment on a new car for you."

Receiving the first new car she'd ever had really picked up Lana's Christmas spirit and made her twenty-three-mile commute to work much easier.

In May, to break up the monotony of her long drive home, she turned down an unknown street and saw a FOR SALE sign on a white brick Bostonian cottage, with green shutters and ivy climbing over the arched door. She stopped her car as she thought, "That's the most beautiful house I've ever seen!"

Even though she had no possibility of buying a home, she decided to go in and take a look thinking, "I'll pretend I'm married and tell the agent I'll bring my husband back later."

She walked in the front door and saw the house was painted a soft gold that exactly matched everything she owned. There was just enough space for the furniture and when Lana stepped out into that backyard and stood on the patio she fell in love with the cobblestone walk out to the ivy covered gate. There were giant elm trees and oak trees all over the fenced-in yard with its perfectly manicured lawn. It was everything she could ever want. Lana went home that night very depressed and bitter because other people could have a house like that and she could have nothing. The next day she talked to her sister on the phone and mentioned that she had found her dream house. Within a few days, Lana's dad called and said, "I understand that you looked at a house."

"Yes I did."

"I'd like to go back and look at it with you."

Lana was floored, but excited. She and her father got in the new car together and went over to the house. Just as a young couple was walking out of the back room to give the real estate agent a check, Lana's dad handed her one first. The agent turned to the couple and said, "I'm very sorry but this gentleman just gave me a check on the house and it's his."

On the first of July, Lana, Rob, and Brett moved in and she went to work on the house. In seventy-two hours without sleep, she unpacked every box, got all the empty ones into the trash, hung all the curtains and pictures, bolted the bookshelves into the walls, put the fish into the aquarium, and even corked a whole wall in the den. Everything was perfect and looked as if they'd lived there for ten years. On the third day after her marathon of decorating, Lana answered the door to be met by Louis from Big Brothers and his friend, Marc.

Lana was surprised that Louis had brought a friend along to take her son on an outing. She hadn't had a date in eighteen months and when she glanced at Marc she knew instantly that this was an exceptional man. As they looked each other over, they both felt an unusual attraction. Marc asked her out and on their first date they knew they were "meant for each other," although there were some obstacles to their relationship.

Marc was a Christian and he shared his faith and some books with Lana. At first she refused to read them. She had been pushed around so much in life that she was not going to have this man tell her what to do. After months of inner rebellion, she sat down one November night and began to read *The Late Great Planet Earth*. [4] She finished it all in one sitting and knew for the first time that God was alive and Jesus Christ was who he said he was. She closed the book and went into the bathroom where she fell down on her knees and cried out to God to save her. Lana confessed her bitterness and anger that she had never faced before, and she asked God to take away the fears that surfaced at the mere thought of another marriage that might also end in failure. She couldn't face the possibility of another defeat.

In December Marc proposed to Lana and at that moment she remembered her prayer from a year before: I need $300—Louis had given her $300. I need a car—her father had made the down payment on a new car. I need a house—her father had bought her dream house for her. I need a husband and father for my boys—Marc had appeared and now wanted to marry her. The bonus to all these answered requests was that Lana had committed her life to the Lord and had tangible evidence that God cares. Lana looks back and marvels at how God answered her prayers, in sequence, when she wasn't even a believer; how he brought her to himself and then showed her the miracles he had done.

On Valentine's Day 1974, Lana and Marc were married in a little chapel in Dallas. As a new Christian, Lana inhaled scripture. Her zeal kept her in the Word and she developed a passion for the Old Testament. She studied and took so many notes she wondered what to do with them all. The obvious choice was to teach what she had learned, and almost overnight she became a Bible teacher. She started at a Hebrew-Christian Synagogue and then added a class for airline flight attendants and one for reservation clerks. A group of Catholic ladies asked her to teach them and soon she had classes going all over Dallas.

At first Marc had been excited about how his new bride hungered for the Word of God and channeled her energies into teaching Bible studies, but at the end of three years of this all-consuming marathon of teaching, Marc seated her on the couch and said, "Those classes have become your God. You love them more than you love your family. You have got to give them up."

"Give them up? How dare you tell me to give up my Bible studies!"

Marc insisted and Lana was furious. "What kind of a Christian is he anyway? Doesn't he know that I'm out serving God? What right has he to make me quit?"

Lana had found self-worth in teaching her Bible studies and to be stripped of her audience also removed the false props that had held her up. The band-aid of Bible studies burst open and the anger, resentment, bitterness, and rebellion that she had suppressed for those three years of marriage came roaring to the surface. The old symptoms that she had shoved aside returned. She had a migraine headache that lasted day and night for two years. She went from doctor to doctor and even had sinus surgery with no relief. One doctor gave her an experimental drug that so increased her appetite she ate round the clock and went from a model's figure of 118 pounds to 170 in six months.

Marc and the boys met strong resistance when they tried to curb her appetite, and Lana remembers looking in the mirror and thinking she resembled a large marshmallow with toothpicks for arms and legs. She wore maternity clothes and would burst into tears when someone would ask when the baby was due. One day she got so angry she made a sign and pinned it on the front of her dress saying, "I'm not pregnant, I'm just obese."

Finally in desperation she cried out to God, "What is wrong with me?" This was a new question, for Lana had been able throughout her life to always put the blame on someone else. Nothing was ever her fault, but suddenly she realized her problems couldn't always be "all them."

The one universal answer Lana got from God, Marc, and the boys was "Lose weight!" She called the doctor who had put her on the medication and asked if it could cause her to gain weight. He told her it had nothing to do with the medicine. "You have a greasy elbow. Just learn to push away from the table." Lana didn't feel right about that answer and she called him again and insisted he read her the side effects of the medicine. As he went down the list, he paused.

Lana asked, "What does it say?"

He quietly replied, "In some cases the patient may have extreme weight loss or extreme weight gain."

Lana never took another one of those pills although she still had the constant migraines. As her pounds began to drop off she joined Weight Watchers and changed her eating habits.

A friend gave her a book on inner peace and letting go of the pains of the past. As she read each page she saw herself and with each chapter she felt that deep need to get to the root of her problems. She knew the author lived in Houston but when she called Information, she found the number was unlisted. Lana felt, "If only I could find that woman, I know I could be made whole."

One day at the reservations desk, Lana spotted an old Houston phone book. Since the airlines changed books every six months, it was unbelievable to find one three years old, but it was there and so was the author's number. Lana called and the lady asked, "How did you ever find my number?"

They made an appointment to talk for an hour on the phone for the following Tuesday, but on Monday Lana decided to take a free ride on American Airlines and show up in person. When she arrived, she took a cab to the lady's house and sat on the front steps waiting for her to come home. In a short time she arrived and was stunned to see a stranger on the steps.

The author explained she had been in her office working when the Lord told her to go home. She had resisted, but the thoughts were so strong she had grabbed her purse and driven home. She took Lana back to her office and cancelled all other appointments explaining, "God sent me a walk-in."

What a day they spent as Lana poured out a life-time of hurts, humiliations, and heartaches. The woman led her step-by-step through a return to those past situations with the Lord Jesus at her side, forgiving those who had harmed her and receiving forgiveness for the selfish wounds she had inflicted on others. Through that special day of counseling and prayer Lana was set free from a life of crippling emotions and started on a path toward maturity.

Lana found herself able for the first time to go to those she had hurt and apologize, but when God told her to call her ex-husband, she adamantly refused.

This is too much Lord. Don't you remember he left me? I didn't leave him. He left me those babies and he didn't even want to see them again. He should apologize to me.

As she set God straight, she tried to put Bob to rest. But his name kept popping up before her. Finally she asked, "What are you trying to tell me, God?"

"I'm just asking you to obey. I'm not proving who's right. You won't get rid of your pain until you do what I ask."

Lana called Bob in California and asked his forgiveness for the bitterness and anger she had expressed over the years for his leaving and for his disinterest in his own children. Bob was floored and kept asking, "Why are you doing this? You don't have to apologize. Why do you care? What do you want from me?"

Lana added, "I just want you to say that you forgive me."

"Well, OK. I forgive you. I wasn't such a prize myself."

That statement was the closest Bob ever got to saying he was sorry for abandoning Lana and never seeing his sons again.

After Lana hung up she felt such relief as she realized she had obeyed what God had asked even if Bob didn't deserve it. How many women I know who would rather die clutching their righteous anger than receive relief by forgiving an undeserving person. God does not reward the logical but the obedient.

Little did Lana know at that time that Bob, a Continental Airlines pilot, had cancer and within two years would die never having acknowledged his sons. At the funeral, one of Bob's closest friends came up to Rob, an identical replica of his father, and said, "If I didn't know better, I'd think you were Bob's son."

Rob replied, "I am."

After her day of counseling and prayer Lana's attitude at home improved so greatly that Marc said to her. "I don't know what that lady in Houston did to you, but I'll pay for you to go down every week if you'll keep going back."

As others began to notice the changes in Lana, they asked her what had happened. She didn't know what to say. Who would believe that one day in Houston could transform her life? Who would accept that the pain and problems of thirty-five years could be prayed away in a day. People kept asking and Lana gave vague answers.

One night God got her attention and said, "Lana I have something in mind for you. You are to comfort others as I have comforted you."

Lana answered, "No, Lord. I've been rejected all my life. I don't want to work with people who might reject me again."

She sat up all night wrestling with God as Jacob had done with the angel. She studied, prayed, and cried. God assured her if she'd be willing to counsel, he'd personally teach her how. She finally agreed under one condition. *You'll have to bring the people to me and they'll have to fall apart right in front of me so I know that's what you want me to do.*

Little did Lana know how fast God could move. Suddenly strangers showed up weeping on the doorstep, people who didn't know her called on the phone for counsel, church members swarmed around her looking for advice. Some would even arrive and say, "I don't know why I'm here, I just felt drawn to this house.

Lana would ask, "Do you have some pains from your past?" and the person would burst into tears. The house was so often full of people that Marc would call home from the bank and ask, "Do you have another surprise guest at the dinner table tonight?"

After Lana had led eight women through a full day of counseling and prayer and their changed lives were apparent to families and friends, they decided to meet together for follow-up and prayer. From these eight packages of past pain, Philippian Ministries was born.[5] Headquartered in Dallas for the last three years, Lana's staff has counseled over four hundred women and is training new staff in other states.

I can personally attest that Lana has only to recite her poem "Child's Song at CLASS and women are magnetized by her every word. They see the radiance of the Lord around about her and they are drawn to her well of healing, hope, and emotional health. We know from the lives of Christian leaders who come to CLASS that God's emotionally crippled children are a growing number. The church can ill-afford to turn a deaf ear to these walking wounded but must learn how to get these lives on the mend.

As our CLASS staff got acquainted with Lana, we saw this special saint had a gift different from our abilities and a perception which we did not have. As soon as we added Lana to our staff, we began to seek her counsel.

Francine, with a lifetime of rejections, was able, through Lana's day of counseling and prayer, to release her past hurts and to look in a new way unto Jesus the author and finisher of her faith.

Patsy, with gaps in her childhood memories and with lengthy bouts of agoraphobia which kept her inside her house for two years at a time, found some missing pieces to the puzzle of her life and was freed from her fears.

Barbara, who had been a victim of attempted murder and who still has a bullet at the base of her skull, spent two days with Lana and found help for her nightmares and a new sense of forgiveness.

Did I need to see Lana? I had not been rejected; I didn't have agoraphobia; I'd never been shot. I asked Lana what she thought and she replied, "You don't come out of curiosity or to run through a new program, you only come if you sincerely want to remove anything that stands between you and what God wants you to be."

For a year I prayed about God's direction and felt increasingly drawn to a day of counseling and prayer with Lana. We met in a Dallas hotel at 8:00 in the morning and Lana led me through a series of questions about my feelings from the past. How amazed I was at childhood incidents that came quickly to the front of my mind and at strong emotions that colored some of these events.

Lana took notes on my answers to her questions and found several consistent problems that had influenced my decisions and attitudes in life. The first was a fear of poverty. Throughout my childhood during the Depression, I frequently heard my mother sigh as she stood by the cash register in our little store and say, "I hope we take in enough money so we can eat next week." I guess we always did, but I had instilled in my young mind that there was a reasonable doubt as to whether there would be food on the table. We used soap until the sliver disappeared in our hands and we had one new pair of shoes each September no matter how fast our feet had grown.

As I thought back on these facts I realized why I was always anxious about Fred's business, why I won't open a new bar of soap until I have two in reserve, and why I love shelves of shoes in every color. More important than these seemingly trivial revelations was the feeling I had that my father had not provided well enough for me.

Though my rational mind knew he did the very best he could under adverse circumstances, my heart ached for a real house, a steady income, and plenty of soap and shoes. Internally, I had held my father accountable for what I did not have.

Because those ladies in my father's store didn't think I had much hope or good looks, I determined to be smart and studied almost compulsively. I didn't like my appearance and blamed myself for not being beautiful.

As Lana and I uncovered the plot of my life, I was fascinated with some filed away memories we found and grieved over those whom I had not forgiven. I had always avoided confrontation and had some unresolved conflicts which needed to be put to rest. We laughed and cried; we talked and prayed. For over five hours we prayed. Lana held my hands and led me back to those people I needed to forgive. She had me picture the Lord Jesus at my side as I went back to the store and forgave each person whom I had held accountable for hurts or deprivation. I found myself as an eight year old on the fold-out couch in the den behind the store crying because I wasn't pretty. I held my childish face in my hands and released myself from the responsibility for my looks in the name and power of the Lord Jesus. As I traveled this path through the past, I felt lighter, and brighter and could not believe we were still praying at one in the morning.

> Sweet hour of prayer! Sweet hour of prayer!
> That calls me from a world of care.

How beautiful to go back through time with Jesus, forgive those I'd held accountable, and forget the pains of the past. How joyful to relive so many happy and humorous hours with the Lord as my special friend.

The results of my day of counseling and prayer are a new lightness of spirit, a freedom of faith, a divine power I've never felt before. I've taken off the old clothes and put on the new.

How about you? Are you still plodding through the pains of the past? Are you still holding others accountable for things that may not have been their fault? Have you not forgiven even yourself for some of your failures? What can you do about it?

If you do not feel this promised peace, if you have headaches, muscle spasms, stomach problems; if you have low energy, frequent depression, or a pervasive feeling of fear or self-doubt, perhaps there's someone you haven't forgiven. Maybe it's you. Don't stuff these disquieting thoughts away to add to your stress level, but deal with them starting today. Begin by asking God to make you open to his direction and willing to hear His voice. "God is always at work in you to make you willing and able to obey His good purpose" (Phil. 2:13, TEV).

If you don't have a "Lana" handy to work with you, perhaps you could follow her steps by yourself or better yet with a supportive friend.

Emotional healing prayer contains several basic ingredients which set it apart from other types of prayer. There are generally two persons involved, the intercessory prayer counselor and the one coming for inner healing. There is a time of discussion or recounting of life experiences and then both counselor and seeker come together in prayer. These nine points describe the elements involved in such a day of prayer and are taken from Lana's book *God's Crippled Children.* [6]

1. **RENOUNCING OCCULT INVOLVEMENT.** Many who come to emotional healing have had some involvement in the occult. The one coming for prayer first seeks God's forgiveness for any involvement in or curiosity about areas of Satan's wisdom and then renounces any hold the enemy may have due to past experimenting in the realm of darkness.

2. **PRAISING GOD.** Time is spent praising God the Father for all he is and for his great love of mankind. Praise is given to our Lord Jesus for his willingness to come into this world as the expression of God's own heart, to face rejection and suffering for us.

3. **MOVING THROUGH LIFE'S EVENTS IN CHRONOLOGICAL Prayer.** Now attention is turned to the earliest memories in childhood and a process of praying through each painful event in life begins. Jesus is visualized walking hand in hand with that hurting child as each event is faced anew—with Christ by her side.

4. **FORGIVING IN GENERAL.** During the course of praying through those years of disappointment or struggle, what appear to be trivial events may rise to the surface. It is then necessary

to stop and both ask and give forgiveness to those who hurt this person at that particular point in life. For instance a well-meaning school teacher may have refused to allow a child to go to the restroom causing a humiliating incident in the classroom. Just thinking of this may bring tears to the adult as she remembers her childhood feelings. This teacher needs to be forgiven for the pain she caused and presented with an apology in prayer for any sinful responses or resentments the child may have harbored as she grew up.

5. **FIGHTING THE SPIRITUAL BATTLE.** At different points during the prayer an interruption for spiritual battling will take place. Each area of oppression sensed by the counselor will be addressed and renounced. For instance, the one praying may still have a root of anger due to an unfair punishment or pronouncement in the past. The leader would stop and renounce any oppression Satan could have used as a tool in this life because of that particular event.

Example: "Spirit of anger, I bind you and cast you out in Jesus name."

The person seeking help respects this verbal stand against the soul's enemy and takes a spiritual stand in the power of Jesus.

6. **FORGIVING IMMEDIATE FAMILY MEMBERS AND CHILDHOOD FAMILY.** Now the one seeking emotional freedom will go with the Lord Jesus to each member of the immediate family to both give and receive forgiveness. After dealing with the present family, the childhood family must be faced.

7. **SEEKING THE LORD'S EYES TO SEE ALL WHO'VE HURT US.** The one coming for prayer counsel now seeks the Lord's eyes to see all who've caused pain.

8. **THANKING GOD THAT NOTHING IS WASTED.** The prayer thanks God that not one moment of the hurting individual's struggle will be wasted but that God will work it all together for good not just for the heart of his child but for the glory of his kingdom. Thank him that you can now say with Joseph, "What they meant for evil, God meant for good."[7]

9. **CLOSING.** Prayer ends as the individual places the pieces of her life into the hands of Jesus and acknowledges that he alone

can repair and make whole that which was damaged and scarred throughout life. Praise is then given for all that will be done in answer to this prayer; thanksgiving is offered for God's healing touch and his desire to bind the brokenhearted and set the captives free!

Who needs this help?

Just this past week I met a pastor who was still grieving over the "No vote" his congregation gave him. A Bible study teacher shared her lack of forgiveness to her father who never "loved" her. When I spoke on the six reasons teenagers give for why they fool around, one being "I can always get an abortion," the altar in the church filled with sobbing women who had terminated babies.[8] One who was about to do it changed her mind. That same message in a different church brought forth a girl who had an illegitimate baby at fifteen, followed by two abortions, and later giving a baby up for adoption. Add these to the marriage miseries, childhood molestations, and incest and you know there are many Christians who need a loving arm around them to lead them through the steps of forgiving others and themselves and healing their pains of the past.

O Lord, we lift up our hands, we ask you to strengthen our feeble knees that we may run the straight path and be healed. We pray that as we weed out the roots of bitterness, you will give us peace, that peace which passes all understanding.

When Lana was twenty-eight she wrote a poem which represented how she felt about herself at that point and titled it "The Winter of My Mind."

> Winter, cold, gray, lonely.
> Thank God it somehow passes into spring
>
> Just as the darkest night gives way to day,
> The great reliever,
>
> When all your sad and lonely thoughts shall pass,
> Will slip away
>
> As does the winter frost
> When spring at last bursts forth
> to soothe the dampened soul.

For some, there are no springs, no quiet dawns.
I can't remember feeling light or free.

I've lived a thousand winters in this cave,
The soul's own prison, locked.
There is no key.

Do I seem to stare beyond you when you speak?
I seldom hear your words.

It's not that I don't want to share your springs,
But while you speak

An icy wind comes drifting through my mind.
I've closed the door.

I build my fires alone.[9]

Lana concludes by telling us:

The winter of my mind lasted thirty-five years, but my God was greater than that prison and he reached down and set me free. Not only did he set me free but he said, "I want you to see the purpose for your pain. For in every struggle and every dark hour and every deep valley I have built a treasure from your pain."

God showed me that he had wasted nothing in my life. He reached down into the darkness of a mind that was emotionally unbalanced, of a mind that was filled with rejection and insecurity, of a mind turned inward with sick introspection and he called me out of that winter of my mind, out into the light and fresh air.

Winter has passed away now, the seasons are changing in my mind, and spring has come. It's a world that I had never known where the sun shines and where the flowers grow. I can see more than myself now; I can see you and your pain and I long to serve you. Because God has healed me, I long to take you from the winter of your mind to the springtime of his love.

Tying Up the Loose Ends

Showing what we can do to mend the wings
of the brokenhearted and give them flight again,
to put a song on the lips of the silent.

No friend like music
    when the last word's spoken
And every pleading
    is a plea in vain.
No friend like music
    where the heart is broken,
To mend its wings and
    give it flight again.

No Friend Like Music
David W. Hicky

16

Helping Mend Broken Lives

There are still troubles right here in River City, but the God of all comfort comforts us in our afflictions not that we would be comfortable but that we should comfort others with that same comfort where withal we were comforted. Each woman in this book has had troubles. Each has been comforted. Each is now comforting others.

No matter what the problem, it's always worse when it's ours. Some of us complain about a headache while some are burdened with the extreme pain of losing every person and possession, as in the life of Job.

Paulette and Georgia suffered in the painful withdrawal from alcohol and drugs so devastating that they wished they were dead. Patsy was in emotional pain when she was gripped by fear and couldn't leave her house because of her intense phobias.

Mona, Shelby, and Bonnie all suffered from the rejection of their mates, an epidemic that is sapping the strength and productivity of so many women today. And Emilie was faced with the overwhelming pressures of family life.

Barbara, Jennifer, and Jan were victims of violent and abusive acts that left them in physical and emotional pain.

Lauren, Marilyn, and I have had that heartbreak of losing children and having that big lump in the throat last so long we didn't know if we could ever swallow again without the physical reminder of our grief.

Evelyn has learned that God puts a warm blanket of love over a suffering body and Lana shows others how to reach for the hand of the Lord Jesus as they take a healing journey through the pains of the past.

Problems of pain persist in every path of life and our purpose is not to wallow in self-pity but to accept the facts and decide what we're going to do about it. Mona states it well when she says, "Life isn't fair."

We don't need to research the reason, but we must get on with the solutions. God isn't out to cause us grief, but when it happens he is there to make the best of it with us. One of my favorite verses asks, "Is your life full of difficulty and temptations? Then be happy, for when the way is rough, your patience has a chance to grow. So let it grow, and don't try to squirm out of your problems. For when your patience is finally in full bloom, then you will be ready for anything, strong in character, full and complete" (James 1:2–4, TLB).

Problems and pain produce patience. When I was holding my second dying child, I didn't have any urgency to preside over meetings or any sense of glory in the trappings of my social world. I learned through my pain to have patience until God showed me what he was going to do with my life.

Paulette and Georgia learned that healing didn't come overnight. It took months of physical and emotional suffering, knowing God was on their side, before they emerged with a deep compassion for others in similar situations.

Barbara went through months of excruciatingly painful therapy and still suffers from the bullet lodged at the base of her skull.

Jennifer and Jan felt shame, guilt, and humiliation at the desecration of their bodies.

It is a rare person in today's world who has not suffered. Paul says:

> We know that the whole creation has been groaning in travail together until now and . . . we ourselves . . . groan inwardly as we wait for adoption as sons, the redemption of our bodies . . . If we hope for what we do not see, we wait for it with patience (Rom. 8:22–25, RSV).

Paul also encourages us by his words, "I consider that the sufferings of this present time are not worth comparing with the glory that is to be revealed to us" (Rom. 8:18, RSV).

How do we handle pain and suffering? The true life stories of these courageous women in this book, all personal friends of mine, have been written not because of their traumas but because of their victories through the Lord Jesus Christ, in order to give HOPE to others so their lives can begin to mend.

As you think over the wide variety of these lives on the mend, you may relate specifically to one or two. If you are a victim, there is HOPE; if you aren't, there is opportunity. Don't close the book and put it on the shelf, but ask the Lord Jesus what he wants you to do to fulfill his purpose for your life.

Be Informed. One of the great needs for Christians today is to gather knowledge on the various problems, traumas, victimizations, and addictions rampant in our society. We must fight fire with fire. So many of the fine Christian ladies and gentlemen who come to CLASS for leadership training have chosen to look the other way and hope the problems will run off also.

I surely wanted to live happily ever after, but the Lord has moved me to the firing lines where I can clearly see the wounded.

Start with the information in this book and begin to gather material on whatever subjects interest you. Even Christian magazines are now including articles on rape, incest, drug abuse, and alcohol. When I first mentioned teenage suicide, people began sending me clippings, pamphlets, and case histories. Within three months I had a large box full of so much material I could easily write a book from it. You have only to mention a subject to have people give you their own true stories which will add to your reservoir.

Learn the symptoms of the various traumas and begin looking into people's eyes to observe the well of pain about to overflow, that you may be of comfort.

Encourage your church or Bible study to assemble information on abuse and addictions and let people know it's available. Have on hand the tapes and resource book designed to accompany this book and suggest that your pastor listen and then lead a study group of those who wish to be alert and aware.

Find out what different support groups, counselors, or hot lines there are in your town and have these lists at home and in the church. So many tell me, "If only I'd known where to turn for help." The church should be the first place problem people go but so often we are uninformed. You be the catalyst remembering

God's word, "My people are destroyed for lack of knowledge" (Hos. 4:6, KJV).

Be Inspired. As you gather information on human problems, also get into the Bible and seek God's direction. Each one of the women in this book reached out for human help, but was given the victory through scriptural inspiration not religious answers. Don't preach to the downcast, don't show them how they could have done it better, don't remind them of the sin in their lives, don't drop condemning verses which will add to their guilt.

Those of us who have suffered know the guilt we bear and we don't need reminders. When we're grieving we are not cheered by Romans 8:28, for at that moment we can't see that anything is working for good. Don't try to jolly up the hurting person. A young pastor stood next to me as a friend told me how her thirteen-year-old son had been killed by a motorcyclist just three weeks before. In an effort to spread spiritual joy, he looked up brightly and said, "Well, God knows best." As her face dropped, I was dumbfounded at his lack of sensitivity and hopeful that he would soon "grow up in Christ."

God doesn't want us to use his word and spirit to condemn, but to uplift and inspire. He wants us to be so close to the Lord Jesus that we radiate his warmth, his concern, and his love. He wants us to take our knowledge and experiences and blend them with his word in such a way that those who listen to us will feel his touch. How grateful I was to receive this note from a woman who had heard me speak in Tulsa at a "Women Caring for Women Seminar" where I referred to some of the problems covered in this book.

> While I was but one in a large audience, a face in a sea of many, there were those times when it seemed to me you sat beside me, took my hand, and with your sensitive, heart-warming words of experience and caring you entered my life as a sister. Somewhat like finding a treasured letter from a long, lost friend.
>
> In the very busy and often hectic days of our individual struggles we seldom find the time to reach out to strangers.

Be Involved. Whatever your knowledge, experience, or spirituality, you won't be used in mending the lives of others until you're willing to take the first step. Being involved isn't always easy and it requires taking risks, but being used to change one life is the greatest thrill we'll ever know. The women in this book didn't go from the pits to the peaks overnight; they put in their time to know their subject matter. They spent time in God's Word seeking his answers, and they were willing to move out, lay their life on the line, and be vulnerable. Each one came to CLASS to sharpen her skills and receive motivation; each one has gone from being a lady with a story to becoming a messenger with a ministry. What about you? Is there something in your life that you should be sharing with others? Do you have a victory that could give someone HOPE? Have you kept quiet long enough?

> A time to rend, and a time to sew;
> A time to keep silence, and a time to speak (Eccl. 3:7, kjv).

Perhaps your time is now!

For information on any help or counseling references, please call or write our office:

Praise Ministries
1814-E Commercenter West
San Bernardino, CA 92408

(Phone: 714–888–8665)

Notes

Chapter 1

1. Dr. Anderson Spickard, Jr., "Alcoholism: Even the Church Is Hurting," *Christianity Today,* Aug. 5, 1983.
2. Ibid.
3. Rev. Joseph L. Kellerman, *Alcoholism: A Merry-Go-Round Named Denial,* a booklet published by Al-Anon Family Group Headquarters, Inc., New York.
4. Lana Bateman, "Ashes to Gold," an unpublished poem.

Chapter 2

1. Texas War on Drugs, P. O. Box 42808, Houston, TX 77042.
2. *The Kind of Drugs Kids Are Getting Into,* pamphlet no. 6841, distributed by Pharmacists Against Drug Abuse.
3. *Los Angeles Times,* Jan. 3, 1984.
4. Jean Seligman et al., "Getting Straight," *Newsweek,* June 4, 1984, 62–69.
5. Dr. Colter Rule with Maxine Abrams, "The Dictionary of Emotional Problems," *Good Housekeeping,* May 1983.
6. *Los Angeles Times,* Jan. 3, 1984.

Chapter 3

1. *USA Today,* Sept. 20, 1984.
2. Jerry Adler et al., "The Fight to Conquer Fear," *Newsweek,* Apr. 23, 1984, 66–72.
3. Ibid.
4. Ibid.
5. Ibid.
6. Ibid.
7. George Sweeting, "Talk It Over," *Moody Monthly,* Mar. 1985.
8. Florence Littauer, *Personality Plus* (Old Tappan, NJ: Fleming H. Revell, 1982).
9. Rule, "Dictionary."
10. Littauer, *Personality.*
11. Rule, "Dictionary."

Chapter 4

1. *USA Today,* Nov. 3, 1983.
2. *The Dallas Morning News,* Mar. 7, 1985.
3. *The Dallas Morning News,* Mar. 7, 1985, quoting from Wendy Leigh, *The Infidelity Report* (New York: William Morrow and Co., Inc., 1984).
4. Ibid.
5. *New World News,* Sept. 1984.

Chapter 5

1. California Civil Code 4801.
2. Ted Gest, "Divorce: How the Game Is Played Now," *U.S. News and World Report,* Nov. 21, 1983.
3. Ibid.
4. A letter written by an anonymous friar in a monastery in Nebraska late in his life. Quoted by Tim Hansel, *When I Relax I Feel Guilty* (Elgin, IL: David C. Cook Publishing Co., 1979), 44–45.

Chapter 6

1. David Gelman et al., "Playing Both Mother and Father," *Newsweek,* July 15, 1985.
2. "They're Living Alone and Liking It," *Los Angeles Times,* Apr. 7, 1985.
3. Ibid.
4. Henry Lee, "How to Live Alone," *Parade,* July 29, 1984.

Chapter 7

1. *Los Angeles Times,* Apr. 11, 1985.
2. Ibid.
3. *Planning for Health,* a bulletin published by Kaiser Permanente Medical Care Program, Southern California region, Los Angeles, 1984.
4. *The San Bernardino Sun,* Apr. 15, 1984.
5. Ibid.

Chapter 9

1. *The Hemet News,* Dec. 21, 1984.
2. Dr. Joyce Brothers, "Why Men Abuse Women," *Parade,* Nov. 11, 1984.
3. Ibid.
4. *How to Protect Yourself Against Sexual Assault,* a booklet published by Consumer Information Center, Dept. 44, Pueblo, CO 81009.
5. Maureen Dowd et al., "Rape: The Sexual Weapon," *Time,* Sept. 5, 1983, 27–29.

Chapter 10

1. "The Offenders," *LIFE,* Dec. 1984, 47–50.
2. Ibid.

3. Ibid.

4. Ibid.

5. California Penal Code 2805.

6. *Help for the Secret,* a pamphlet published by The Recovery Assoc., Box 821453, Dallas, TX 75382.

7. Harold Myra, "The Glamorous Prostitute," *Christianity Today,* Oct. 5, 1984, 14–19.

8. Betty Baye, "Incest, True Stories of Women Who Suffered and Survived," *Beauty Digest,* Jan. 1985, 22–23.

9. Susan Forward and Craig Buck, *Betrayal of Innocence: Incest and Its Devastation* (New York: Penguin Books, Inc., 1979).

10. *USA Today,* Sept. 17, 1984.

11. *Newsweek,* May 14, 1984.

12. D. Finklehor, from a study cited in "Ethics and the Problem of Sexual Abuse," *American Journal of Orthopsychiatry,* vol. 49, 1979, 292–7.

13. Roland Summit, M.D., and J. Kryso, "Sexual Abuse of Children: A Clinical Spectrum," *American Journal of Orthopsychiatry,* vol. 48, 1978, 231–51.

14. Baye, "Incest."

15. Dr. Dennis Bull, *The Long-Term Effects of Childhood on Adult Women,* a pamphlet published by The Recovery Assoc., Box 821543, Dallas, TX 75382.

16. Myra, "Prostitute."

17. Ibid.

18. Russell Watson et al., "A Hidden Epidemic," *Newsweek,* May 14, 1984, 30–36.

Chapter 11

1. ALIVE, Inc., 12141 Lewis Street, Garden Grove, CA 92640.

2. Charlotte Ross, *Youth Suicide and What You Can Do About It,* a pamphlet distributed by The National Committee for Youth Suicide Prevention, 1811 Trousdale Drive, Burlingame, CA 94010.

3. Seligman, "Getting Straight."

4. David Gelman et al., "Teenage Suicide in the Sunbelt," *Newsweek,* Aug. 15, 1983, 70–74.

5. Ibid.

6. *Dallas Times Herald,* Oct. 12, 1984.

7. "Trouble in an Affluent Suburb," *Time,* Dec. 25, 1978, 60.

8. Ibid.

9. Alfred Del Bello, "Federal Help Is Needed to Reduce Teenage Suicide," *The Arizona Daily Star,* Sept. 16, 1984.

10. Florence Littauer, *Blow Away the Black Clouds* (Eugene, OR: Harvest House Publishers, 1981).

11. Quoted by John Wesley White during an appearance on the television program "100 Huntley Street."

Chapter 12

1. 97th Congress by National Institute on Alcohol Abuse and Alcoholism, Division of Prevention.

2. Alan Parachini, "Daytime Drunk Driver; Unsuspected Menace," *Los Angeles Times*, Dec. 14, 1984.

3. Ibid.

4. *Hemet News*, Dec. 21, 1984.

5. Parachini, "Unsuspected Menace."

6. Ann Japenga, *Los Angeles Times*, Dec. 14, 1984.

7. Don Kirkman, "Young Drivers and Drinking a Deadly Mixture on the Road," *Los Angeles Times*, Dec. 14, 1984.

8. Joni Eareckson Tada and Steve Estes, *A Step Further* (Grand Rapids, MI: Zondervan Publishing House, 1978).

Chapter 13

1. Lauren Briggs, *What You Can Say . . . When You Don't Know What to Say* (Eugene, OR: Harvest House Publishers, 1985), 20.

2. "For Those Who Hurt," Christine Wyrtzen Ministries, 1982, CWM, Inc., Loveland, Ohio. All rights reserved. Used by permission.

3. Heart to Heart, Oak Grove, Oregon. All rights reserved. Used by permission.

4. Ibid.

5. Charles R. Swindoll, *For Those Who Hurt* (Portland, OR: Multnomah Press, 1977).

6. Amy Ross Mumford, *It Hurts to Lose a Special Person* (Denver: Accent Books, 1982).

Chapter 14

1. "It's All in Your Head," distributed by National Center for Health Statistics, quoted in *San Antonio LIGHT*, Dec. 9, 1984.

2. Ibid.

3. Philip Yancey, "The Question God May Not Answer," *Worldwide Challenge*, June 1983.

4. David Gaw, "Backward and Forward," *American Way*, Apr. 2, 1985.

5. Joan Tedeschi, "Health Today," *MS*, May 1985, 114–16.

6. C. Austin Miles, "In the Garden," Rodeheaver Co., 1940.

Chapter 15

1. William Shakespeare, *Julius Caesar*, act 3, scene 2, line 75.

2. Steve Scott and Brooks Alexander, "Inner Healing." *SCP Journal*, Apr. 1980.

3. Ibid.

4. Hal Lindsey, *The Late Great Planet Earth* (Grand Rapids, MI: Zondervan, 1976).

5. Philippian Ministries, P.O. Box 31122, Dallas, Tx 75231.

6. Lana Bateman, *God's Crippled Children* (Dallas: Philippian Ministries, 1981).

7. Genesis 45:5, paraphrased.

8. Florence Littauer, *Out of the Cabbage Patch* (Eugene, OR: Harvest House Publishers, 1983), 6.

9. Bateman, *God's Crippled Children*.